PIPE POLITICS, CONTESTED WATERS

Embedded Infrastructures of Millennial Mumbai

LISA BJÖRKMAN   Duke University Press   Durham and London   2015

Designed by Courtney Leigh Baker
Typeset in Minion by Westchester Publishing Services

Library of Congress Cataloging-in-Publication Data
Björkman, Lisa, [date]–author.
Pipe politics, contested waters : embedded infrastructures of millennial Mumbai /
Lisa Björkman.
pages cm
Includes bibliographical references and index.
ISBN 978-0-8223-5950-0 (hardcover : alk. paper)
ISBN 978-0-8223-5969-2 (pbk. : alk. paper)
ISBN 978-0-8223-7521-0 (e-book)
1. Water-supply—India—Mumbai. 2. Waterworks—India—Mumbai. 3. Infrastructure
(Economics)—India—Mumbai. 4. Mumbai (India)—Politics and government. I. Title.
HD4465.I5B57 2015
363.6'10954792—dc23
2015010921

Cover art: Photo by Lisa Björkman.

Duke University Press gratefully acknowledges the American Institute of Indian Studies,
2014 Joseph W. Elder Prize in the Indian Social Sciences, which provided funds toward the
publication of this book.

FOR CAROL BRECKENRIDGE

Awarded the
**JOSEPH W. ELDER PRIZE
IN THE INDIAN SOCIAL SCIENCES**
by the American Institute of Indian Studies
and published with the
Institute's generous support.

PIPE POLITICS, CONTESTED WATERS

CONTENTS

ACKNOWLEDGMENTS

The idea for this book emerged in 2004 during a graduate seminar with Professor Carol Breckenridge, an early mentor whose deep affection and curiosity for the city of Mumbai was contagious. Over the following years the project came to life under the guidance of my advisors and mentors at the New School for Social Research, especially that of Vyjayanthi Rao, Timothy Pachirat, Sanjay Ruparelia, Michael Cohen, Arjun Appadurai, and Victoria Hattam, each of whom influenced the project in distinct and important ways.

I owe tremendous thanks to the American Institute of Indian Studies (AIIS) for their consistent support for my research over the years. Fieldwork in Mumbai between 2008 and 2011 was made possible by an American Institute of Indian Studies Junior Research Fellowship, and Hindi training in Jaipur was supported by language fellowships in 2004 and in 2007–8. I would like to thank Elise Auerbach, Philip Lutgendorf, Purnima Mehta, the AIIS trustees, as well as the extraordinary faculty at the AIIS Hindi Language Program in Jaipur. Early support for this project was provided by a New School India China Institute Fellowship in 2006, and a New School for Social Research Dissertation Fellowship in 2007–8. I am grateful to the Tata Institute of Social Sciences in Mumbai for providing affiliation during the period of my fieldwork, and to the Institute of Advanced Studies in Lucca for providing a warm and welcoming work environment in 2011. Much of the writing of this book took place while I was a postdoctoral fellow at the Max Planck Institute for the Study of Religious and Ethnic Diversity in Göttingen, which offered an intellectually invigorating and exceedingly pleasant atmosphere in which to read, think, and write.

At Duke University Press I owe particular thanks to Miriam Angress and Susan Albury, who have worked with me on this book since 2012. The three external reviewers that Miriam recruited to read the manuscript provided tremendously valuable feedback. I would like to extend my gratitude as well to Brian A. Hatcher and to two anonymous reviewers from the American Institute of Indian Studies' Elder Prize selection committee for their very insightful comments and suggestions. Thank you as well to Bill Nelson for his help with the diagrams, and to Dave Prout who prepared the index.

This book benefited tremendously from the insights of an extraordinary community of interlocutors in Göttingen, at the Max Planck Institute and at the Center for Modern Indian Studies. I am especially grateful to Nathaniel Roberts and Uday Chandra, each of whom read the manuscript in its entirety, and whose critical engagements have been an extremely enjoyable source of provocation and insight—thank you. I would also like to thank Ritajyoti Bandyopadhyay, Anderson Blanton, Devika Bordia, Jayeel Cornelio, Ajay Gandhi, Radhika Gupta, Weishan Huang, Annelies Kusters, Sumeet Mhaskar, Srirupa Roy, Roschanack Shaery, Shaheed Tayob, Sahana Udupa, Lalit Vachani, Peter van der Veer, Rupa Vishwanath, and Jeremy Walton for their encouragement, feedback, and suggestions.

The book has benefited as well from the generosity of friends and colleagues over the years who have offered their thoughts on various ideas and chapter drafts. I am especially grateful to Jonathan Shapiro Anjaria, Amita Bhide, Noelle Brigden, Patton Burchett, Michele Friedner, Andrew Harris, Giammario Impullitti, Devesh Kapur, William Mazzarella, Colin McFarlane, Savitri Medhatul, Lisa Mitchell, Philip Oldenburg, Anastasia Piliavsky, Anupama Rao, Mark Schneider, Simpreet Singh, Neelanjan Sircar, Rahul Srivastava, Natascha van der Zwan, and Leilah Vevinah. Many of the ideas and formulations presented here were tested out during the marvelous series of Water Workshops between 2006 and 2014 at Harvard University's Center for Middle Eastern Studies, graciously hosted by Steve Caton. Among the many participants and interlocutors who offered provocative and insightful feedback, I wish to extend particular thanks to Jessica Barnes, Namita Dharia, Gareth Doherty, Tessa Farmer, Toby Jones, Martha Kaplan, Mandana Limbert, Benjamin Orlove, Catarina Scaramelli, Anand Vaidya, and above all to Steve Caton.

The research for this book was made both possible and pleasurable by the tremendous generosity and open-mindedness of a great many people in Mumbai. For their advice, guidance, and assistance during my fieldwork in Mumbai, I wish to extend thanks to Amita Bhide, Anita Patil-Deshmukh, Medha Dixit, Leena Joshi, and Deepak Dhopat. My deep and heartfelt appreciation goes to the Municipal Corporation of Greater Mumbai's Department of Hydraulic Engineering (particularly those of the M-East Ward), whose engineers and staff not only made this book possible, but whose extraordinary graciousness, patience, and unshakable good humor made the research immensely enjoyable as well. I am especially grateful to S. R. Argade, S. R. Bidi, R. B. Bambale, D. P. Joshi, A. N. Kadam, N. H. Kusnur, V. R. Pednekar, S. M. Shah, and T.V. Shah, who provided invaluable feedback and critical comments on various chapters and ideas presented here. Countless interlocutors and research participants in Mumbai will remain anonymous; the thanks I express here can only hint at the debts I incurred and at the depth of my gratitude.

INTRODUCTION

Embedded Infrastructures

In 1991, in conjunction with India's liberalizing economic reforms that year, the chief minister of Maharashtra announced a plan to transform the city of Bombay into a global financial service center modeled on Singapore—and to let the market do much of the work. Animated by an international policy discourse recommending market solutions to all manner of political, social, and material conflict, a coalition of Bombay's planners, politicians, landowners, and business elites put markets to work in arbitrating long-standing political conflicts over access to urban land and resources—conflicts on which a generation of urban development planning had faltered. Institutionalizing a new set of regulatory instruments and market mechanisms, liberalization-era policymakers enlisted private-sector participation in the city's transformation. The years since have seen Mumbai gripped by a fever of construction, demolition, and redevelopment: working-class neighborhoods and older built forms are making way for shiny new malls, office towers, mega-infrastructure projects, and luxurious residential compounds, while sprawling townships of low-income housing sprout up along the urban periphery.

Yet the dazzling decades of urban development and roaring economic growth have not been without cost: Mumbai's transformation has presided over the steady deterioration—and sometimes spectacular breakdown—of the city's water infrastructures.[1] Water troubles plague not only the more than

60 percent of city residents now reported to live in slums (where basic infrastructural services like municipal water supply are often both legally tenuous and practically unreliable),[2] but city elites too have seen their taps grow increasingly erratic and prone to drying up. Well-heeled Mumbai residents increasingly supplement spotty taps with piecemeal purchases and deliveries, while private-sector actors resort to infrastructural self-provisioning, hiring transport companies, digging wells, and investing in enormous on-site water recycling plants and filtration systems. Every day hundreds of water tanker trucks drip their way along Mumbai's traffic-clogged streets, delivering water to slums and up-market hotels alike. For their part the city's major political parties—in high-profile displays of antimigrant one-upmanship—have taken to blaming erratic pipes on the city's poorest residents themselves (accusing them of overburdening the city's infrastructures with their very presence) as well as on one another (for supposedly allowing the poor to plunder the pipes in a clientelistic exchange for votes). The tanker trucks, parched pipes, and political theatrics fuel the imaginations of Mumbai's legions of news reporters, who respond with a steady stream of often fanciful stories about "water mafias," "thieving plumbers," "patron-politicians," and "corrupt engineers."

Mumbai's dry taps are puzzling. The city is India's financial and commercial capital, accounting for some six percent of GDP, 40 percent of foreign trade, and over a third of the country's income tax revenue.[3] With a per capita income almost three times the national average, Mumbai boasts real estate values that can rival those of Manhattan. The city, in other words, suffers no dearth of financial resources with which it might redress infrastructural shortfalls; indeed municipal records suggest that a significant proportion of the city's water and sewage budget regularly goes unspent. As for water, city engineers explain that there is no aggregate water shortage in Mumbai, where per capita availability (as well as estimated levels of leakage) is on par with that of London (if not quite that of New York).[4] With no shortage of resources, how might Mumbai's fitful taps be made sense of?

This book is about the encounter in Mumbai between liberalizing market reforms and the materially and symbolically dense politics of urban infrastructure. While above-ground landscapes have been rapidly reconfigured by "world class" city-building efforts,[5] market reforms to facilitate the transformation have wreaked havoc on the city's water pipes. The just-in-time arbitrage temporality of market exchange has resulted in geographies of built space—and thereby of water demand—that deviate wildly from what is projected (and permitted) by the city's development plan and control rules. The city of Mumbai is thus characterized by a growing incongruence between its above-ground form and its below-ground flows, with the result that its water pipes have become increasingly volatile. As engineers explain, there is no aggregate water shortage in the city of Mumbai; the challenge rather is how to make water flow to the unpredictable (and constantly changing) *location* of demand. The result has been an improvised, constantly fluctuating, often unreliable, and little understood configuration of water flow in the city. In contemporary Mumbai water is made to flow by means of intimate forms of knowledge and ongoing intervention in the city's complex and dynamic social, political, and hydraulic landscape. The everyday work of getting water animates and inhabits a penumbra of infrastructural activity—of business, brokerage, secondary markets, and sociopolitical networks—whose workings are transforming lives and reconfiguring and rescaling political authority in the city. Indeed Mumbai's illegible and volatile hydrologies are lending infrastructures increasing political salience just as actual control over pipes and flows becomes contingent upon dispersed and intimate assemblages of knowledge, power, and material authority. "Pipe politics" refers to the new arenas of contestation that Mumbai's water infrastructures animate—contestations that reveal the illusory and precarious nature of the project to remake Mumbai as a world-class city and gesture instead toward the highly contested futures of the actually existing city of Mumbai.

World-Class City

The project to transform Mumbai into a global financial service center modeled on Singapore must be considered in light of broader macroeconomic, ideological, and intellectual trends of recent decades. "The period of urban revolutions has begun," wrote Henri Lefebvre (2003: 43) a half-century ago, turning Marxist orthodoxy about the reorganization of industrial production in cities on its head,[6] insisting instead that the production of urban space was *itself* becoming the primary means by which capitalist accumulation was advancing. Lefebvre's insight was itself revolutionary, inspiring a generation of thinking on the relationship between global processes of urbanization and the universal movement of capital. Neo-Lefebvrian urban geographers have thus theorized how structural inequalities and macro-level capitalist power geometries have underpinned the historical production of highly uneven patterns of "planetary urbanization" (Brenner 2013; Merrifield 2013) as well as inequitable distributions of resources (Harvey 2001; Swyngedouw 2004).[7]

While neo-Lefebvrian thinkers have drawn attention to planetary patterns of urbanism as global capital's "spatial fix" (Harvey 2001), political economists of "global cities" have emphasized the renewed importance of cities to new forms of global economy, with cities said to play a crucial role as "command posts" (Sassen 1991) in spatially dispersed but economically integrated international economic systems.[8] While large-scale industrial *production* is moving out of urban centers, global cities theorists argue, producer *services*—banking, finance, education, high-tech, entertainment, real estate—are moving in. These kinds of extremely profitable service industries cluster in urban areas, where they benefit from, among other things, the extremely dense material networks of infrastructural connectivity (electricity, fiber optics, airports, water pipes) that cities have to offer. The idea that national economic fortunes lie in the extent to which a country's economy is linked—through its cities—to global networks of finance and commerce has inspired planners, policymakers, business interests, and funding agencies the world over to formulate strategies for making cities attractive to transnational service-sector firms and competitive in the global marketplace for investment. Recent decades have thus witnessed the alignment of state- and private-sector actors in a bid to build "entrepreneurial" internationally competitive global cities, either (as in Dubai or Pudong) by creating cities from scratch or (as in Mumbai) by transforming existing urban landscapes in such a way that global firms might be inclined to set up shop there.[9]

The globally mobile development discourse and policymaking framework exhorting countries to reconfigure cities to attract international investment capital—and to use market mechanisms in doing so—has met with both scholarly and popular critiques pointing to the negative distributional effects and democratic deficit seen to inhere in the global city project.[10] The imperative to attract global investment capital, it is argued, renders urban infrastructures and built spaces more responsive to the imperatives of global finance and business than to the needs of resident citizenry. In this way macroeconomic shifts become inscribed in the fabric of the city itself, leading to sociospatial segregation and deepening inequality. Liberalization and globalization is thus charged with undermining the material and ideological basis of a "modern infrastructural ideal" (Graham and Marvin 2001: 35) by unbundling the relationship between citizens and cities. While global city infrastructures might provide connectivity among spaces that are relevant to the new economy (the IT parks, gated communities, airports, and call centers), it is argued that they do so to the exclusion of people and places that liberalization and globalization has rendered economically obsolete: the defunct factories, the working classes and their housing, and the hazy world of urban informality and illegality commonly known as the "slum."

These kinds of metanarratives about what liberal capitalism does to urban space seems to fit well with much of what we see in Mumbai. It is precisely through these kinds of large-scale efforts to reconfigure urban environments with massive investments in urban infrastructure, Harvey (2001) tells us, that surplus capital finds its "spatial fix."[11] The infrastructurally mediated devaluation of economically unproductive urban spaces like slums is precisely what allows for their profitable demolition and redevelopment. Dry taps in poor neighborhoods can apparently be explained by the logic of capital, whose workings will likely soon see such neighborhoods razed and reconfigured for some higher-value use; this is all part of capital's creative-destructive tendency.[12] Indeed Sassen (2010: 85) notes that economic deregulation to attract investment is of a piece with informalization in the lower echelons of the economy and society—part of the same global movement of capital.[13] Capitalism is infinitely adaptive, Marxists might say; relations of production have simply been reconfigured and reworked in Mumbai in this particular way. All these informal infrastructural arrangements—these "mafias" of tankers and plumbers—are all just doing their part to advance the universalizing impetus of capital.[14]

Marxist political economy accounts have been critiqued by scholars, particularly postcolonial theorists, who note that infrastructures cannot be described as *splintering* in cities like Mumbai since such cities never approximated any modern, networked ideal in the first place. Contemporary infrastructural and spatial disjunctures are better explained, it is suggested, by looking at how patterns of rule and relations of governance with roots in a *colonial* past continue to inform contemporary patterns of citizenship. Theorists have described how colonial administrative divisions of populations into "citizens" and "subjects" have contemporary manifestations in the ways that postcolonial societies have been governed since independence (Chatterjee 2004; Mamdani 1996). In contemporary Calcutta, for instance, Chatterjee details how "population groups" constituting the urban poor are not treated on par with "proper" citizens, whose claims to infrastructure and urban amenities are made in a language of democratic citizenship *right*. Chatterjee (2004, 2013) suggests that because the lives and livelihoods of the urban poor hinge on "illegal" occupations of land and "informal" commercial and productive activities, the preservation of a formal legal structure has precluded the extension of formal rights to things like shelter and water to the slum-dwelling poor, who—unable to make legal, rights-based claims—resort to *negotiation* for substantive goods and entitlements from the state.

While Chatterjee explicitly positions his formulation as a response to Benedict Anderson's (2006) theorization of a universal ideal of civic nationalism (Anderson's "imagined community"), his argument joins those of Scott (1998), Ferguson (1990), Escobar (1995), and Simone (2004) in offering a critique of the Eurocentric and universalizing assumptions of generations of urban planners and development professionals more generally. The imperialist designs of "high-modernist" social order, Scott suggests, have repeatedly failed to "improve the human condition" because they have neglected to take into account the various and multiple (non-Cartesian) epistemic forms already operating within the social spaces that development experts and urban planners aim to "improve" through rational knowledge. The infrastructural ideal of a fully networked city is thus cast as a value-laden formulation, whose claims to moral and empirical superiority rest on a Eurocentric conception of the "good" that is centered around the rights-bearing individual and his or her relation to a sovereign state—a conception that more often than not functions as a platform for the consolidation of state power and imperial domination.

Understandings of "infrastructure" that consider only large-scale, state-directed technical and engineering feats—pipes, concrete, wires, and bulldozers—are thus criticized as both limited and misleading. Infrastructure might rather be understood to comprise the multitude of practices and elements that facilitate access to what Simone calls "spaces of economic and cultural operation" and that function as "a platform providing for and reproducing life in the city" (2004: 407–8). *Formal*, state-led efforts to extend or upgrade urban service provision, in other words, undermine already existing, *informal* arrangements and disrupt socially and culturally embedded frameworks of access and belonging. This line of antiplan theorizing emphasizes how the grand designs of capital are interrupted, particularly in the postcolonial context, by cultural solidarities and life forms that thrive in the informal interstices of markets and states, subverting these structures from within. Universalizing metanarratives are alleged to hit a roadblock in the postcolonial city, where communitarian identities and solidarities subvert the grand designs of capital. Thus rather than interpreting the informal urban economies, spaces, and practices as signs of modernity's failure to fulfill its promises, antiplan theorists *celebrate* urban informality, reading the disorderly city not as *dystopic* but as a possible *alternative* to the totalizing politics of planned, state-led modernity. Urban informality, it is suggested, might be understood to comprise forms of sociality and economy born of traditional modes of life and livelihood with roots in non-Western cultural and social forms. As the architect Rem Koolhaas wrote as he soared above Lagos's slums in a helicopter, "From the air, the apparently burning garbage heap turned out to be, in fact, a village" (quoted in Gandy 2005: 40). Alternative forms of habitation, conviviality, and infrastructural connection, in other words, should not be read as spaces of oppression or exclusion but as urban instantiations of modes of life rooted in indigenous cultural practice—what Koolhaas characterizes as "ingenious, alternative systems" of "very elaborate organizational networks" (quoted in Gandy 2005: 40)—native to the Global South; it may simply be the case, in other words, that the apparent disorder of Lagos or Mumbai is simply what urban modernity *looks* like in the non-Western world.

This attention to the historical, political, and sociocultural dimensions of urban form and fragmentation is a welcome intervention. Yet reading infrastructural informality as a space of resistance to the totalizing dynamics of global market forces does not explain the hydraulic puzzles posed by Mumbai, where the "formal" status of one's home does not go far in predicting what comes (or does not come) out of one's pipes and where water does not flow readily along class lines. For instance, in the middle-class housing society where I lived during my research, between 2008 and 2010, we received only forty liters of municipal water per person per day—roughly a third of the municipal supply norm for residential consumption and a quantity that is on par with some of the poorest, legally precarious, and politically and socially marginalized localities in which I did research. Our society's supplementary, by-the-tanker water purchases, Marxists might counter, is perfectly explicable within a capitalist logic: with purchasing power rather than citizenship right determining access, water has simply been reconfigured as an *economic* good, one that our society was fortunately able to afford.[15] Those unable to pay for water at the market rate (i.e., the urban poor), by contrast, are forced into informal infrastructural arrangements. By this reading, what antiplan celebrates as *opposition* to the totalizing forces of the bourgeois-capitalist state becomes indistinguishable from dispossession, informalization, and criminalization of the poor; what antiplan describes as authentic forms of sociality uncolonized by capital is in fact entirely compatible with the exigencies of capital accumulation and dovetails with pro-market celebrations of entrepreneurial liberal subjectivity. One might even say that what antiplan does is simply redescribe everyday efforts to live with the effects of capital in rather more celebratory terms. In championing makeshift or informal infrastructural arrangements as agentive resistance to the bourgeois state, antiplan theory not only lacks explanatory power but (as we see in chapter 4) takes as a point of analytical departure the conceptual categories of the very liberal market logic it professes to critique.

Indeed it may very well be true that capital is perfectly happy in Mumbai, that the power of capital is not at all at odds with forms of power and authority operative in and through urban informality—infrastructural or otherwise. Capital might be said to work much like water itself, channeling and pooling, making and remaking the landscapes through which it flows, reconfiguring the contours of sociomaterial worlds that it inhabits. Yet what Marxist economic geography does not tell us is why water pipes have become so erratic in capitalist Mumbai but not in, say, Shanghai, Seoul, or Jakarta. Mumbai's hydrologies cannot be deduced nor their future predicted by a theory of the universalization of capital; appeals to capital's infinitely adaptive workings (which are by definition always true) are therefore, for our purposes, not particularly illuminating. To make sense of the relationship between economic markets and Mumbai's water infrastructures we must push past these conventional categories of analysis—class and community, rights and rules—to pay attention to water infrastructures themselves: to the sociopolitical and material landscapes through which water flows are produced and within which infrastructures are embedded.[16]

Embedded Infrastructures

More than a half-century ago the economic historian Karl Polanyi (2001 [1944]: 3) described "the idea of a self-adjusting market" as "a stark utopia." Challenging a cornerstone of neoclassical economic theory—Adam Smith's (2001 [1776]: 16) notion that mankind's natural "propensity to *truck, barter,* and exchange one thing for another" results in internally animated, self-regulating markets[17]— Polanyi used the example of England to show how markets are in fact the highly artificial creations of an interventionist state. Far from natural, Polanyi (2001 [1944]: 3) argued, markets are produced through radical institutional and legal changes that, if left unchecked, pose a dire threat to the "human and natural substance of society." His theoretical intervention was twofold: it belied dominant economic thinking, first, by demonstrating that actually existing markets are "embedded" (2001 [1944]: 130) in society and, second, in showing how economic theory *itself* can affect societally embedded markets in ways that have dramatic sociopolitical implications. Polanyi's book demonstrated the tremendous social disruption that resulted from this state-directed project of creating land and labor markets in nineteenth-century England. In what he calls a "double movement," he shows how these social dislocations animated a political "countermovement" that curtailed the expansion and operation of England's newly created markets. While he shows the operation of a market economy to be a result of deliberate state action, this political response to the project of disembedding markets from society and the subsequent restrictions on the implementation of laissez-faire economic theory is characterized as spontaneous. The utopian project to mold actual economies in the image of free-market theory, Polanyi (2001 [1944]: 136) argued, "attacked the fabric of society" and thus gave rise to fierce resistance to this impossible project.

With a global resurgence of neoclassical economic thought since the 1970s animating a wave of popular and scholarly interest in the free market—both as an ideology and a political project—Polanyi's lessons are as timely as ever. Scholars have adopted the term *neoliberalism* to refer (on the one hand) to the idea that, when left to their own devices, markets are efficient, self-correcting, and fair in the way they allocate resources, as well as (on the other hand) to the multiplicity of policies and programs that invoke the efficient-market idea as a legitimating rationale. Of course a theory about how the market mechanism works is not the same thing as concrete policies that cite these ideas as their justification and motivation.[18] The necessary divide between efficient-market *ideas* and the various policies and practices *animated* by these ideas means as well that there is no necessary correspondence between the two as far as *ends* are concerned. Ethnographers have thus shown how efficient-market logics have been put to work by politicians and policymakers in trying to address *all manner* of social and political problems, from environmental pollution to political deadlock (e.g., Collier 2011). In his discussion of infrastructure in post-Soviet Russia, for instance, Collier (2011: 25–26) shows how the market logic of individual "calculative choice" was deployed by Russian planners "in a way that could be accommodated to the *substantive* orientations of universal need fulfillment." "We should not move too quickly," Collier cautions, "from the identification of neoliberalism with a microeconomic critique and programming to any assumption about the formations of government that neoliberal reform shapes."[19] Indeed the globally ascendant form of political rationality that emerged at the end of the twentieth century was less a call to *liberate* market relations "from their social shackles" (Rose 1999: 141) than a call to *restructure* techniques of governance such that social goals are pursued via market mechanisms—through the aggregation of calculated, interest-maximizing choices of individuals and firms.

In liberalization-era Mumbai the efficient-market idea found a receptive audience among an odd-bedfellows coalition of urban development planners, international experts, populist politicians, landowners, and real estate developers who saw in "the market" a seemingly magical solution to a long-standing and intractable urban problem: how to reconcile sky-high urban land values with the need to acquire land for social purposes like infrastructure, amenities, or public housing. While this puzzle had stumped a generation of urban planners, in the 1990s the problem took on particular salience, animating a broad political coalition of actors united by the imperative to transform Mumbai into a "world-class city." As a matter of national importance, Mumbai's transformation became a cause célèbre that would see policy experts, private-sector interests, and popular politics join hands to put market logic to work in pursuit of Mumbai's makeover. A new set of regulatory instruments institutionalized in conjunction with the country-level liberalizing reforms of 1991 and expanded in a series of amendments over the following two decades (the subject of chapter 2) attempted to resolve Mumbai's perennial land puzzle by creating a market in urban development rights. The new rules created incentives for private-sector actors (landowners and developers) to hand over land and build amenities for social purposes by offering compensation not *monetarily* but *in kind*—with market-responsive rights to develop above and beyond heights and densities allowed by the city's development plan. While markets for development rights of course exist in other cities (e.g., New York), the way and extent to which liberalization-era Mumbai has operationalized this market mechanism may well be globally unprecedented;[20] in what one centrally involved planner ruefully recalled as "our special innovation,"[21] Mumbai's liberalization-era planning regime effectively severed the right to build from land itself.

In order to make sense of how liberalization-era Mumbai's marketization of urban development rights has affected the city's water infrastructures, we must briefly return to the Polanyian question of what markets do and how they are made. Markets work as a "coordination device" (Guesnerie 1996, quoted in Callon 1998: 3), resolving conflicts over terms of exchange. To create a market in something, that something must first be reconceptualized as an abstract thing—a commodity—so that a price for such things can be agreed upon.[22] To describe something as a commodity is thus not to identify any particular *quality* of that thing that distinguishes it from other, noncommodity things but rather to identify a particular *situation* of exchangeability.[23] Creating this kind of exchange requires measuring some object's value vis-à-vis the value of other objects.

Calculating something's exchange value is complicated by the fact that objects of exchange are not *really* abstract objects but are invariably "caught up in a network of relations, in a flow of intermediaries which circulate, connect, link and reconstitute identities" (Callon 1998: 17). The process of reckoning involved in the creation of a commodity situation therefore involves a process of systematically sorting through these dense networks of relations within which any particular actually existing thing exists. While some properties, attachments, and associations will be included within the ambit of calculation of some object's exchange value, others will not make the cut. The process of adjudicating which properties and relations will be taken into account in valuation and which will not is accomplished by means of rules, laws, and accounting procedures—acts of measurement that define the boundaries of the commodity situation of any particular thing. The process of conceptual cutting off and inclusion—of extricating objects from the dense networks of sociocultural, political, and material relations in which they are in actuality embedded—allows for the possibility of calculation. It is this process of "framing" (18) that sits at the heart of marketized exchange.

The marketization of development rights in world-class-era Mumbai commoditized urban development rights by conceptually unbundling rights to build from the materialities of the city; development rights, as one planner put it, were "brought out of thin air, not related to land in any fixed proportion" (Phatak 2007: 47). The market-driven, rapidly changing form of Mumbai's built space has thus been unbundled from the planning trajectories and regulations governing the city's land-bound water infrastructures.

Notwithstanding the conceptual cutting off of marketized things (i.e., development rights) from the material, social, and political worlds in which they are in actuality embedded (i.e., land and land-based infrastructures), the relational ties that are formally excluded from market framing do not, of course, simply disappear. The problem is well understood by mainstream economics, where the afterlives of these relational ties are referred to as "externalities." A common example of market externality is industrial pollution: when toxic waste discharged by a manufacturing plant into a local river affects the health of local residents, these health costs—which were not taken into account when setting the price of the industrial good—would be considered market externalities. Similarly in cities the marketization of built space can have all sorts of infrastructural externalities that are well understood by urban planners the world over: the construction of a tall residential tower on a narrow road in a prime neighborhood, for instance, might lead to many hours wasted by third-party actors in traffic snarls—costs that were not factored into the market price of a new flat in the big building.[24] The marketization of development rights means that logics animating the production of Mumbai's built space have been severed from those governing its water infrastructures. The market in development rights, in other words, is remaking the face of Mumbai without consulting the pipes.

Life in the city is of course not possible without water; notwithstanding the institutional unbundling of the city's built space (where people live and work) from its water pipes, the political and bodily exigencies of life in the city mean that Mumbai's businesses, residents, and industries *do* get water—in some way or another—every single day. In this context the interesting question becomes that of access: How *does* the growing and globalizing city of Mumbai meet its daily water needs? What is at stake, and who are the stakeholders in various configurations of flow and access? What kinds of politics, power relations, modes of governance, and practices of citizenship are produced, animated, or constrained by these configurations? In this book I show that what flows or does not flow out of this or that pipe depends on highly dynamic intersections among the multiple regimes of knowledge and authority that water inhabits, as well as the ways flows are configured and reconfigured across space and over time. Making water flow requires continuous and often contentious efforts to direct and redirect flows across the rapidly changing built space of the city. As one astute observer quipped when I asked why her tap had gone dry, "Look, when water comes, it's because of politics, and when water doesn't come, it's because of politics."

Pipe Politics

What can we learn from studying infrastructure? What analytical leverage does an infrastructural perspective allow? Infrastructures are dualistic, Larkin (2013) notes; they are not only things in themselves but are also relations among things. When doing their relational work, the properties of infrastructures as things in themselves can become invisible, hiding behind the associations that they mediate in a disappearing act that social scientists sometimes call "black boxing" (Latour 1999: 183). For instance the relationship between people and water in Mumbai might be said to be mediated by material things (pipes, trucks, valves, pumps) and forms of knowledge (maps, work tenders, hydraulic models, news reports), as well as less tangible, larger-scale forces (financial instruments or interest rates). Such things appear significant only insofar as they enable or impede a relationship between people and water, and so they tend to be overlooked until moments of breakdown or blockage. It is when water stops flowing that the pipes *themselves* come into focus. At these moments attention is pulled upstream and underground, toward maps and models and toward power and politics. It is at such times that relationships that might have been taken for granted, naturalized, are revealed instead to be rather "precarious achievements" (Graham 2009: 10). Moments or locations of interruption work as a methodological entryway to the sociopolitical and material forces underpinning otherwise taken-for-granted urban processes and geographies—a means by which to explore the technologies, materialities, and politics that infuse everyday life in the city.

While promising insight into these multiple layers of interaction and mediation, thinking about infrastructure relationally can also be mystifying, as it blurs the boundaries of what might "count" as infrastructure. For instance, while pipes, pumps, and valves are of course part of the assemblage that connects people and water,[25] water itself is what allows pipes, pumps, and valves to work in this particular way: a pipe will not convey just any water, for instance, but requires water of a certain pressure in order to perform its transporting job. Here a particular *property* of water—pressure—becomes part of water's infrastructure. A machine to produce water pressure, a suction pump for instance, might for this purpose be introduced into water's infrastructural ambit, but then of course without water to prime it, a suction pump will not coax water from the end of a pipe at all but might instead blow up—a situation that, needless to say, might require water to remedy. Certain properties of water thus become part of water's infrastructure.

Indeed infrastructures are not only relational but are also things with lives of their own. The materiality of infrastructural objects can have affective dimensions, producing "sensorial and political experience" (Larkin 2013: 12). Infrastructural things can be highly symbolic: the construction of airports, bridges, and even water pipes can be animated by logics that intersect only tangentially with official, stated purposes. In contemporary Mumbai large-scale infrastructural projects (both highly visible ones like bridges and airports and less charismatic ones like water pipes) are often conceived (and indeed admittedly so) first and foremost as a way to signal and perform the city's world-class character to potential investors. Similarly (as we see in chapter 7) a water distribution main laid with much pomp and show by a politician in the run-up to an election might work as much to demonstrate a political aspirant's capacity to mobilize the apparatus of the state as it does to improve water supply to a neighborhood. Moreover while the symbolic and material lives of infrastructures as *things in themselves* might be indifferent to infrastructure's *mediating* role (i.e., to connect water with people), activity related to infrastructure's *affective* register will invariably have hydraulic implications, impacting (often inadvertently) the relationship between people and water. An account of how water is made to flow through Mumbai will thus need to consider not only (on the one hand) the networks of material, technological, and ideological interactions that mediate relations between people and water, or (on the other) the affective dimensions of infrastructures, but also how these material and symbolic lives interact in sometimes complementary and sometimes contradictory ways.

These multiple dimensions make water infrastructures unwieldy and extremely porous, their meanings and operations constantly exceeding the designs and hopes of any particular author. Mumbai's water infrastructures animate and inhabit manifold and layered regimes of knowledge and authority that are put to work in producing flows. These networks operate within three registers: first, the abstract logics of planning, modeling, regulation, finance, and management; second, the real-time material processes and activities that constitute the everyday work of making (or trying to make) water flow; and third, a semeiotic register in which water and its infrastructures are performative of power, knowledge, and authority.[26] The ineluctable materiality of water infrastructures means that the various registers fold in on one another: hydraulic *spectacles* are, for example, necessarily underwritten by the very real and material work of making water *actually* appear. By the same token the material exigencies of bodily hydration or of hydraulic spectacle destabilize and challenge abstract, ideological domains of planning and regulation.

This book focuses on *water* with attention to the specificities of the material itself.[27] Water is a medium with which to explore material and symbolic dimensions of political contestation at the intersection of large-scale infrastructural dynamics (flows of finance, technological expertise, global management discourses) and intimate forms of knowledge, power, and authority. Water is extremely heavy and unwieldy, extraordinarily time consuming and expensive to move; once it has reached a resting point—once gravity has done its work—water tends not to go very far without significant financial, technological, and political investment. By the same token water's materiality means that actually *getting* it has necessarily spatial and temporal dimensions. Attending to water's materiality thus invites a broader conceptualization of power and politics than suggested by neo-Marxian formulations (where power is a structurally given resource wielded in the interests of capitalist elites), attending instead to how power and identity are materially produced, contested, drawn and redrawn through space and across time.

While all infrastructures mediate and interact with spatiotemporal relationships and divides, water has physical properties that make it particularly good to think with: water has a tendency to flow downhill, thereby informing relationships not only among localities at higher and lower elevations but between upstream and downstream points of access on particular pipes; water has a propensity to be siphoned off and to disappear without a trace, giving rise to rumor and speculation over the paths along which water may or may not flow; water has a capacity to distribute pathogens and refuses to respect social boundaries, meaning that water not only produces social divides but bleeds across them in complex ways; water requires bulky, high-cost, labor-intensive transport infrastructure, and as a result network extensions are often fraught with enormously time-consuming processes resulting in material configurations that can prove somewhat "obdurate" (Bijker 2007: 122) once in place; water's weighty infrastructures provide a lens into the importance of time and space, as pipes sink deep into swampy ground (thereby challenging gravity-fed flows, as we see in chapters 4 and 5), while remaining buoyant as they pass through bedrock-supported neighborhoods (chapter 6); relatedly since water is a necessary and time-sensitive substance (no one survives long without it), access practices are informed not only by exigencies of hydraulics, finance, or practicality but by strategies and socialities of risk mitigation (chapter 6); finally networks of water pipes and below-ground flows (as opposed to, say, transport infrastructures) are often hidden from view, buried under the epidermis of the city, illegible and opaque and thereby pregnant with possibility (chapters 6 and 7).

A pipe-political approach to urban water is first and foremost a matter of method, one that requires us to both follow the water (Deleuze and Guattari 2004) across space and through time and to follow the inquiries of the actors we encounter along the way (Farias 2011).[28] The material, place-specific, and meaning-laden qualities of water and its infrastructures invite (even require) a holistic, ethnographically grounded research approach (Orlove and Caton 2010). The research for this book was carried out over eighteen months, focusing on a geographically contiguous region of Mumbai—the M-East Ward—which is simultaneously an administrative, electoral,[29] and a *hydraulic* unit: the neighborhoods, businesses, and industries of M-East are supplied water from a single local reservoir. Working with this unit of analysis allows for an exploration of hydraulic relations between different locations: who or what is upstream or downstream from whom, for instance, on a particular distribution main. Accounts and insights emerged from myriad social, political, and geographic positions within the water distribution network, each location functioning as a particular lens through which broader political and social processes are explored. The narrative builds on insights gathered at the neighborhood level (ethnographic research and oral histories with individual families and businesses, local plumbers and water vendors, neighborhood leaders and political aspirants), at a sociotechnical level (involving rounds with water department engineering staff, municipal valve operators, tanker drivers, licensed plumbers, and meter readers), at an institutional and more explicitly political level (interviews with senior-level water engineers, state ministers and legislators, technical experts, and international consultants and lenders), as well as from textual analysis (of current and archival policy documents, development plans, project reports, and maps). Working with such a broad range of sources allows

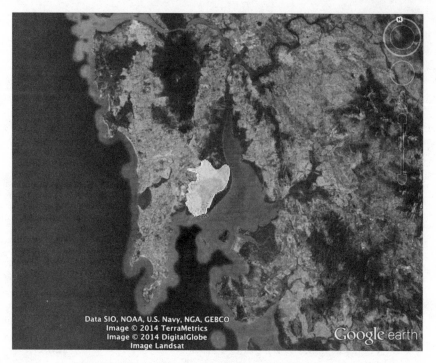

FIGURE I.1. Mumbai's M-East Ward. Google Earth: Data SIO, NOAA, U.S. Navy, NGA, GEBCO. Image ©2014 TerraMetrics, Image © 2014 DigitalGlobe, Image Landsat.

for an account of the city that is both ethnographically rich (in both thickness and duration) while also historically grounded—not only attending to contemporary politics of water but also providing insight into how the pipes came to be so unpredictable in the first place.

Organization

The book begins with the arrival in India of an internationally mobile discourse extolling "the market" as the best and most efficient allocator of resources and provider of urban services. The opening chapter traces the career of this idea in Mumbai, revealing a surprising history of how the water department's century-old system of careful mapmaking and record keeping was abandoned—a decline in which the debates over privatization are shown to have themselves been deeply implicated. Having undermined the water department's ability to do its job, this ideologically driven reform agenda (pushed by Mumbai's world-class-city boosters) then sought to render the distribution network knowable—its market risks calculable—as per the exigencies of a privatization contract. In an effort to produce these kinds of data, a series of high-tech (and labor-saving) calculative tools were introduced into Mumbai's infrastructural ambit. This knowledge-production project, however, was fundamentally incoherent; the new measurement tools were simply incommensurable with the material and technological specificities of Mumbai's actually existing, historically inscribed water infrastructures. New, mechanized devices thus produced a steady stream of discordant (even meaningless) data, while the department's long-established, human-centered systems of mapping, monitoring, and recording fell into decline. The privatization debates thus presided over the decimation of the department's informational infrastructures—a dynamic that, in an ironic twist, would derail a privatization initiative when it finally arrived. While the two-decade arc of debate over the benefits and pitfalls of privatization would conclude with Mumbai's water infrastructures squarely in the public domain, the chapter shows how market logic unmapped Mumbai's water distribution network.[30]

Chapter 2 turns to the political project to transform Mumbai into an investment-friendly world-class city by using market mechanisms to reconfigure the built spaces and upgrade its infrastructures. The market presented a utopian solution to long-standing and intractable political struggles over land—struggles in which the city's landowners, policymakers, and popular politicians had locked horns at least since independence. Animated by the idea that these deeply political conflicts could simply (and indeed quite profitably) be adjudicated by the market, Mumbai's liberalization-era policymakers approved a set of new regulatory tools, thereby creating a market in urban development rights. The chapter analyzes how this market actually works—how it has unmoored the geographies and economies of the city's built space from its material infrastructures both theoretically (in order to create the market) and in practice (as the market-fueled built space of the city is rapidly reconfigured). Animated by the high-risk volatilities and high-return possibilities of real estate, Mumbai's marketization of urban development resulted in a temporal and material mismatch between its above-ground built space and its below-ground pipes, flows, and pressures.

While the disjuncture between the city's built form and its water pipes seems to suggest that the world-class city would also be a *dry* city, this is not the case; the new malls, gated communities, shimmering office towers, and glittering hotels do, generally speaking, get water. The imperative to make water available to the world-class city—notwithstanding the linear constraints of time and the material constraints of pipes—has, in the words of department engineers, thrown "the entire infrastructure in a shambles." Chapter 3 is concerned with "the shambles": the technologies, hydrologies, and imaginaries that work to make (or attempt to make) water available to the rapidly changing space of the city notwithstanding the materialities of the pipes.

Chapter 4 shows how the market in development rights—what Mumbai's water engineers disdainfully refer to as "the slum and building industry"—is tied up with the historically layered and materially inscribed political landscapes within which the city's working classes have made claims to urban land and resources. The narrative follows the material, ideological, and legal transformation of a municipal housing colony, a neighborhood called Shivajinagar-Bainganwadi, into a "slum" that could be surveyed for redevelopment.[31] The reimagining of Shivajinagar-Bainganwadi as a slum was itself the result of the politically mediated deterioration and criminalization of its water infrastructure in the context of liberalization-era policy shifts, which position the unplanned, illegal or informal slum as the self-evident conceptual counterpoint to the planned, formal, world-class city. Shivajinagar-Bainganwadi's story reveals the deeply political and highly unstable nature of the world-class/slum binary and demonstrates the shifting political and economic stakes imbued in these categories.

The second half of the book turns ethnographic attention to the everyday work of making water flow and to the sociopolitical and material landscapes that flows of water both produce and inhabit. Chapter 5 describes the everyday infrastructural practices devoted to making water flow and hedging the ever-present risk of breakdown. These practices in turn give rise to whole landscapes of rumor, speculation, and stealth—on pipe locations, on water pressures, and on the timings and operations of valves as well as on the networks of power and influence that underpin these volatile flows, appearances, and disappearances of water. Various kinds of knowledge about water are attained or hidden, leveraged or blocked through elaborate and power-laden activities of knowledge exchange. The opacities that infuse the distribution system animate constantly shifting sociopolitical and relational networks and fuel practices of "knowledge brokering." Given the inexorable necessity of water—everyday access being quite literally a matter of survival—water knowledge is power. And controlling the dispersed networks by which that knowledge is accessed and mobilized become the stakes over which thus empowered political players battle.

Despite water engineers' best attempts to explain water trouble as the result of technical difficulties (such as airlock), natural disasters (such as insufficient rains), or shortages (increasing demand from population growth), dry taps are overwhelmingly described—in private conversations, in popular discourse, and in media narratives—as the result of an all-knowing, all-powerful state that is riddled with corruption. Notwithstanding the fragmentation of knowledge and hazy legalities that department engineers themselves must navigate in providing water to the rapidly changing city, Mumbai residents remain convinced that the water department possesses complete knowledge of and exercises precise control over the water distribution system. Dry taps are thus assumed to be the deliberate designs of wayward officials. Chapter 6 demonstrates how everyday experiences of the ever more erratic distribution system are effectively rendered comprehensible largely through these ever more fantastic ideas about corruption.

Chapter 7 outlines the relationship between water infrastructure and political authority in Mumbai. The chapter begins with a cholera outbreak in the slum neighborhood of Rafique Nagar in the run-up to the 2009 parliamentary elections, focusing on the response of the area's elected councilor, a man named Patil.[32] Politicians like Patil face a dilemma: whatever flows or does not flow out of his area's pipes will be interpreted as a sign of power and authority over the omniscient and corrupt state apparatus—either his own authority or someone else's. Yet given the intractability of the distribution system, the volatile discourses of legality that permeate water supply especially to slums as well as the very real hydraulic challenges of actually convincing pipes to produce water, evidencing this kind of material authority is exceedingly complex and politically risky. Given that no one is quite sure who or what makes the water come, but everyone knows that it comes "because of politics," much effort was made by local-level knowledge brokers (who tend to become party workers at election times) to provide concrete (or rather aqueous) evidence of this or that political party's material sovereignty over the pipes. As elections are fought and won or lost largely on the strength of local knowledge networks, those who can demonstrate command of hydraulic knowledge become—through the electoral process—politically powerful players in the city. While the project to transform Mumbai into a world-class city has thus presided over what the water department describes as hydraulic "chaos," the disembedding and reconfiguring of infrastructural knowledge has rescaled political authority in the city. Pipe politics is producing urban forms and opening up possible futures that, as we see in the conclusion, diverge quite starkly from those envisioned by a world-class urban imaginary.

ONE

"WE GOT STUCK IN BETWEEN"

Unmapping the Distribution Network

Hunting for Maps

At the outset of my research in Mumbai, getting my hands on the water department's official maps of the distribution network seemed the most sensible way to begin; once I had maps, I reasoned, I could tack them up on my walls and refer to them as I proceeded. I envisioned pressing colorful, meaning-laden pushpins into these maps, whose patterns would reveal to me important geographies of flow and access and blockage. But getting hold of the kind of maps I had in mind proved to be somewhat less straightforward than I had anticipated. While I had imagined that procuring maps would be a jumping-off point in my exploration, instead the processes of locating, gaining access to, and attempting to make sense of various maps of Mumbai's water supply network became themselves fertile and generative research sites.

Within the first months of my arrival in Mumbai, my repeated requests for maps from the Mumbai Municipal Corporation's Hydraulic Engineering Department (the water department) produced a stack of five or six enormous blueprints. I collected my coveted stack from the department's head office downtown one sweaty afternoon in November 2008. Pleased with my acquisition, which seemed to signal the real beginning of my research, I loaded the carefully folded treasures into a large tote bag and jealously guarded them close to my chest throughout the hour-long, bone-jarring ride back to the eastern suburbs in the ladies-only compartment of the Mumbai local train, while business-women and fisherwomen—pressed against one another in the sticky, angular embrace of rush hour—sighed their annoyance at my bulky bag. At home my landlord and downstairs neighbor, Dilip, who had taken a keen interest in my somewhat unconventional but possibly very useful network of contacts inside the Municipal Corporation, joined me for the initial unfurling on the floor of my apartment. We crawled around excitedly on the smudgy blueness, identi-fying familiar landmarks—There's the slaughterhouse! There's the Atomic Re-search Center!—but after a few minutes the thrill of recognizing things wore off as it became apparent that my maps did not correspond in some very sig-nificant ways to what I had seen (and what Google Earth imagery suggests) on the ground in M-East. The cluster of seven-story Slum Rehabilitation buildings that I had visited the day before was represented on the blueprint as an open expanse labeled "bone factory" (later I learned that there used to be a bone-grinding facility on the site, but it had been closed for over twenty-five years); a neat row of small squares signaling residential blocks and a larger square labeled "recreation ground" trespassed in the space on my blueprint where the all too real Deonar dumping ground should have been depicted; the site of a well-established, three-decades-old working-class residential neighborhood was identified on the western half as a "playground," and on the eastern half as, somewhat cryptically, "Nazara Godown."[1] Perhaps most puzzling were the stretches of road depicted on the blueprint that had absolutely no counterparts on the ground.

Conversations with senior engineers over the following weeks and months offered an explanation for these confounding noncorrespondences: the blue-prints I was given were not "maps" in what I had unthinkingly taken to be a shared or conventional understanding of that idea—a visual representation of things that might be presumed to actually exist in the world.[2] Rather, it was ex-plained to me, the blueprints are a variety of *plan*. The water department's of-ficial procedure for keeping track of the city's ever-expanding network of pipes and valves, I was told, is to continually draw them onto the city's development plan sheets. The blueprints from M-East that I was given (which, needless to say, are the most recent available) were dated between 1976 and 1980, meaning that they are copies of the 1967 Development Plan. These blueprints, in other words, are representations not of any present or past arrangement of things in

the plan

the world; rather they are historically imagined possible futures onto which information about the present city is supposed to be depicted.

I say *supposed to be* depicted because the water department abandoned these practices sometime in the 1980s. Until the mid-1980s the water department had a functional survey section whose sole responsibility was to "update the plans" when a new water main was commissioned. There was a "set rule," a retired senior engineer named Kulkarni explained to me, that any time a new water main was laid, the local ward office would tell the survey department, who would send someone to go and survey the new line—to actually go to the site and see, "with their own eyes," the physical location of the new pipe. Members of the survey section known as "tracers" would then draw the new main onto the plan. This practice, Kulkarni explained, was inherited from British engineers, who used to keep track of water mains on colonial-era "survey sheets." These older, colonial-era sheets differed from the current development plan sheets in three important ways: First, colonial-era survey sheets were much more detailed—approximately eighty-two times larger in scale than the present-era plans. The sheet I had, which was labeled "surveyed in 1919; corrected up to 1927," even depicts trees, with symbols differentiating coconut from palm. Second, the colonial-era sheets existed only for the Island City; since the suburbs were annexed only in the 1950s, the Municipal Corporation has no survey sheets for suburban areas like M-East Ward (see figure 1.1). Indeed the only existing survey for the area now comprising the M-East Ward is the 1833 land revenue survey, which shows the boundaries of area *gaonthans* (agricultural settlements) and *koliwadas* (fishing villages). Third, and perhaps most important, unlike survey sheets, which profess to visually represent things presumed to actually exist in the world, development plan sheets depict a not yet realized arrangement of space in an imagined *future*. Senior engineers would become animated recalling how they had overseen the laying of new distribution mains along the routes of proposed "DP Roads" (development plan roads) that were never constructed (or sometimes that were constructed with dimensions unrelated to those indicated on the plan). One engineer described his attempt to later access one such pipe, the laying of which he had supervised in the mid-1980s, only to find that a high-rise residential complex had been constructed in place of the road.

The Brihanmumbai Municipal Corporation's (BMC) survey and tracing system seems to have been at least formally operational until the early 1990s. Each ward had a fitting book (see figure 1.2) into which data about new mains were to be entered: the name of the street or neighborhood where the new main was

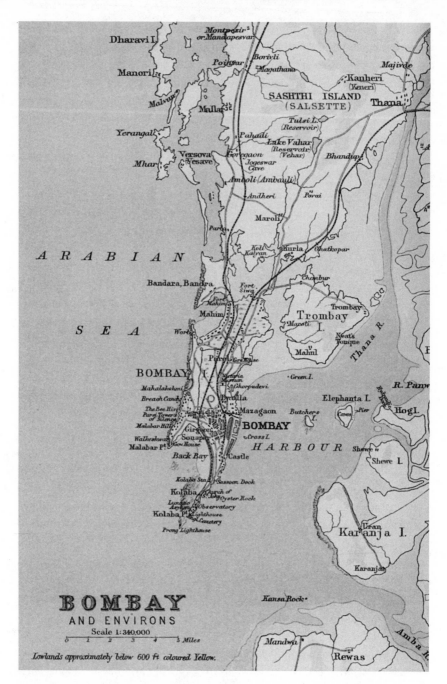

FIGURE 1.1. Bombay Island City, Trombay Island, and Salsette Island, 1893. J. G. Bartholomew, Archibald Constable, and Company, *Constable's Hand Atlas of India*, 1893 edition.

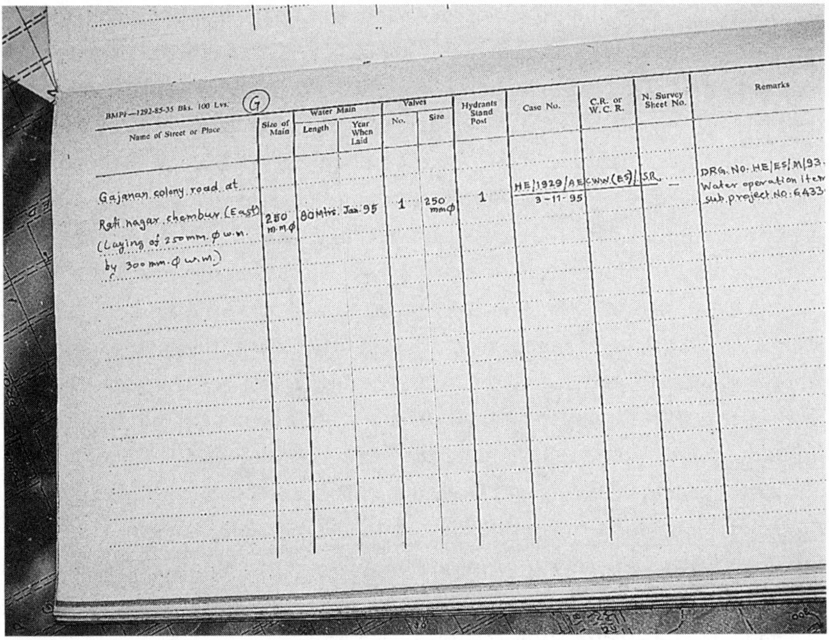

BMPJ—1292-85-35 Bkl. 100 Lvs. (G) Name of Street or Place	Size of Main	Water Main Length	Year When Laid	Valves No.	Size	Hydrants Stand Post	Case No.	C.R. or W.C.R.	N. Survey Sheet No.	Remarks
Gajanan colony road at Rafi nagar, chembur (East) (Laying of 250 mm. ⌀ w.m. by 300 mm. ⌀ w.m.)	250 mm ⌀	80 Mtrs.	Jan. 95	1	250 mm⌀	1	HE/1929/AE 3-11-95	CWW(E9)	SR.	DRG. NO. HE/ES/M/93. Water operation item sub project No. 6433

FIGURE 1.2. M-East Ward logbook. Courtesy of Municipal Corporation of Greater Mumbai, Department of Hydraulic Engineering. Photo by author.

laid; the diameter and length of the main; the number and size of any valves controlling water pressure, timing, and flow into the main; the number of public outlets (standpipes or hydrants) that would be fed by the new main; the case number of the new main; the number of the survey sheet onto which the new main would be drawn; and information about the funding source for the new main. The current M-East Ward's logbook that I was shown in 2010, however, had only one entry: a listing from 1995. The evidence and memory of this now defunct system of recording and updating information about the water supply network thus presents a needed corrective to much current writing about urban infrastructure in the Global South—which tends to depict cities like Mumbai as somewhat timeless in their infrastructural dysfunction—and also a puzzle: Why did the Mumbai water department stop mapping its work?

The decline of formal mapping practices, this chapter shows, intersected in the 1980s and 1990s with a highly mobile, globally empowered development policy discourse extolling market logics and encouraging the involvement of private-sector actors in municipal services while condemning government-run systems as inherently corrupt and inefficient—ideological battles that would effectively colonize the political and discursive space around water-related questions for nearly two decades. While Mumbai would emerge from the decades of debate over privatization with water infrastructures still squarely in the hands of the municipal bureaucracy, the years of anticipation and speculation on the seemingly inevitable forces of privatization have nonetheless had serious and lasting hydraulic effects, particularly in the havoc wreaked on the department's informational infrastructures. In step with a globally ascendant audit culture hoping to render market risks knowable and quantifiable (as per the exigencies of private-sector contracts) and in response to an increasingly acute shortage of manpower, the water department adopted a series of labor-saving tools and calculative technologies. Yet these new measurement instruments were largely incommensurable with the material and technological particularities of the city's water infrastructures; the data-collection tools ultimately generated a constant stream of meaningless facts and figures. With the department's long-institutionalized, human knowledge–centered informational infrastructures (of surveying and mapping pipes and of monitoring and auditing pressures) falling into disuse, the calculative fantasy of market management effectively unmapped Mumbai's water infrastructures.

Waiting for Privatization

Beginning in the 1980s concerns about water access in the world's growing and globalizing cities were increasingly refracted through the lens of the privatization debates. Official discourses of various international lending institutions increasingly sidelined conceptions of water provision as a state-provided service in favor of a notion of the urban resident as a consumer who makes individually reasoned, calculated choices regarding "infrastructural goods." After water was famously declared "an economic good" at the 1992 United Nations International Conference on Water and the Environment in Dublin, the notion that the full "costs" of water provision should be recovered from consumers came to infuse international debates on water management. "Water has an economic value," the World Meteorological Organization proclaimed in a statement released at the conference's conclusion, "and should be recognized as an economic good."[3] With international lending and aid organizations (particularly the World Bank) increasingly advocating marketized conceptions of water and recommending private-sector involvement in its management as a way to extend and rationalize services (and to stem the alleged inefficiency of public utilities),[4] the Dublin Conference both reflected and sparked global debates on the most appropriate roles and responsibilities of states and markets in allocating and distributing water.

Privatization and *marketization* are of course not the same thing. Marketization (as outlined in some detail in the introduction) describes a process of framing something as a commodity as well as the management principles and logics animating commodity framing.[5] Privatization, on the other hand, refers simply to *who* provides water and may or may not involve various elements of marketization. Moreover privatization can describe a huge variety of legal-contractual agreements between governments and private actors; the content, terms, and duration of contracts described by the term *privatization* can vary dramatically, from an agreement in which the private company is granted short-term responsibility and authority over aspects of operations and maintenance, to the complete divestiture of the utility, including sale of the asset or resource to be provided. In between are a range of options, which can involve many different kinds of risk- and investment-sharing arrangements; the commonly heard term *public-private partnership* refers to the wide range of possible arrangements falling short of complete divestiture. Between the 1980s and the first decade of the twenty-first century the policy framework advocated by World Bank consultants shifted focus somewhat, from the privatization question of *who* provides water (state institutions or private sector actors) to the rationality underpinning its delivery: from a "state-hydraulic" (Bakker 2005: 546) model of infrastructural development planning to a logic of marketization (Bakker 2005, 2010; see also Rose 1999). During these interim years, however, while the theoretical, political, and material-hydraulic stakes of these multidimensional debates were being fought (both in pipes and on paper), cities across the globe were transformed into high-stakes laboratories of policy experimentation.

The multidimensional conceptual shifts in international policy discourse set the stage for a handful of high-profile privatization debacles; in 1999, for instance, the signing of a forty-year concessional contract for municipal water operations in the Bolivian city of Cochabamba led to spectacular price hikes when the U.S. corporate consortium Bechtel attempted to implement an ideologically driven full-cost pricing scheme.[6] Bolivians poured into the streets to protest the contract, which was reviled not only for its price increases but for allowing the contractor to collect charges even on rainwater harvested in local wells and for going so far in protecting corporate interests and shielding the company from financial risk as to give Bechtel the right to actually seize the property of delinquent consumers (Finnegan 2002). The dramatic popular uprisings in the face of brutal police and military violence against the demonstrators led the Bolivian government to withdraw the contract and became a powerful symbol and inspiration for the growing ranks of antiprivatization activists worldwide.[7]

By the time the Delhi Jal Board, the capital city's water utility, approached the World Bank for a loan in 2002 to fund a citywide water audit to be used in the writing of an operation and maintenance contract, activists were thus primed for battle. One prominent Indian nongovernmental organization, headed by the world-renowned environmental activist and writer Vandana Shiva, charged, for example:

> The various policies of the World Bank related to water have already created acute water shortage throughout the country. Today, bowing again to World Bank and WTO [World Trade Organization] pressures, the government is rushing to privatize water and hand over its ownership to giant corporations. Privatization of water will totally bypass people's needs, sustainability and equity in the use of water. The government is signing away the water rights of the people to giant MNCs [multinational corporations] like Coca Cola, Pepsi, Monsanto, Mitsubishi, Hyundai, Suez, and Vivendi. (quoted in Navdanya 2011)

Using the newly implemented Right to Information Act, Indian antiprivatization activists acquired thousands of pages of documentation pertaining to ongoing negotiations between the Delhi Jal Board and the World Bank that revealed egregious irregularities in the bidding process (Singh 2006). The media spectacle that ensued led to the withdrawal of the Delhi government's loan application, and activist organizations celebrated the shelving of the restructuring project as a victory for democracy (Bhaduri 2005).

Meanwhile in Bombay international ideological trends since the 1980s had fueled a wave of discussion and speculation on how and whether to increase private-sector involvement in urban water distribution, a set of conjectures that coincided in India with national-level debates over pension reform. According to rules framed at the time of India's independence in 1947, jobs within the Bombay Municipal Corporation are pensionable according to the central government's pension scheme. In the 1980s, however, in response to increasing life expectancy among the laboring classes, the government of India began to push for amendments to pension laws—an effort that met with overwhelming political opposition, due at least in part to the enormous size of the public sector. In the 1980s senior sources inside the Corporation recalled, the BMC's recruitment office was instructed by Delhi not to fill vacant engineering and laborer posts unless absolutely necessary.[8] As a former additional municipal commissioner explained to me, "We were thinking to outsource these activities, so the municipal commissioner made a unilateral decision to ban the recruitment of staff." He continued, "If it's going to go private, and we've hired all these people, we're going to be stuck paying pensions until they die."

It was in this context that, in 1997, World Bank officials in Delhi informed the Bombay Municipal Corporation of the existence of a surplus from a sanctioned but unutilized loan left over from a sewage department project and suggested that the BMC appoint a "world-renowned consultant" to study the management of the city's water supply. Senior engineers, who welcomed the Bank's suggestion, agreed happily to both the project and to taking over the restructured sewage project loan.[9] Thus in 1997 the international consultancy firm M/s Binnie was appointed to conduct an overall assessment of the municipal water department's management structure.

When the survey results were presented to the department, however, the engineers were dismayed; the survey's main conclusion was that the department was "inefficient" because it was overstaffed. Coming in the wake of the decade-old hiring freeze, the assessment seemed absurd to department engineers, suggesting a lack of rigor and attention to the specificities of Mumbai's water supply and management system: "They looked at our number of connections and said 'You've got to cut back to world norms.' But they didn't take into account the reality of Mumbai!" The assessment, a senior engineer named Gupta explained, was based on a deeply flawed comparison with Singapore:

> [The Bank] told us that Singapore was operating with just two workers per connection, and we've got forty workers per connection. But you can't just look at connections! In Bombay we count one connection per *building*—or sometimes one per *housing society*; in Singapore they have separate connections to each apartment in the building, to each house in a housing society. But if there are seventy flats in a building, then we're doing a lot better than Singapore![10] They could have looked instead at persons employed per million liters of water supply, but they didn't, they only looked at connections. The amount of *water* that we're dealing with suggests a much bigger system—they didn't look at that. Statistics can always be manipulated to say whatever you want. I wrote a letter to the municipal commissioner about this, but he didn't listen. He cut staffing—which is what they wanted to do in the first place. You know what they say: "Before you shoot a dog, call it mad."

While from the 1980s the water department was subsumed into a corporation-wide hiring freeze, by the late 1990s international development experts had provided legitimizing data shoring up the ideological coherence of the staff-reduction policy.

Before You Shoot a Dog

1999 -
2009
population
growth

Between 1999 and 2009 (the decade preceding the period of research) Mumbai's water supply itself grew by 30 percent and the (official) city population by 20 percent. Yet as of 2009 during that same period the department staff did not increase at all; on the contrary, as the existing crop of engineers and laborers reached retirement age, the department staff dwindled. I met with the acting deputy hydraulic engineer (Planning and Control), a man named Gurav, one day when a correspondent for the English-language daily *Times of India* came for a weekly press conference. Gurav, a man in his late fifties with an acerbic wit and the good-humored bluntness of someone who no longer sees a need for euphemism, introduced himself to the reporter, a woman in her midthirties named Mariam whose blue jeans, natural-fiber kurta, and lack of shawl announced her private social views (environmentally and socially progressive) and socioeconomic standing (not poor). Gurav explained to Mariam that he is not *actually* the deputy hydraulic engineer (Planning and Control); he is really only the man *in charge* of the deputy position. His actual position is executive engineer (Central Control), but because of understaffing he is the acting head.[11] "We're supposed to have ten deputy hydraulic engineers in the department," he explained, but since all but one of the positions were empty, in practice each of the remaining nine deputy positions was staffed by an executive "acting as the in-charge." Mariam, stunned, asked for an explanation, and Gurav, amused, obliged: "See, our staffing schedule is based on figures from 1973—the population, the size and lengths of water mains, the number of municipal councilors. . . . The official numbers of engineers and laborers are based on those outdated figures—but even *those* posts aren't all filled." Mariam's request to see a copy of the schedule that Gurav mentioned produced confusion among staffers. When Gurav explained to a young clerk what it was that the reporter was requesting, she looked baffled and replied (in Hindi) that she had heard of no such schedule, a statement Gurav then translated into English for us as "She doesn't know where the schedule is." (The question of whether or not a schedule actually exists is revealed by this exchange as entirely irrelevant; there is in practice no relationship between any official and actual numbers of engineers and laborers.) I left Mariam while she was quizzing Gurav on the relative numbers of "scheduled" and filled posts for a story to be printed over the following days. While I suspect that she wrote the article, it was never printed; the next day's paper instead offered a piece about a burst water main in an upscale neighborhood of central Mumbai—apparently a more newsworthy subject than that of empty posts from a rumored staffing schedule from the 1970s.

Schedule or no schedule, by the 1990s (the heated years of the privatization debates) challenges posed by staffing shortages inspired senior water engineers themselves to look into possibilities for subcontracting various aspects of water distribution. When unionized laborers went on strike in October 2000, senior department engineers were left unable to manage the openings and closings of the city's more than eight hundred daily opened valves, whose operation allows water to flow intermittently through Mumbai's 110 water supply zones.[12] Indeed while BMC engineers repeatedly told me that *inertia* explained the continued functioning of Mumbai's water distribution system in the face of described challenges (understaffing, inadequate maps, outdated equipment, and political malfeasance), Mumbai's taps do not produce water without a stunningly elaborate choreography performed on a twenty-four-hour basis by water department laborers who produce the city's constantly shifting landscape of water pressure and flow by means of the opening and closing of valves.[13] Mumbai's water distribution network, in other words, is not configured to provide continuous pressure but rather works as a "sump and pump" system; the department supplies water on a rotating basis, pressurizing the network first here, then there for a few hours per day. Water that comes out of taps during these times is stored and further distributed as needed for use throughout the day by means of myriad configurations of tanks, pumps, pipes, and hoses.

Since, formally speaking, it is the responsibility not of the laborers but of the deputy hydraulic engineer (Planning and Control) to orchestrate the operations of the city's valves, the laborer strike in 2000 should not have posed such a problem.[14] The official system works like this: Every year, a senior engineer named Sharma tells me, on the first of October (after the monsoon has subsided), the Planning and Control department "takes stock" of the supplies in the lakes that supply Mumbai's pipes. After assessing the capacity of the lakes, the deputy hydraulic engineer (Planning and Control) draws up a plan according to a calculated per-day availability of water. Based on that assessment he decides how much should be drawn from these sources, how much will be filtered every day, how much will be supplied to each of the master balancing reservoirs and to each of the city's twenty-seven service reservoirs, and how much will be released daily from each service reservoir. The implementation of the supply plan is the responsibility of the city's three assistant engineers (Control) who sit in each of Mumbai's regional offices: the Eastern Suburbs,

Western Suburbs, and the Island City. It is thus—formally—the responsibility of the team of engineers under the command of the deputy hydraulic engineer (Planning and Control) to calculate the precise number of valve turns and timings according to which the water will be allowed to flow through the network of pipes.

Yet because of the complexity of the system of valves and the absence of official data on the valves' precise location, size, and number (and even direction) of turns required to open each valve to the required degree, the task of deciding on valve choreography has informally devolved to the ward-level offices. The frequency with which ward-level engineering staff are transferred, however, combined with the general abandonment of documentation practices due to grievous understaffing in the department, has meant that practical knowledge of valve operations resides almost exclusively with each ward's three or four laborers known as *chaviwallas*, or "key men." Indeed while engineers are transferred every few years, laborers generally spend the entirety of their career in a single ward and thus acquire an intimate knowledge of the internal workings and flows of the water distribution system. Thus during the union strike, Sharma recalls, it was "impossible for engineers to operate the system. So many [valves] were broken, and each one had its own characteristics—the diameter, type, operating torque required, number of turns of the key required to open and close, size of its cap and fitting key."[15] Outraged by the water department's failings, angry Mumbaikars stopped traffic on arterial roads, blocked trains from running, besieged the BMC headquarters, and even burned one of the union offices to the ground. Sharma, who joined the water department in the 1960s, described this episode as the "first time in history" that Mumbai's water supply was "in chaos."

After the strike incident in 2000, Sharma explained, "we decided to replace all the valves with identical characteristics" so that the system could be "operated with a machine." The department floated a tender, "but we weren't able to choose the valves that we wanted! We had to give the contract to the lowest bidder who could provide valves that met the standards of the Indian Standard Institute. We had to go with the cheapest—it's public money, after all, so we have to pick the cheapest, and they were no good." In the end eighty valves were replaced; most of them have since failed for various reasons. So the department decided to try to "give the whole valve business to a private operator and then *they* can buy whatever materials they want to keep the system functional."

The strike incident, it seems, finally gave political impetus to the idea of expanding private-sector involvement in the city's water distribution system, a notion that had already been taking shape among senior engineers throughout the late 1990s. As Sharma recalls:

> There were things that were inefficient—things that we couldn't make efficient inside the department. So we said maybe we can have private people do this. For example, because I'm the government, I can't decide what kind of pipe to use. A few years back I wanted to switch to ductile iron pipes; we were using cast iron pipes, not ductile iron.[16] The world over, no one uses cast iron anymore! It cracks too easily. But the problem is that there was only one manufacturer in Mumbai. And I couldn't depend on just one manufacturer, because we'd have a political problem; the current manufacturers of cast iron pipes would accuse the ductile pipe manufacturers of corruption, monopoly, et cetera. So I couldn't do it. The department couldn't make these decisions, but maybe a private operator could.

argument for privatization

The department's interest in restructuring its relationship with the municipal and state governments was inspired not only by this kind of longer-standing problem of political interference in the department's functioning but also, by the late 1990s, by growing challenges posed by chronic understaffing. The shortage of engineers, Gupta explained, meant longer and more challenging work hours for existing staff. Sharma told me that these days "no one wants to work in the [water] department; people only come here if they're forced." By contrast, in his earlier years in the department the senior engineers would select and recruit engineers at the assistant level and then "groom them" over the course of many years. "We would request people early in their careers, back when there was a functional human resources department." These days, Sharma explained, any new staff recruited into the department quickly managed to arrange for transfer into another department. Now that the human resources department has "collapsed, we don't have experts in the department anymore."

"interference"

In response to these challenges, by the late 1990s senior department engineers had begun a series of conversations with the acting additional municipal commissioner (AMC), Subhod Kumar, about the possibility of creating a "water and sewerage board," modeled after the publicly owned Brihanmumbai Electricity Supply and Transport, which would be owned and managed by the Corporation.[17] Sharma told me, "We said [to the AMC], [water] is a specialized job; we wanted to have a separate HR department because then our staff wouldn't be transferrable." While Kumar seems to have been intrigued by the proposal, he was soon transferred, which resulted in the shelving of the

AMC

issue—which, Sharma told me, is still pending with the state government: "It's been ten years, but now no one is bothered [to pursue it]."

now pro- privatization

While the idea to reorganize of the water department as a public undertaking seems to have been put into cold storage, the idea of increasing private-sector involvement was greeted with a much warmer response; the idea of reorganization was effectively crowded out by debates over privatization. In order to investigate private-sector possibilities, in 1999 senior water department engineers formed a "privatization cell" whose four or five members conceived of a pilot study in Mumbai's K-East Ward. The pilot project was, in essence, to be a privatization *experiment* in which various aspects of K-East Ward's water distribution system would be contracted out to a private operator.[18] The privatization cell quickly realized, however, that in order to draw up a contract, they would need new kinds of data about the K-East Ward—data that the department did not currently collect. In order for tender documents to be floated and the scope of the work to be specified, it became necessary to conduct a water audit that would pinpoint precisely how much water was consumed by the residents, industries, and commercial enterprises of K-East.

Audit

Until the late 1980s, a senior engineer named Kulkarni told me, the department used to routinely audit each of 110 isolated water zones. Using a "low-tech" system known as "pito gauging," every six months the department would measure the pressure and quantity of water traveling through certain water mains. The zones were known and defined in those days: it was a "regular program. We had a system for finding out how much water went to the wards with the pito gauges. It was an old technology, but it worked." In the 1990s, however—in the context of the staffing shortage—the water department purchased a set of high-tech, labor-saving flow meters, abandoning the pito-gauging system. "Pito gauging involves manual recording," Kulkarni explained, "whereas in the case of new meters, recording is done automatically and transmitted electronically to the central control station." Such labor-saving devices promised much relief to overworked engineers and laborers. Furthermore "pito gauging is a primitive method and the accuracy in such measurement is limited. New techniques in flow measurements became available where flows can be measured more accurately." However, as Kulkarni explained, the new high-tech meters—largely for technical reasons but also because the new meters were hugely expensive—could not be provided at all of the locations that had previously been monitored by the manual pito-gauging system. Kulkarni shrugged helplessly: "More flow meters are still required to measure the flows in each ward or in each water supply zone." As of 2009 the department still had plans to install more meters, but in the interim years the status of knowledge about water flows became even more fragmented. "The new meters are more accurate, but at this point we know very little about how much water flows into and out of each zone." The department thus long abandoned the practice of regularly auditing the water supplied to the zones. "Honestly, we don't know how much water we give [to each of the 110 water zones] because we have no way of measuring."

In order to carry out the water audit in conjunction with a privatization pilot project in the K-East Ward, the department would need to overcome these informational deficits, not least with significant investments in expensive equipment. Sharma recalled, "We needed four- or six-foot-diameter meters *expensive* that work within 1 percent or 2 percent accuracy—magnetic meters—which *material* are very costly." Since the materials would have to be purchased from overseas, *for* the BMC, which at that time did not have sufficient foreign currency to acquire *pilot* the materials on its own, again contacted World Bank officials in Delhi in 2001.

Department engineers' decision to pursue a pilot project in K-East Ward coincided with the World Bank's International Water Year of 2001. "There were ☆ all sorts of seminars" in Delhi, Kulkarni explained, and various officers of the Indian Administrative Service (IAS) were invited and encouraged to attend.[19] During this period of seminars and workshops touting the virtues of continuous water supply, fancy high-tech equipment, and increased private-sector involvement in management and distribution, World Bank officials in Delhi responded enthusiastically to the Mumbai water department's request for help in funding their experiment in the K-East Ward. But rather than offer the department a loan to purchase the materials it wanted for its in-house audit, Sharma explained, Bank officials in Delhi encouraged the department to engage private-sector experts to draft a management contract for the whole K-East Ward privatization experiment, with the BMC engineers simply deciding the terms of payout. While this was not what they had wanted, Sharma told me, department officials agreed to the plan:

> We suggested [to the Bank officers] that the payment be linked to some kinds of parameters of result. If the contractor achieves some result, then they'll get paid; if they don't, they'll get less. We wanted there to be safeguards—because anyone can manipulate a survey! So I said, "We'll put pressure recorders"—this would be an independent assessment. We would identify points in the network and put automatic meters

there. Then we'd pay according to pressure. Pressure is the only neutral measure—if pressure goes up, it means that leakage has been reduced, and we would pay accordingly. But this idea was shot down by [the World Bank officer]. He said that no one will be interested in such a contract.

The issues at stake in this particular standoff—how to measure leakage reduction given the fragmented state of knowledge about water flows and pressures; who should bear the not insignificant financial and political risks of assuming responsibility for a system characterized by so many unknowns; and the extent to which the sometimes incommensurable imperatives of cost recovery (if not outright profit), consumer rights, and social welfare should dictate patterns of investment in municipal infrastructure—describe the contours of the social and political debates that would preoccupy the department engineers for the following decade.

The standoff was temporarily resolved when, as a result of various improvements in the department's billing system in 2002, the water department no longer needed a loan to pursue its pilot auditing project; by the end of 2002 the department budget was, as Sharma described it, "huge."[20] Department officials thus decided to go ahead with the pilot project in K-East Ward with its *own* funds rather than using World Bank funding to contract a private operator. But the project was stalled once again when the proposal encountered internal opposition, this time from the Municipal Corporation's new additional municipal commissioner, an IAS officer named Kannade. He had just emerged from what one engineer described as "a very bad experience of privatization," having served as CEO of Maharashtra's Electricity Board when a highly politicized contract involving the U.S. multinational Enron resulted in huge losses for the government of Maharashtra in 2001. The World Bank officers in Delhi, not to be deterred, approached Mumbai's Municipal Corporation once again in 2003, this time with a proposal not for a loan but for a grant, earmarked for hiring a consultant to conduct an audit and prepare the water audit contract.[21] Department engineers, who no longer saw any need to involve international experts in their pilot experiment, recalled that at this point the World Bank simply "decided" to fund the privatization initiative. "It was *our* project," Sharma explained, "but we had a huge budget by then, and the Bank had its eye on it."

I told the people at the Bank, "I don't want your grant." But others—the additional municipal commissioner, the government of Maharashtra, the people in Delhi—they were all saying "Take the free money!" The AMC was supposed to go to Delhi to represent our department and get the grant approved, but he said to me, "I don't know anything about the water department, so you go." I didn't want to go. I told him, "But I oppose the grant!" He said, "Personally, you oppose it, but go there representing the Corporation's view." I finally said, "Okay, as long as there are no strings attached, as long as there is no commitment to implement the recommendations of the study." He agreed. So I went to Delhi, and the grant was approved.

According to documentation acquired by antiprivatization activists, on March 25, 2003, the government of Maharashtra's Ministry of Finance approved an application for a grant from the World Bank's Public-Private Infrastructure Advisory Facility (PPIAF) in the amount of $300,000 for a Water Distribution Improvement Program (WDIP) in Mumbai. The funds, which were given in the form of an unconditional grant, were to be used to pay a Bank-appointed private sector consultant to prepare "documents for privatization of Water Supply operation in K-East ward" (CASUMM 2008).

Notably nothing in the terms of the 2003 PPIAF grant required that the Municipal Corporation actually act on the consultant's recommendations in any way. Yet the Ministry's acceptance of the grant, the arrival in Mumbai of the corporate consultants, and the increasingly unpredictable and volatile nature of the city's water flows[22]—coupled with the near complete colonization of policy discourse by the privatization debates—resulted in a situation wherein privatization took on an air of inevitability. The arrival in 2006 of the Bank-appointed consultants seemed to be the culmination of two decades of discussion about the possibility of privatization in the water department, which had begun with the debates over pension reform in the 1980s. By the time the consultants finally arrived, two decades of speculation on the likelihood and desirability of private-sector involvement had already produced a series of processes and dynamics with very real implications for the department's informational infrastructures: staffing shortages had led to the abandonment of the survey section, resulting in the increasing fragmentation and personalization of knowledge about the pipe locations, pressures, timings, and flows; the regular practice of auditing the city's 110 water zones using the labor-intensive pito-gauging system was (in conjunction with overzealous enthusiasm for high-tech gadgets) another casualty of understaffing; increasingly stressful working conditions resulted in frequent requests for transfers by engineers who sought placement in other departments or in the private sector;[23] the rapid and dramatic transformation in the built space of the city meant that decades-old blueprints had a decreasing resemblance to anything that might be found on or under the ground; and the criminalization of water access for many of the city's residents animated a range of infrastructural practices that were neither on the map nor had any clear place in the conceptual and regulatory framework through which water was—officially speaking—supposed to be provided.

Ultimately the unreliability of the department's maps and flow-meter readings as predictors of where, when, and how much water might flow would render it exceedingly difficult for the consultants themselves to produce data shoring up the case for privatization. When Castalia submitted its audit report on the K-East Ward to the Municipal Corporation in June 2007, the findings and recommendations sparked angry debates among department engineers, activists, politicians, NGOs and in the media. The report, which attempted to pinpoint figures on efficiency, leakage, bill recovery, contamination, and customer service, made four basic claims: first, that intermittent water supply in K-East led to contamination during monsoon months; second, that distribution was inequitable across neighborhoods; third, that customer complaints were not promptly attended to; and fourth, that approximately 40 percent of water supplied in the ward went "unaccounted for" (Castalia 2007). Castalia recommended a three-phase set of reforms that converged on the goal of phasing out Mumbai's intermittent water-distribution system and introducing "24x7" water supply in Mumbai. The first phase would involve an in-depth water audit of the whole city, during which geographic information systems (GIS) technology would be used to map and keep track of the network of pipes, valves, and flows in various water zones. Flow meters would be installed at selected points, which would allow for the monitoring of water volume and pressure. Phase 2 would focus on leakage reduction, pipe upgrading, and a public education campaign to reduce household consumption. Phase 3 would involve maintenance of the now upgraded system: informational inputs into the GIS programs, responding to consumer complaints, streamlining leakage repair.

Department engineers were incensed by the report's findings, particularly its claims that an estimated 40 percent of the water supplied to K-East was "unaccounted for." The figure on which the consultants and the engineers finally agreed (20 percent was the generally accepted number discussed in a 2009 meeting that I attended), while still large enough to inspire the consultants to point to "high levels of leakage,"[24] had the unfortunate quality of being on par with estimated leakage levels in water distribution systems of some of the world's most respected water distribution systems, for example, those of New York and Paris. The leakage rationale, in other words, did not hold much water among Mumbai's engineers.

Indeed while senior engineers readily acknowledged that they had "no way of measuring" with any precision the water supply to each of the 110 zones, they did know *some* things. Calculating based on outflow from the city's master balancing reservoirs, department engineers expressed confidence in their knowledge of how much water they provided on a daily basis to the city *as a whole*; it was only once the water flowed in across the city lines that the accounting became somewhat dodgier. According to the careful data on the inflows to, outflows from, and water levels in the city's master balancing reservoirs—data collected and maintained by the Planning and Control wing of the department—Mumbai's water department (as of 2009) claimed to distribute somewhere between 3,300 and 3,500 million liters of water per day to the city.[25] Subtracting from this overall supply estimate the aggregate billed water, the department calculates that around 20 percent of the water they distribute goes "unaccounted for."

However, engineers expressed little faith in the precision of the 20 percent estimate; while they were confident in aggregate *supply* estimates, water is trickier to track once in the city. This is the case, engineers explained, for a few reasons, two of which I will highlight. First, as already mentioned, mapping had not kept pace with the changing above- or below-ground city, rendering it difficult to hydraulically isolate areas of the city for auditing purposes. But second, even if engineers could isolate zones for auditing purposes (i.e., even if engineers could pinpoint exactly how much water was provided to each zone),[26] the way consumer connections were metered and billed did not correspond to the calculations governing supply. That is, the *kind* of data that was collected and maintained about the quantities of water released from the master balancing reservoirs into the enormous trunk mains that conveyed water into the city was simply incommensurable with the knowledge produced and maintained by the various ward-level offices (record keepers, meter readers, bill collectors, etc.) about how much water flowed out the ends of hundreds of thousands of water taps across Mumbai. It is thus not simply the case that the department needed more or better consumer meters but that the way auditing had been operationalized since the decline of pito gauging had become fundamentally incoherent. This situation had to do with three peculiarities about billing in Mumbai: a large number of connections (particularly but not exclusively in the older part of the city) predate the practice of metering; nearly half of the *existing* meters were reported to be nonfunctional; and partially as a result of the first two points, the way consumers were actually billed had little relation to any information about actually used water.

To account for this situation we must travel back in time. Until the annexation of the suburbs in the 1950s, water charges were collected according to Section 141 of the 1888 BMC Act, which provides for a variable "water tax" to be levied according to property value. The idea of billing according to the *quantity* of water consumed was not introduced until the 1950s. With the annexation of the suburbs (first in 1950, followed by another extension of city boundaries in 1957) the water department suddenly became responsible for providing water to an area over six times the size of the original Island City.[27] But whereas in the Island City of Bombay water was billed as a *service* to be paid as a tax, residents of the suburbs—most of whom relied for water on the area's abundant freshwater wells at the time of annexation—would be connected to the piped distribution system only incrementally, over time, according to demand. Thus in the 1950s the BMC Act was amended to provide for "a water charge in lieu of a water tax, based on a measurement or estimated measurement of the quantity of water supplied" (BMC Act 1888: Section 169). This need for an "estimated measurement" in order to calculate bills for water provided to newly incorporated areas led to the introduction of water meters. Beginning in the 1950s, in other words, water charges were levied based on a dual system: some recipients paid according to the *amount* of water they received, while others paid for water as a *service* provided to them as users of a particular property. Since the pito-gauging system of water auditing did not require comprehensive knowledge of *end-use* consumption (pito gauging measured *pressures* in hydraulically isolated zones), the dual-billing system did not pose a problem for keeping track either of the water supplied to each of the 110 water zones or of pressures in the distributions mains.

The dual-billing system was phased out in the early 1990s, when, as a condition for a World Bank loan (for capital investments in the distribution system that required foreign-currency purchases), flow meters became mandatory on all consumer connections. This condition was part of the international paradigm shift toward thinking of water as a market good—a shift that required precise measurements of flow and quantity. Holders of preexisting, taxed water connections were instructed by the BMC to register with one of the newly constituted ward-level water department offices (housed in the freshly decentralized administrative ward offices across the suddenly much bigger city) and to purchase the prescribed variety of meter for their connection. As of 2010 engineers and departmental records pinpointed the official number of metered connections (for industrial, domestic, and commercial purposes) in Mumbai at somewhere between 330,000 and 400,000. More than 100,000 unmetered connections (domestic, industrial, and commercial) remain in older parts of the city (primarily the Island City).[28]

A second, related obstacle to conducting regular (post-pito) audits now has to do with the state of existing meters. While the majority of contemporary Mumbai's water connections are officially metered (meaning they receive bills that are ostensibly calculated according to metered consumption), the department reports that only 50 percent of the city's estimated 330,000 meters are functional (if even present). Moreover engineers maintain that even the functional meters do not give reliable readings; since domestically manufactured meters are easy to "tamper with," untold numbers of meters underreport actual consumption. In M-East ward-level engineers report that only 30 percent of the connections are actually metered. "Of the remaining 70 percent," one engineer explained, "30 percent *used* to be metered, but now those people don't pay bills—maybe the meter is gone or there's no water, who knows." The remaining 40 percent never had meters to begin with.

A third obstacle, the official absence of meters on at least 20 percent of the city's documented connections—combined with the high rates of absent or broken meters on the rest—has created particular challenges for the water department's billing section. The meter reading staff in M-East reported that 75 percent of the documented meters in their ward are either missing or broken. Of the remaining 25 percent, many are on commercial and industrial connections (which, due to differential rates, generate over half of departmental revenues), so meter readers spend their time attending to those. The M-East metering section draws up bills for the majority of the department's connections (most of which are documented as "slum" connections),[29] not according to calculated supply but rather according to water supply *norms*. "For each slum residence," one meter reader explained, "we assume five members, and there are supposed to be about six houses per connection. So we bill for thirty people at a supply norm of forty-five lpcd [liters per capita per day]."

Indeed when I asked a resident of the "slum" neighborhood of Shivajinagar-Bainganwadi to show me the meter she had purchased along with her newly laid water connection, she led me not outside but upstairs into the attic, where she produced a shiny, brand-new meter, still in the box. When I asked her why she had not attached it to her connection, she replied, "Our pipe is plastic, so we can't put it on the pipe; it will be too heavy."[30] Another man present nodded, adding, "And if we put it on it slows down the water." He opened up the meter to show me the net-like flow-measuring screen stretched across the mouth of the meter. "No one will put that on their pipe when it's already so hard to get water to come out, so no one uses them." In any case, he continued, "if people put them out, they just get stolen." I asked him if he knew of any connection in the neighborhood that had a meter connected to its pipe. Pausing, he responded that yes, he knew one person who had the meter on his pipe. Leading me up the uneven lane to the adjacent plot, he stopped in front of a block of concrete hunkering outside a doorway. Pointing at the block, he said, "The meter is in there. He packed it in concrete so that no one will steal it." Baffled, I asked, "But if it's packed in concrete, how can the meter readers read it?" He shook his head and said, "They can't."

"But if it can't be read, why doesn't he just keep it inside?"

"It's the law that you have to keep it outside; this fellow, he's very honest."

"But you can't *read* it!"

"It doesn't matter," he explained, "no one comes to read it anyway."

"Then why did he *buy* it?"

"We *have* to buy it—the BMC won't send their crew to make the connection until we show our meter."

"So if you don't put it on, how will the BMC know how much water to bill you for?"

"Well, they come once, usually a few months after we get the connection. We pay them a few hundred rupees and they go away."

A senior engineer confirmed that estimates of water supplied to still unmetered (formerly water-taxed) connections in the Island City (an aggregate estimate of 500 million liters per day) are indeed calculated without consulting any flow-measuring device: the "estimate [is] based upon the number of such buildings and families occupying them." In other words, the idiom in which bills are articulated (charges are levied per 1,000 liters consumed) bears little resemblance to the kinds of information that the water department actually collects and maintains. Subtracting total billed water from aggregate citywide supply therefore gives a number that is utterly meaningless.

The factors—the absence of meters, the nonfunctioning of meters, and the mixed-methods billing procedures—have important implications for the department's ability to estimate and pinpoint leakage. In the add-up-and-subtract method of auditing, leakage-related losses are indistinguishable from *other* kinds of unbilled water—water for firefighting, for instance. Official department supply estimates are broken down in table 1.1.

Individual engineers differed on their descriptions of a few aspects of how these various components of supply break down. The clearest among the table numbers and percentages is the 8 percent (approximately 270 million liters per day [mld]) for industrial and consumer connections. The 57 percent for

TABLE 1.1. Citywide Water Consumption

	Domestic	Slum	Unmetered	Unaccounted-for water	Industrial and commercial
Million liters per day (mld)	1,400	700	500	600	270
Percentage	40	20	14	17	8

These figures were given to me in 2008 by the Office of the Hydraulic Engineer, Department of Hydraulic Engineering, Municipal Corporation of Greater Mumbai. In 2009 Mumbai's supply increased by an additional 78 mld (as part of the pumping station project Mumbai 3A), further complicating the calculations and increasing the stakes over measuring the distribution of where this additional water would go.

residential connections (also referred to as either "domestic consumer" or "planned homes") is less straightforward: senior engineers disagreed, for instance, on whether this number reflected connections to Slum Redevelopment Authority (SRA) buildings (which are technically "planned homes" but are supposed to be billed for the first ten years of occupancy at the "slum rate"). Furthermore while the department is aware of the number of unmetered, formerly taxed connections, it does not have any way of calculating the volume of water provided to them, so it bills instead (as already mentioned) based on supply *norms*—an estimate, needless to say, that bears no necessary connection to actual water supplied, not least because the norms themselves are constantly changing. When I asked for clarification of the official norms, which are spelled out in the Water Charges Rule Book but are regularly revised up and down for various categories of consumers, I received the following explanation: "As we had good rains last season now we have relaxed norms for supply of water. "Humanitarian Grounds" connections and slums are still 'designed' to give forty-five lpcd.[31] The rest of residences are given ninety lpcd. SRA buildings are generally given ninety lpcd, but in case SRA has come up in areas where there is acute shortage of water, they are given forty-five lpcd. Our official norms are 135 lpcd for planned constructions including SRA buildings and forty-five lpcd for slums. But depending on the situation each year, we decide the quantum to be supplied." Nevertheless the estimated quantity of water supplied to these connections is pinpointed at 500 mld—or 14 percent of total distributed water.

The remaining 35 percent balance is accounted for in significantly disparate ways: one engineer said that "slum consumption" accounted for as much as 20 percent and that the remaining losses are reported as "unaccounted-for water" (UfW), a term that is commonly used to refer to losses from underground leakages and burst pipes. Another engineer suggested that the *entire* 35 percent was provided to "slum consumers," thereby lumping together at least four distinct categories of water use: consumption by residents provided water at subsidized (slum) rates; "unauthorized" (unbilled) water connections; nonrevenue water (NRW), comprising water used for firefighting, for public fountains and toilets (e.g., in train stations) and as bulk supplies distributed by tanker;[32] and UfW. Gupta summed up his assessment of the water department's ability to estimate leakage in the distribution system: "You can hardly come to any correct figure for leakage for [the] whole of Mumbai. . . . But as even developed nations cannot contain leakage below 22 to 25 percent, our figure [of 17 percent] looks unbelievably low."

Another senior engineer, a man named Bilimale, expressed more palpable disdain for an activity that he readily offered was an exercise in the absurd. As I was sitting in Gupta's office one afternoon, Bilimale entered and placed a piece of paper on the desk. "What's that?" I asked. "It's rubbish," he replied, handing it to me. On the sheet was written:

100% population served with piped water
150 lpcd
NRW 18%; UFW [Unaccounted for Water] 20%
19% unmetered connections; 48% meters broken
2,600 mld sewage generated, 1,500 mld treated
65% slums connected underground

He continued, "We have to submit this to the central government in Delhi a few times per year."[33]

"What will they do with it?" I asked.

"They'll throw it in the garbage. They have a very big garbage bin in Delhi."

Their Data Was a Little Faulty

Although engineers readily voiced their lack of faith in these official numbers, this did not translate into a lack of faith in the department's capacity to manage leakage at an acceptable level. While Gupta expressed concern that the department's official 17 percent UfW estimate seemed a bit low, Castalia's estimate of 40 percent struck him as implausibly high. Shaking his head, Sharma laughed as he explained that Castalia's estimate of losses in K-East could not possibly be correct:

They said that K-East consumes 240 mld, but is only billing 160. That's an 80 mld loss, 50 percent of what's billed! So I said, "Okay, let's check the next ward over—K-West—they're supplied downstream on the pipes from K-East." So if 400 flows into K-East and 240 is consumed, then 160 flows out into K-West. How much of that is billed? We're billing 160 mld in K-West—so that means there's no loss at all! I asked them, "Are you telling me that we're losing half of what we bill in one ward, and just next door we're not losing a drop?" They responded that what happens in K-West isn't their concern.

Sharma became animated as he spoke about the episode: "It's ridiculous! If we start from a figure of 40 percent leakage, then the private operator will come in, do nothing, and collect the money!" Since they were not familiar with the intricacies of inflow and outflow in K-East, the consultants did not manage to hydrologically "isolate" K-East, which resulted in "some faulty measurements"; they were unable to account for the precise quantities of water that pass through K-East on the way to the neighboring K-West, or H wards. "Flow meters all have to be adjusted . . . for each main," Kulkarni told me, "but [the consultants] seem not to have carried out the adjustments." Another engineer present during my interview with Kulkarni, a younger man named Athawale with a penchant for high-tech gadgets and a palpable disdain for city politics, became visibly angry discussing the report: "We gave them all the information! It was their responsibility to check the accuracy of the meters and take the measurements; the meters were given by us as well as all the relevant information about main sizes." Kulkarni nodded and diplomatically repeated, "Their data was a little faulty." Gupta sighed as he explained, "[Castalia's project leader] is not an engineer; he's an economist. So they didn't really know what they were talking about. When these economists talk we just nod. We're used to having to nod when economists talk, even when they say absolute nonsense."

Ultimately the fragmented state of official knowledge about the pipes made it impossible for the consultant and various engineers to agree on a set of figures on which a tender could be written. For Castalia the opaqueness of the water distribution network presented significant financial risks—risks that any contract would have to offset with guaranteed payments from the BMC. For the department engineers the consultant's figures presented evidence of the challenges and even absurdity of transferring responsibility for water distribution to private actors who have no access to socially embedded networks of knowledge about water pipes and flows and whose profit orientation was interpreted by department insiders as evidence of bad faith.

Attracting equal disdain from department engineers was the Castalia report's pronouncement that there was no contamination in Mumbai's water—a finding that contradicted one of the report's own recommendations: that in order to *prevent* contamination, the water department needed to do away with its intermittent system, patch leaks, and pressurize its pipes continuously. Anyone who has spent any time at all in Mumbai, it was pointed out, can attest that popular complaints and reports of water-borne illness regularly appear during the annual monsoon season, when Mumbai's groundwater rises high enough to intermingle with the contents of centuries-old sewage pipes and seeps into cracked consumer connections—which are frequently laid in open drains themselves.[34] Engineers complained that water quality samples were taken only during the winter months rather than during the monsoons, when there would have been a more accurate measure of contamination. Castalia spokesmen sought to account for this contradiction by citing data collected by the BMC itself during the previous monsoon of 2005, during which Mumbai had experienced record flooding and extraordinarily high rates of water-borne illness.[35] But, as Gupta explained, neither measure was an acceptable representation of the extent of contamination in the city—not the dry-season finding of zero contamination and certainly not the sample taken during Mumbai's most destructive flood in recorded history. Gupta and his colleagues pointed to Castalia's use of these two measures as further evidence of the cynicism with which the Bank-funded study was carried out—a study, they insisted, in which the recommendations had already been decided upon before the study was even commissioned.

The audit affair was recalled by many senior department engineers with the bitterness of betrayal. Sharma confessed, "My personal views are that the World Bank gives [funds] which we are required to use in generating business for the companies which belong to the donor countries of the World Bank fund." Because he was so vocal in his criticism of the Castalia report, he said, activist organizations incorrectly concluded that he and his colleagues in the department were against *any* sort of private sector involvement in distribution. "Bringing in private-sector actors was my idea in the first place! We wanted to bring efficiency, but not on a flimsy ground where only a private operator would be benefited." The consultant's flawed numbers were evidence to these senior department engineers of the profiteering motives of the foreign lenders, whom some engineers—citing the Delhi Jal Board scandal—accused of pursuing the interests of the foreign corporations whose home governments occupy primary positions of power in the World Bank.

The Truth

"Do you want to know the truth about the K-East Ward water audit?" The question was posed to me in July 2009 by a retired senior water engineer. Of course I wanted to hear "the truth." He began, "See, because [the consultants] didn't understand the network, they subcontracted the study. Not officially of course, but they gave the project back to the ward staff—not to the assistant engineers of the ward, but to the subengineers, the junior engineers, and the laborers."[36] He explained that since the ward staff had neither the time nor the interest in "doing a good job" with the study, they too subcontracted the work, to some neighborhood-level contractors. "Just their friends, local people in the area that they may have known."

In her 1993 monograph, Anna Tsing (1993: 93) discusses the complexities of dealing with the epistemological status of the category of knowledge commonly referred to as "rumor." During her research in the mountainous regions of Indonesia, Tsing encountered a wave of popular reports that government "headhunters" were stalking the mountains. While she admits to having initially dismissed the importance of the headhunter rumors because of the unlikeliness of their truth value, she later realized that "by suspending disbelief, even for a moment, it becomes possible to find structural elements" that help to explain the "power-laden cultural negotiations" that mediate relations between, in her case, the Indonesian state and the "peripheral" people that she studies. By giving "a little more room" to the rumors, Tsing is able to learn a great deal about the dynamics of uneven development and core-periphery relations in Indonesia. The stories of headhunters, she concludes, offer "clues" to understand, not by providing verifiable knowledge but by revealing how state-directed development schemes are experienced by marginal peoples not as integrating forces but as shoring up existing sociopolitical fault lines and power structures. Indeed as Fujii (2010) points out, rumors are often less interesting for their veracity than for what they can reveal about available and relevant categories of meaning. As Fujii explains, people use preexisting concepts to make sense of the world. Rumors can thus be illuminating insofar as they render visible and intelligible the available ideas through which experience is made meaningful. It is in this spirit that I present the following accounts of the Castalia report and of the political feuding that resulted—a series of understandings and conjectures, much of which can best be described as rumor. What were the stakes of the K-East pilot project? How did the people either directly or indirectly involved with the audit and its undoing make sense of the project's spectacular failure? The opacity of the distribution system fueled widespread suspicion regarding the circumstances and results of the audit. The following accounts offered by World Bank and Castalia consultants, journalists, engineers, activists, politicians, and bureaucrats reveal the contours of the political and discursive landscape animated by the audit affair.

A Consultant's Tale

"This project has not been a moneymaker for us," Castalia's thirty-one-year-old director of Asian infrastructure, Alok Joshi, sighed when I caught up with him for breakfast at a café in downtown Mumbai in February 2009. "Believe me, it hasn't." Alok was born and raised in Sydney, but his parents grew up in Bombay; his work during the week-long visit to the city thus competed for his attention with familial obligations to aunts, uncles, and cousins. "Bombay is *my* city," he told me, which is why he had chosen to work on the project. "If [Castalia] can do anything to help, that would be just fantastic!"

When I asked Alok to tell me about the much-disputed findings of the K-East Ward audit, he became animated. The department engineers turned against the project, he explained. "The BMC sabotaged our survey. I *knew* the leakage-estimate results were problematic—I sent the subcontractor back for five retrials!" The problem was that the local department office did not provide the subcontractor with accurate maps of the distribution network. Moreover the subcontractor requested a thousand flow meters for the audit, but Sharma gave only 400. "[Sharma] said it would be too complicated to take measurements from so many at once."[37] And the lack of contamination? Also the subcontractor's fault: "I told them, you have to test during the monsoon! That's when contamination happens because the whole city is underwater. But they refused to test during the monsoon" because the meters do not work underwater.[38] Alok's presumption that senior engineers themselves had access to maps and meters reveals the landscape of suspicion animated by the opacity of the underground system of pipes and flows in which the consultant perceived the audit having become enmeshed. The department, he insisted, sabotaged the audit because career engineers felt threatened and insulted by the prospect of a management contract. Alok shook his head imploringly. "But the K-East Ward audit was not necessarily about a management contract anyway; we were just hired to figure out what was wrong with the system!"

The project's descent into political infighting, Alok maintained, was the department's own fault because it was they who selected the K-East Ward for the pilot study: "It's one of the most profitable wards! So of course the research ended up showing that the department was making a lot of money, that there were no leaks, that there is no contamination. So the engineers could say, 'What do we need a consultant for? We can conduct improvements on our own.'" Indeed the issue of the selection of the profitable K-East for the pilot study became something of a Rorschach test during the heated years of the audit, as contending perspectives vied to interpret the selection. A widely held understanding among activists and the media was that K-East was intentionally selected not by the water department but by the World Bank itself since a pilot project there would invariably demonstrate the success of private-sector involvement in public goods management. The antiprivatization activist Afsar Jafri (2007), of the advocacy group Focus on the Global South (one of the organizations that spearheaded a media campaign against the K-East pilot project) proclaimed, "The K-East ward is one of the most profitable wards for the [Brihanmumbai Municipal Corporation] where the operating cost of water is Rs. 65 million, while revenue collection is Rs. 400.43 million per annum. The [World Bank's] choice of K-East ward is therefore strategic because it is bound to result in successful implementation of the management contract."[39]

"The whole affair became entangled in politics," Alok complained, especially the issue of prepaid water meters: "I told [the AMC] from the beginning that it was a horrible idea—that it was politically unfeasible."

Prepaid Meters: Global Discourses and City Politics

The real problem was the NGOs—and God knows where they came from!
—**WORLD BANK SENIOR SANITATION SECRETARY**, field notes February 2009

By the time Castalia released its report, Mumbai's globally connected antiprivatization activists were prepared for battle. In a stakeholders meeting called by the Municipal Corporation on June 3, 2007, NGOs and civil society representatives united under an umbrella group calling itself Mumbai Pani (Mumbai Water) attacked the study and the report for its "privatization agenda."[40] Blow-by-blow accounts of the rowdy meeting were reported by the city's English-language media, whose reporters were unashamed in their sympathy for Mumbai Pani's position on the matter. A few months later the Municipal Corporation, under the enthusiastic leadership of a new pro-reform additional municipal commissioner, announced a set of reforms based on the Castalia report recommendations clubbed together under the name Sujal Mumbai.[41] Another stakeholders meeting was called, and this time the heated conflicts became confrontational. Sujal Mumbai's expressed objective followed on the Castalia report's umbrella recommendation that Mumbai should aim to supply round-the-clock water pressure to the city's water distribution network. In pursuit of this goal, Sujal Mumbai offered a set of policy initiatives. Demand-side reforms would include the introduction of telescopic billing rates,[42] prepaid metering for slums that did not meet a pre-1995 residency "cutoff date" for municipal water supply, and a contract for the replacement and upgrading of the city's thousands of individual (postpaid) water meters. Supply-side reforms would involve the contracting of a consultant project manager who would oversee a citywide water audit and manage the contracted laborers who would be brought on board for leakage reduction and pipe repair.[43] Mumbai Pani activists and their sympathizers in the English-language press were particularly animated by the proposal for prepaid metering in slums—an idea that was nowhere mentioned in the Castalia report but that antiprivatization activists nonetheless described as part of the World Bank and Castalia's "sinister" and "antidemocratic" privatization agenda.

Activist opposition to Sujal Mumbai was galvanized by the proposal for prepaid metering, which became the symbol and rallying point around which claims that neoliberal and neocolonial forces were threatening India's control of its most basic and sacred resource. The hullabaloo over Sujal Mumbai's prepaid water meter proposal is significant for what it reveals about the ways global flows of information among activist organizations and social movements interact with local and particular social and political reform contexts. In the wake of a handful of high-profile cost-recovery initiatives (notably in South Africa), the prepaid water meter has become something of a global symbol of the ways neoliberal economic and policy logics are said to be colonizing water resources the world over—resources that antiprivatization literature often describes as a naturally occurring, commonly owned public good.[44] As a group of antiprivatization activist-researchers in Soweto writes:

> The prepaid water meter is perhaps today's starkest expression of this commitment to the profit motive above the needs of people. In addition to entrenching the logic of payment for a basic resource, the prepaid meter individualizes the relationship of people to water and makes any notion of individual right dependent on individual ability to pay. "Responsibility" also becomes individualized (away from the state and society) as water provision is made the responsibility of a private company to a paying individual. (Coalition against Water Privatization 2004)

Armed with theorizations and language lifted from this globally mobile activist discourse, the November stakeholders meeting in Mumbai turned violent, resulting in the arrest of six Mumbai Pani activists, who accused the BMC of being a "World Bank agent" (Mumbai Pani 2007). A journalist named Sanjiv Dixit of the English-language *Daily News and Analysis*, a sympathizer of the antiprivatization activists (who made no pretense of neutrality either in his coverage of the events or in our private conversations), explained his theory: "The AMC knew that the prepaid meter initiative would not be passed alone, so he lumped it together as part of Sujal Mumbai which was about 24x7 water, and about privatization—they call it partnerships, or contract work, but it's privatization." Dixit credits an activist media with the defeat of the prepaid meter initiative; the proposal was dropped because "the media fraternity" opposed the meters.

Dixit accounted for the Mumbai activists' opposition to the prepaid metering project using phrasing that reflects transnational antiprivatization discourses: "You see, here in India water is not a commodity, it's a right. You ask anybody, in the slums they protest for water, they demand water because it's their right! The World Bank is trying to privatize water everywhere, but here in India water is a right, not a commodity." Dixit's comment is intriguing for the assumptions it makes about the existing modes of water access available to slum residents and for the dramatic divergence between these assumptions and the political landscapes I encountered in my own research. In Mumbai some of the city's poorest residents regularly pay up to seventy-five times the legal municipal rate for water and make significant inputs of labor and time into the transportation of their daily supplies. It seemed to me that, far from being a disciplinary extractive technology and means for commoditizing a common resource, prepaid meters offering municipal water at the official unit rate might be a welcome relief.

Let Them Bring Meters!

Curious about this disjuncture between my research findings and the discourses employed by activist groups claiming to represent the poor, I asked a housing rights activist named Suraj, whose organization is active in some of the M-East neighborhoods where my own research was focused, for his take on the prepaid meter episode. He told me a very different story:

> The Mumbai Pani people were waging a media campaign against the prepaid meters, but it almost all happened in the English-language media. They don't have any mass connections;[45] mostly they sit in front of their computers. So when they wanted to have a protest on Azad Maidan [a location in downtown Mumbai], only about two hundred people came

out. That's not a protest! During the protest one of their organizers called me and said, "*Bhai*, mobilize your slumdwellers, come out in protest of the meters." Because, see, we had been keeping silent. The journalists were involved too. [Sanjiv Dixit of *Daily News and Analysis*], even he called me because he too thought that I should be opposing the meters; he was writing articles in opposition, he was on the side of the Mumbai Pani people. Sanjiv asked me, "Why are you keeping silent?" I said, "Okay, I'll talk to people and see what they have to say." So I did, and they didn't seem to be too bothered. They said, "Let them bring meters! We'd like meters, we're prepaying to private people anyway, by the month."

Suraj was in support of the prepaid meter idea as long as the people affected were in favor, but personally he believed that the meters should be provided by the BMC rather than by a private provider. On these grounds, he explained, he attended the protest. Only a handful of his slum-dwelling colleagues, however, chose to join him.

One of the most committed, fearless, and respected housing rights activists in the city, Suraj does not generally take such wishy-washy positions. I pushed him to explain his tepid response to this particular issue—one that might have wide-ranging implications for the neighborhoods in which he works. Nodding slowly, Suraj chose his words carefully: "I also didn't want to get involved because the metering issue was very political; Shiv Sena was opposing it, Congress was supporting it.[46] We didn't want to take sides, didn't want to throw our weight behind either of them." Indeed prepaid metering cut to the heart of the city's most politically volatile issues: housing rights, land claims, and ethnolinguistic chauvinism. In proposing to provide prepaid metered water connections to city residents who could not meet a pre-1995 proof of residency requirement for municipal water connections, the municipal commissioner waded head-on into cutoff date debates over which Mumbai's two largest political parties, the Congress and Shiv Sena, had been locking horns for over a decade. Following the Shiv Sena government's unfulfilled 1995 electoral promise to provide "free housing" to the city's more than 4 million "slum dwellers," in 2000 the Congress Party swept the 2000 Maharashtra State Legislative Assembly polls on a pledge to update the cutoff date to 2000.[47] The Shiv Sena, which retained its firm control of the Municipal Corporation despite losing the State Legislature to Congress in 2005, came out in strong opposition to updating the cutoff date, arguing that the move would reward lawbreakers (by giving "squatters" a free home) and would thereby encourage migration to the "already overcrowded" city. Congress responded by accusing Shiv Sena of bald-faced vote banking, claiming that Sena's opposition to the cutoff-date change stemmed from a simple (and cynical) calculation that the more recently settled north Indian and Muslim neighborhoods that would be helped by the shift were simply not their voter base. Shiv Sena responded in turn, accusing Congress of encouraging the so-called influx of illegal Bangladeshi migrants (migrants, Sena maintained, with possible terrorist connections) and of pandering to their *own* vote bank (of north Indians and Muslims), thereby overburdening civic infrastructure at the expense of the city's "real" citizens: the Marathi-speaking working classes. By 2006 the whole issue had become mired in a high-profile and somewhat bizarre series of public interest litigations. The prepaid metering issue arose just in time to exacerbate this already festering political wound.

Shiv Sena jumped on the prepaid metering issue, with the party's senior leadership proclaiming the proposal to be "unconstitutional" since it went against a government rule directing the water department not to "approve" municipal water connections without proof that a structure met the 1995 cutoff date. Shiv Sena Standing Committee Chairman Ravindra Waikar articulated his party's opposition to the water metering proposal using the very same terms in which his party had been opposing the extension of the cutoff date. "It means that anyone coming to Mumbai can erect a hutment and the BMC will provide them water," he told the Standing Committee. "This is wrong as we will only encourage mushrooming of slums." Waikar went on to point out that the prepaid meters, which were to be attached to continuously pressurized water lines, would be doubly unfair to residents of older, *pre*-1995 slums whose own pipes produced water only intermittently for a few hours per day.[48]

Suraj told me that at the height of the Standing Committee debates on the prepaid metering—which incidentally were furiously covered by the English-language media but barely acknowledged by vernacular presses—he received a phone call from the additional municipal commissioner himself. "He called me and said, 'Suraj, we're trying to help *your* people,[49] why won't you come out publicly and endorse [the prepaid metering proposal]?'" Suraj responded by proposing a meeting: "I told him, 'You're making us an offer. We're not just going to accept it and say thank you; if you want to talk to us, we'll sit down at a negotiating table and we'll talk about it.'" Unfortunately the meeting never happened because the Sena-controlled Standing Committee simply threw out the proposal. The AMC was extremely keen on the Sujal Mumbai project—"It was his baby," as Suraj puts it—and he was very disappointed when it was thrown out. Suraj explained his theory about the origins of the prepaid metering proposal (which incidentally was not among the Castalia report's recommendations): the AMC himself came up with the idea because he thought it would generate broad-based political support among the masses and thereby discredit the antiprivatization Mumbai Pani activists who were causing so much trouble at the stakeholders meetings and getting so much attention from the English-language press both in Mumbai and internationally. "That AMC," Suraj said, shaking his head, "he was from Delhi; he didn't understand politics here in Bombay." As I stood up to leave, Suraj was pensive, a playful grin tugging at the corners of his animated eyes. "Maybe we should start a citywide agitation in favor of prepaid water meters."[50]

A Commissioner's Account: World-Classing the City

Suraj's account invites a question: Why were the various additional municipal commissioners so committed to the Sujal Mumbai initiatives? Suraj's claim that the Sujal Mumbai reforms were dear to the AMC is echoed by many of the senior water department engineers who were involved in the episode, four of whom independently described to me the strong, seemingly personal investment that the AMC displayed in the Sujal Mumbai project. The issue is puzzling: after all, AMCs are officers of the national-level Indian Administrative Service and are not known to be beholden to local political imperatives; it was unlikely that the AMC was doing the bidding of a particular party in pushing the reforms. Why did Mumbai's AMC care so much about this seemingly mundane and somewhat parochial set of reforms? My conversations with senior engineering staff converged on a compelling observation and conjecture: in the wake of the liberalizing reforms of the 1990s there emerged a consensus among international lending institutions, development consultants, and management experts extolling the virtues of private-sector involvement in municipal infrastructure. Privatization seemed inevitable; it was just a question of when and how it would be implemented. This consensus and already determined future, the engineers surmised, probably inspired IAS officers to compete to join (and thereby take credit for) the winning side of history. As Gupta explained, "The additional municipal commissioner at that time, he was ambitious; he wanted to leave a legacy. And he also probably hoped that, if he did the [World] Bank's work, then after his retirement, he could get hired [by the World Bank] for some time and earn a pension in dollars. That's every IAS officer's dream!" Indeed a number of engineers referenced a rumored World Bank policy, wherein as a conditionality (or perk) of Bank loans, borrowing countries are required or entitled to send a certain number of their top bureaucrats for periods of deputation to the Bank. The supposed purpose of this policy is both to indoctrinate IAS officers into the ideologies that will advance the profiteering goals of multinationals from fund-investing countries and to provide an incentive for IAS officers to ease the path of Bank-friendly reforms. Intrigued by this hypothesis, I spent countless hours combing documents for some reference to this so-called policy—to no avail.[51] In the end, whatever the formal or informal mechanisms by which IAS officers can join the Bank, our AMC's motives were suspect by virtue of the very notion and possibility that he _might_ pursue private ends by endearing himself to the Bank (by pushing the Bank's goals regarding private-sector involvement) with an eye toward an American deputation—and a dollar-denominated pension.

In the spring of 2009 I met with the former AMC who had presided over the Sujal Mumbai episode.[52] I began our conversation by asking him about the history of the K-East pilot project and his role in bringing it about. He took a deep breath, assuming an air of seriousness as he began his explanation: "There's another project that you should know about, a project called Mumbai Transformation, which is going to make Mumbai into a world-class destination for investment."

> [In 2004] the central government in Delhi put together a committee to study the possibility of creating world-class cities in India. They did a study of Mumbai and said that Mumbai should become a financial services center. To achieve this, the city needed to create international-quality infrastructure. Not just the roads and water to keep the city moving, but to create an international-quality lifestyle. That means social and lifestyle infrastructure too: theaters, auditoriums, libraries, sports, education. . . . If we want expats to come and live here, we've got to provide a quality of life that they're used to—that they would get in a comparable city! If people are going to be stuck in traffic jams all day, they won't want to live here.

When the World Bank "mission" arrived in Mumbai for the first time in 2005, the commissioner recalled, they "strongly recommended" transitioning from an intermittent to a continuously pressurized water distribution system—a process that, first and foremost, would require auditing the existing distribution network. He decided to approach the World Bank to fund the audit rather than just hire a consultant directly using the water department's own resources, reasoning that "when you go through the Bank, there's a sense of seriousness on the part of the implementing agency. If we do it ourselves, [the contracted auditing agency] can tell us anything. We went through the Bank so that our tender would have credibility." Thus under his leadership tenders were floated in 2005, which resulted in Castalia's appointment.

Risk's Revenge

"The study is finished," Gupta said with resignation. "[Castalia's] work is complete; the scope of the K-East Ward project was simply to carry out a study." Kulkarni's account echoed Gupta's: "We were going to prepare a document for all of Mumbai based on the experience in that pilot project . . . but we never floated an [expression of interest] document. We held a few public meetings, interactions with stakeholders, and . . . there was resistance from the public, especially from the corporators [municipal councilors]. They questioned the data generated by the Castalia study." He shrugged, indicating the straightforward-ness of the whole affair. "The consultants gave a bunch of recommendations, and the Municipal Corporation threw out the recommendations." Another engineer in the room nodded silently.

The commissioner, however, had concluded our interview with a rather different impression: most of Castalia's recommendations, he insisted, would be implemented. He handed me a letter addressed to the BMC Standing Committee dated November 2007, in which he wrote, "In the context of Mumbai's aspirations to emerge as a truly world class city, it is necessary for the Municipal Corporation of Greater Mumbai to give adequate and pure water to the citizens on a 24x7 basis." "We're taking up both demand and supply reforms," he explained, "100 percent metering and telescopic rates on the demand side, and on the supply side we are replacing pipes, increasing supply, and going in for a management contract for a water audit." I demurred, pointing out that the Standing Committee had *rejected* most of the Castalia recommendations; he clarified that the reforms were being carried out "departmentally." Indeed while the privatization craze subsided, the utopian fantasy of calculative precision—which itself had decimated the water department's century-old in-formational infrastructures (mapping and pito gauging)—lived on.

While Sujal Mumbai's strongest recommendation in 2007—for a project manager who would carry out a citywide water audit and leakage repair program—did not happen that year,[53] the idea did not disappear. Sometime in the following year World Bank consultants in Delhi once again approached the department, pointing out that some of the PPIAF funds from the K-East Ward project were still available; why not use this remaining money to bring in an expert to write a tender document for a city water audit?

Thus it happened that, in February 2009, Castalia's team of consultants returned to Mumbai to attend a World Bank–sponsored series of discussions on the preparation of bid documents for a Water Distribution Improvement Project—a series of workshops and meetings that I was fortunate enough to attend. In an air-conditioned conference room inside the Municipal Corporation headquarters, a senior water department engineer flanked by a team of consultants from the World Bank and Castalia beseeched his skeptical colleagues to be open-minded about the WDIP's goal of providing round-the-clock water across the city. Mumbai, he pointed out, had a domestic per capita water availability of 180 liters but was making that water available to consumers for only two to four hours per day. Other large cities provided round-the-clock water with much less availability! London provided a 24x7 supply with only 150 lpcd; Kuala Lumpur with only 120. All we needed to do was "incentivize" a project manager to incrementally increase the number of consumers provided round-the-clock water. Other senior engineers were skeptical: Why should we aim for round-the-clock supply? Our goal should be to improve the distribution system—to patch the leaks! Can we not incentivize some measurable indicator that is more directly related to leakage reduction? The consultant pleaded; with 24x7 supply you get it all: better quality, quantity, pressure, and duration. (The tautology of this claim seemed to baffle the room into silent assent.) Furthermore much new technology is designed for 24x7 pressurized systems: ground-penetrating leakage-detection radars, high-tech meters and automatic meter readers—they only work on twenty-four-hour pressurized systems. And this technology, the consultant argued, is much less vulnerable to political pressures than the "human-centered" approach that the department currently took.

The February meeting generated another year's worth of conversations about contracting a project manager to implement a three-phase series of programs, united by the goal of providing 24x7 water pressure to Mumbai's consumer connections: the first step would be to update the maps; the second would involve using GIS technology to keep track of the maps; the third divided the city into two hundred or so hydraulically distinct zones, each of which would be equipped with state-of-the-art flow meters. "With the new technology," Gupta (who at this point was still optimistic about the project) explained to me, "we'll be able to do a water audit every day!"

Within a year, by February 2010, the conversations had collapsed, and the senior engineers who had been supportive of (or at least open to) the project had grown disillusioned. "I told [the World Bank official in Delhi] that I have lost faith in the management project," Gupta sighed. "If you ask me [the project] should have been named 'How to Cheat Third World Countries.'" The problem, he explained, was that the terms of the contract that Castalia came up with transferred all of the risk to the BMC, while consultants would be "guaranteed payment . . . regardless of whether they do anything at all!" The sticking point stemmed from the incentive structure on which the proposed contract would be based, which would include performance-based bonuses for each additional "connection" to achieve continuous water pressure without increasing overall supply. The presumption of this incentive structure was that such increases in duration of water pressure could be achieved only by the reduction of leakage. This very basic idea, it should be noted, was complicated by the fact that each "consumer connection" in Mumbai provides water to entire housing societies, including anywhere from five to five thousand families. Further complicating the issue was Mumbai's sump-and-pump system, in which water provided on an intermittent basis by the municipality is then further distributed through society-level mechanisms and household-level pumps and tanks. For practical purposes, most households already have water continuously available, if not in their taps, then in other kinds of storage containers in their homes. Castalia's one-size-fits-all concept of 24x7 water was thus essentially open to multiple levels of interpretation in light of Mumbai's more complex hydrology.[54]

After a series of disagreements the engineers and experts in the meeting decided that, for the purposes of the contract, 24x7 pressure would apply only to the pipe that feeds a society's below-ground sump (rather than to each consumer tap). Yet since many of the city's popular neighborhoods do not have belowground sumps, slums were proposed to be excluded from the 24x7 requirement altogether. Indeed among the many complications that the negotiations encountered, a major sticking point involved the tricky business of slums. A suggestion was made to incentivize the project manager to increase the number of "authorized" connections in slums by rewarding the manager for each new connection, regardless of the number of hours the connection would be pressurized; in the absence of augmented supply, it was reasoned, new connections could be granted only in conjunction with reduction in leakage. Yet from the first moment that the question of slums was raised, it was clear that the tidy dreams of the consultants would be very difficult to reconcile with the messiness of the city's political landscape. The meeting's first mention of slums functioned as a kind of comic relief from the otherwise abstract and somewhat esoteric discussions of the day. The Castalia consultant asserted, "Half of this city is slum dwellers, and we want to be sure that this program genuinely helps everyone in the city. So slum upgrading is part of the program. We want slum upgrading in authorized slums." After a pregnant silence, Gupta, fighting a smile, asked, "Can you clarify what you mean by 'slum upgrading'?" The fifteen or so municipal engineers erupted in laughter, while the foreign experts looked at one another in confusion.[55] Each time during the two-day meeting that an issue emerged gesturing toward the challenges of trying to reconcile Mumbai's deeply political hydrologies with the tidy rigidity of a contract, the engineers responded to the intrusion of reality into the conversation with laughter. While seeming to welcome such reality checks into the discursive space of the workshop, the laughter did not translate into any substantive discussion or attempt to deal with these challenges:

> *World Bank Representative:* In Andheri I once saw a big protest rally for a bigger pipe. When someone explains to [the poor] that they'll get more water another way, they don't believe it.
> *Castalia Consultant:* (sarcastically) Oh, so they're all engineers now!
> *World Bank Representative:* This has to be addressed, but not in an ad hoc manner.
> BMC *Engineer A:* Politically initiated proposals you're referring to . . . ?
> BMC *Engineer B:* (smiling) Maybe we can find a way to figure it into the contract! (laughter among the engineers)
> *Castalia Representative:* You're laughing, but we're taking note.

Toward the end of the workshop, during a conversation regarding expected water-augmentation projects, an engineer again raised the issue of how to reconcile Mumbai's legally complex hydrologies with the exigencies of a fixed contract. Addressing his colleagues in Hindi—thereby excluding the foreign experts—he raised a concern regarding the question of the cutoff date: a shift in the cutoff date from 1995 to 2000 was "on the [state government's] agenda [and] could happen anytime." The ambiguous nature of the hundreds of thousands of water connections whose already hazy legal status would become even more contested was clearly not something that would be easy to work into a contract. The comment was not translated into English.

In the months following the February 2009 meeting, a core group of senior engineers continued to communicate with the World Bank office in Delhi and Washington, sending amended versions of the tender document back and forth. By July, however, the initiative had run out of steam: "[they] used to [email] every day," Gupta reported, "but now [they hardly write] at all. If we want the document, we need to show more interest, but the department's not interested, so [the Bank has] lost interest too." I asked him to explain why the department engineers have lost interest, and replied that, really, there was never much interest to begin with. Much of the original impetus for the audit was political:

> [The politicians] see this as a big contract—as a big game really—so they yell "Leakage! Leakage!" These are big contracts—the Standing Committee just approved a metering contract worth Rs 880 crores! See, the contracts come first, *then* the name of the program. Sujal Mumbai grew out of the conversations between [IAS officers and Bank consultants]. They decided what they wanted to buy and sell and said "Okay, let's call this set of reforms 'Sujal.'"

In the end Castalia never sent Gupta a final version of the tender document. "The Bank thinks that we won't have any offers after we finish amending the documents," he explained. The central sticking point had to do with the system of payouts and bonuses and with who would assume the considerable financial risks inherent in a system so fraught with unknowns: unknown pipe locations, unknown pressures; unknown—and unknowable—numbers of "authorized" (present and future) connections. The consultants, he said, sought to transfer all of these risks to the department, insisting on guaranteed set payments to the contractor, who would be rewarded for each additional connection that was made to produce twenty-four-hour water pressure regardless of whether the contractor could demonstrate that the feat had been achieved by a reduction of leakage. "They really just prioritize the companies. We can edit [the tender document], but we cannot change the tone." By way of emphasis he referred to a line in the tender document draft stating that if the project manager does not fulfill the goals according to the standards of the hydraulic engineer, then the project manager will receive no bonus. "The implication of course is that they will get their regular payments even if they accomplish nothing at all! But of course they won't get a *bonus!*" He concluded, "See, here in India, we know these things, we're very alert. When the World Bank goes into Africa or something, those people aren't as alert, so they get fooled. But Indians are alert."

In the end the privatization storm blew over in Mumbai. Or, as Gupta pointed out, perhaps it never really arrived to begin with. While the decades of the 1980s and 1990s saw lenders and development consultants strongly encouraging (and sometimes requiring) Mumbai's water engineers to involve market mechanisms and private-sector actors in its infrastructural ambit, the various initiatives and policies did not add up—in either theory or practice—in any sort of coherent way, resulting instead a somewhat bizarre amalgamation of contracts, high-tech gadgets, and half-formed initiatives that would combine in unanticipated ways to unintended ends. The sorry state of the department's maps and flow-meter readings as predictors of where, when, and how much water might flow ultimately rendered it exceedingly difficult for the consultants themselves to produce data that might have made a convincing case for privatization. The whole affair was ultimately refracted through contentious and high-stakes political battles concerning giddy efforts to remake the city into a world-class financial services center and the complex and contested policy frameworks pertaining to slums. Indeed while the privatization boosters eventually threw up their hands and went home, the protracted period of privatization debate has had lasting hydraulic implications. Perhaps the most important legacy has been the deinstitutionalization of official departmental procedures for producing and recording official knowledge of the water distribution system: surveying, mapping, leakage detection, and auditing.[56] The senior water engineers who had presided over the privatization years concluded that the idea of conducting a citywide audit was a largely futile project. "We either have a [mapping and water-auditing] system, or we don't," Sharma admitted. "Anyway, even if we *could* do [an audit], we'd just know [about pressures and volumes] for that particular *moment*—but these things change again and again."

↳argument for high-tech meters.

Nice repetition of key themes and facts

TWO

"THE SLUM AND BUILDING INDUSTRY"

Marketizing Urban Development

In October 2008, on the heels of a generous monsoon that left Mumbai's upstate water reservoirs brimming, Municipal Corporation Standing Committee
Chairman Ravindra Waikar "stormed out" of a committee meeting in protest
of continuing water shortages across the city. "Even posh buildings in the suburbs are not getting water!" Waikar fumed. "Every time we complain, [the municipal authorities] have an excuse ready" (*Times of India* 2008). While the
subject of water shortage is hardly news in Mumbai, where politicians stage
periodic marches, sit-ins, and hunger strikes to demand augmented supplies
and additional distribution mains for their constituencies in the city's popular
neighborhoods and slums, Waikar's statement made headlines: What was to be
made of dry taps in "posh buildings"?

Waikar's Walkout, while certainly theatrical, also expressed a genuine question and a straightforward demand for an explanation. Over the following
months, at the request of the Standing Committee, Mumbai's senior water
department engineers prepared a White Paper detailing "the present water
supply scenario, the constraints, remedial measures and future" (Municipal
Corporation of Greater Mumbai 2009: 1). The water department's account
in the White Paper, which was presented to the Standing Committee a few

months later, was not quite what anyone seems to have expected—least of all the municipal commissioner, who, apparently thinking he was already familiar with what a report on such a familiar topic as water shortage might say, appeared not to have actually read the report before distributing it to the Standing Committee in the spring of 2009. A senior water engineer who was present during that particular meeting recalled the tense (and somewhat humorous) exchanges that followed when an elected councilor asked the municipal commissioner whether, as the chief executive of the Municipal Corporation, he "agreed" with the White Paper. The commissioner replied that of course he agreed; why would he present a report with which he did not agree? The councilor then pointed to a section of the White Paper that blamed not the slums (which, as the locus of so much shortage, serve also as something of a popular go-to explanation for the city's water problems) but rather the state and central governments, whose two-decades-long effort to transform Mumbai into a world-class city was accused of creating "chaos" in the water distribution system. Two decades of "random building activity," the report fumed,

"random activity building"

> [has] put too many constraints on water planners and forced [them] to take makeshift water supply arrangement, smaller water zones, curtailed supply hours and . . . inconvenient water supply timings. . . . All this haphazard and indiscriminate development has stressed the available infrastructure creating a chaos and agitating situation on water front. . . . The water supply distribution network, the reservoirs, inlets-outlets and feeder network are designed on certain assumption of growth with specified [floor space index] in [the development control rules] and [development plan] reservations for various activities.[1] The slapdash development threw the entire infrastructure in shambles (Municipal Corporation of Greater Mumbai 2009: 7).

The water engineer who had witnessed this particular Standing Committee standoff laughed as he described how the municipal commissioner, caught off guard, grew embarrassed and became defensive, pulling an about-face on his early pronouncement that he "agreed" with the White Paper. "This is nonsense!" the flustered commissioner proclaimed. "I've been to Shanghai—they have a [floor space index] of fourteen!"

Comparing and contrasting the economic growth experiences and development trajectories of India and China is something of a cottage industry not only in Mumbai, where such references to Shanghai are increasingly standard fare in political circles, popular discourse, and in the media, but in academic and policy debates the world over. In discussing the divergent development trajectories of India and China, the development economist Pranab Bardhan (2000) writes, "A major difference between China and India in terms of preconditions for job creation and general economic growth is in the area of building and maintenance of infrastructure." Chinese investment in physical infrastructure, Bardhan argues, has resulted in lower production costs for manufactured goods and dramatically shorter factory-to-floor times, while "glitzy airport terminals and transportation, industrial parks and multi-lane highways" impress investors and inspire confidence. In India, by contrast, populist politics and corruption are accused of interfering with proper distribution and pricing of infrastructural goods, limiting investment and forcing the private sector to "self-supply" basic needs like power, water, and transportation. This kind of theorization—in which India's messy democracy and bloated, inefficient, and corrupt bureaucracy are said to fetter the energies unleashed by liberalization, stunting economic growth and crippling development—has emerged as a kind of common sense across the political and socioeconomic spectrum.[2] There is thus a particular kind of directionality commonly ascribed to the relationship between the described failures and inadequacies of public sector planning and infrastructural provisioning and the heroic flourishing of the market *in spite of* these limitations. The conflict during the Standing Committee meeting, however, suggests a rather different kind of relationship between markets and infrastructures, one that, as this chapter shows, has to do with the way economic transformations have played out in urban space.

Marketizing Planning

[Transferable Development Right] has now become a regularly traded
commodity like any other asset.
—SENIOR PLANNER, Brihanmumbai Municipal Corporation

In order to understand how marketization of urban development has affected water infrastructures, it is helpful to start with a little history of development planning in the city. Even before Bombay's postindependence population surge following Partition,[3] colonial administrators had been inspired by industrial Bombay's "desperately overcrowded" (Moduk and Mayer 1947: 3; cited in Shaw 1999: 4) conditions to appoint a commission charged with exploring possibilities for expanding the city limits and with preparing a master plan whose recommendations would control urban growth. While this report had no official status, prepared as it was on the eve of Indian Independence, its recommendations would inform planning initiatives for decades to come.[4] Foremost among the report's recommendations was the directive to "include a larger area within the urban limits of Bombay, so as to provide space for further expansion of the city" (Pacione 1981: 211). In line with these recommendations, in 1954 a newly independent Bombay state government passed the Bombay Town Planning Act, directing the Municipal Corporation to create the city's first master plan for the city, as well as to be responsible for implementing it within a set time frame.[5]

The approval of Bombay's first development plan in 1967 brought into being a set of macro-level planning tools—land use zoning and development control rules—to be used in shaping urban land use and controlling population densities. The 1964 *Report on the Development Plan* (Government of Maharashtra 1964) identifies 15,202 acres of land to be designated for "public purposes." Of this, approximately 23 percent was for housing, primarily low-income housing: the *Report* identifies "requirements of tenements to meet the housing shortage" based on projections of "natural increase," "slum clearance and house collapse," "overcrowding," displacement due to reservations, and zoning in the new development plan. Next the *Report* estimates percentages of this anticipated housing requirement to be met by various public- and private-sector agencies: the Maharashtra Housing Board (to provide subsidized low-income housing), private and public employers (railway employees, for instance, and industrial labor), the Municipal Corporation schemes for "rehousing the dishoused as a result of Municipal policies and actions," and cooperative housing societies. As for the private sector, the *Report* expects that such actors can be relied upon to provide housing only for "higher-income group people" (Government of Maharashtra 1964: 88).

Lands zoned for social housing or amenities were to be acquired by the Municipal Corporation (in accordance with the 1954 Bombay Town Planning Act), with landowners compensated at market rates as per provisions laid out in the 1894 Land Acquisition Act (LAA).[6] The 1964 *Report on the Development Plan* thus exudes a palpable optimism that proper zoning, combined with methodical surveying and accurate population projections, could solve Bombay's spatial and infrastructural problems once and for all: "If the problem of housing the industrial labor, which by far forms the bulk of Bombay's population is successfully dealt with, the housing problem of Bombay would be within sight of solution" (Government of Maharashtra 1964: 90). Greater Bombay, the *Report* proclaims, "experiences no difficulty of land requirements to meet its housing programs. The Suburbs and Extended Suburbs provide a vast field and can accommodate any ambitious housing program in contrast to the City" (88).

After the approval of the development plan in 1967, the Municipal Corporation's water department set to work preparing its own plan. Extrapolating from population estimates, development controls on floor space index (FSI), population density, and land-use zoning regulations of the development plan, water supply planning engineers projected future patterns of spatially distributed water demand, with the water needs of the various zones (industrial, commercial, residential) estimated according to supply norms. Postindependence Mumbai's first Master Plan for Water Supply, which was finalized in 1971, envisioned a dramatic restructuring of the city's water distribution system, conceived of as part of the effort to meet increasing demand from newly annexed suburban areas.

Indeed until the late 1950s, the BMC provided water to taps only within the Island City limits. Of course the enormous water mains conveying bulk supplies from the upstate reservoirs to the Island City passed through suburban regions of Salsette Island to the north, but the municipalities and village administrations (*gram panchayat*) in those areas met their water needs primarily using the abundant local water supplies in area wells and creeks. Before the annexation of the suburbs, water supply to the Island City functioned in a relatively straightforward manner, as a "transmission system." Water conveyed to Bombay from lakes far north of the city arrived through enormous trunk mains; upon reaching the city the water fanned out "like a tree" either into storage reservoirs or directly into the smaller-diameter pipes feeding the city's water taps, which at that time were pressurized continuously (Totade 2008: 56). The more than doubling of the city's geographic area with the annexation of the suburbs in the 1950s complexified the system dramatically. In order to supply water to the newly annexed areas, particularly to the large industries that had been relocated from the Island City to Trombay Island (M-Ward) in accordance with development plan zoning in 1967, the water department made a piecemeal series of "tappings" into the trunk mains (the trunks of the distribution tree), diverting water to the suburban areas upstream (the newly annexed areas north of the Island City). These tappings, however, caused water pressures downstream to drop significantly during hours of heavy usage, sometimes drying up Island City taps completely. To manage this problem of meeting peak demand, department engineers began to experiment with periodic openings and closings of valves to supply the suburban tappings, providing water only intermittently, during nonpeak hours, to the suburban areas, with industries and individual consumers storing water in privately constructed underground storage tanks for use on demand throughout the day.

In order to systematically address the provision of water to the growing suburbs, the 1971 Master Plan for Water Supply outlined a two-pronged set of interventions: supply augmentation and distribution system reconfiguration. To address the problem of peak demand, water supply planners conceived of a system whereby water would be provided entirely through a network of service reservoirs located at higher-elevation points across the city and suburbs. Only the service reservoirs were to be supplied directly from the master balancing reservoir, with all of the city's end-users falling under the hydrological jurisdiction of one or another service reservoir. The idea was that storing the water in local reservoirs would minimize fluctuations in demand placed on the master balancing reservoir. The challenge was less one of limited resources than of the hydrological and technological problem of how to maintain water pressure during times of the day when so many taps were open at the same time by allowing water to be provided to the service reservoirs at nonpeak timings. Water engineers would be able to maintain desired pressures in the trunk mains while controlling the precise volumes of water flowing to each service reservoir.

Responsibility for distributing water to the various parts of the city thus came under the jurisdiction of the various service reservoirs, with water dispensed by gravity to the various neighborhoods and industries of the city, which were divided into supply districts (or supply zones). In drawing the zones and designing the distribution system, supply planners thus needed to project demand in various parts of the city. This was accomplished by compiling data on current and future patterns of urban development articulated in the 1967 development plan—population estimates, industrial growth, commercial demand—and then calculating the zone-level water requirements given by water consumption norms and requirements for residential, industrial, and commercial uses as indicated in the plan. The 1971 Master Plan for Water Supply thus envisioned not only the network of service reservoirs but, in order to meet estimated future demand in the various zones, also planned a series of extensions to the secondary transmission system (the network of mains, or "inlets," conveying water from the master balancing reservoir to the service reservoirs) as well as source augmentation projects to meet demands projected according to the development plan.

The vision articulated in 1971 was pursued with mixed results. Of the three components of the plan—primary source augmentation, secondary transmission extensions, and a tertiary distribution system to provide water to the newly articulated supply zones—the first proved to be the easiest to actualize. The Upper Vaitarna Project, completed in 1972, saw the construction of two dams on the Vaitarna River, seventy-six kilometers north of the city, which provided an additional 680 million liters per day to the master balancing reservoir. Subsequently supply-augmentation schemes dubbed Bhatsa I (completed in 1981), Bhatsa II (completed in 1989), and Bhatsa III (completed in 1996) each contributed an additional 455 mld to the master balancing reservoir. The other two components of the Master Plan for Water Supply proved somewhat more challenging: acquiring the land necessary for new service reservoirs and for the construction of additional water transmission mains took longer than anticipated,[7] while increasingly heavy traffic on city roads made it difficult to secure permission for construction and road breaking, thereby preventing the laying of mains on time and according to plan. In one instance, securing all the required permissions—in this case even from the salt commissioner in the north Indian state of Rajasthan, a central government body that owns a piece of the land through which the pipe in question was to pass—took so long that in the interim years the price of steel changed such that the contract had to be scrapped and a new tender floated. The trunk main, which was finally contracted in 1999, was still not commissioned in 2011.

Meanwhile the city changed in ways unaccounted for by the development plan. As a retired senior-level planner named Phadke explained, the authors of the 1967 plan were "obsessed with decongestion," leading to unrealistic density norms and projections. The aim was to reduce the population in the center city by lowering the allowable FSI in areas where buildings were so dilapidated that they would soon need to be reconstructed. Then those high-density areas would be rebuilt with low-density housing. Phadke attributed this "obsession" to an overeager embrace of planning norms and ideologies coming out of North America. "But it made no sense," he explained, shaking his head in defeat, because two years after the sanctioning of the development plan and development control rules in 1967—which were supposed to *reduce* FSI—the state government set up the Bombay Repair and Reconstruction Board with the express aim of keeping these very same buildings in good repair. Not only did the Repair and Reconstruction Board work at cross purposes with the development control rules, but it actually *increased* allowable FSI in order to encourage investment in redevelopment of rent-controlled buildings: while the existing ground-plus-three-story buildings had an FSI of around 1.66, the new Repair and Reconstruction Board rules provided for redevelopment at 2.4 times greater, for a new total FSI of 4. "It completely undermined the entire purpose of lowering the FSI to promote decongestion."

Water supply engineers thus faced a twofold set of challenges in the wake of the 1967 development plan: first, whereas the 1971 Master Plan for Water

Supply envisioned a city provided exclusively by service reservoirs, the disjunctures between *anticipated* and *actual* configurations of built space and population density meant that water department engineers were frequently compelled to provide direct supplies from the secondary system. Second, a transmission system inadequate to convey additional water from supply augmentation projects (Upper Vaitarna and Bhatsa) forced supply planners to experiment *further* with intermittent supply timings.

Indeed the tertiary distribution system (from the service reservoirs to the taps) is described by engineers as having been from the outset the site of much improvisation. Department engineers explain that the tertiary system is extremely complex, characterized by "many networks (loops) of small dia[meter] water mains taking off from the outlets and/or major feeder mains, laid in roads, cross roads etc." (Totade 2008: 56). Designing and operating the new distribution system thus required trial-and-error mathematical modeling of the networks governed by each of the service reservoirs in order to simulate the demands made on the system during peak hours.[8] The simulations require inputs of data on each and every component of the distribution system: pipe diameters, distances, friction coefficients, flow estimates in each section of the system, details of each pipe junction (or "node"), and estimated daily and peak demands for each node in each water supply zone. This analysis of pressures, timings, and flows must be reworked every time a water main is enlarged or introduced into the system in order to ensure adequate supply across each zone. The work of water engineers thus became increasingly improvisational and experimental, based on trial and error. One senior engineer related a story in which a young engineering student sought his advice on how to resolve a hydraulic problem. The engineer described to the woman one practical solution to such a problem that he had often used during his four-decade career in Bombay's water department. When entered into the student's computerized model, the engineer laughed, the practical solution crashed the program.[9] Thus while the 1971 Master Plan for Water Supply had projected demand and planned for supply through 2001, by the early 1990s it was clear that the vision set out in the plan had been derailed by unforeseen delays and unpredicted patterns of urban development and water demand. It was time for a new plan.

In 1992 the government of Maharashtra appointed an expert committee charged with the task of projecting future water demand across the city and with identifying possibilities for source augmentation. Extrapolating from the 1991 population census as well as drawing on the new 1991 development plan, the Chitale Committee (chaired by one Dr. Chitale) estimated wardwise water demand.[10] Reasoning that any new industrial growth would occur only in "hi-tech non-polluting industries" (Government of Maharashtra 1999: 3–9) with limited water requirements (while existing industries would be incentivized by high tariffs to increase efficiency or reuse water), almost all of the projected increase in demand was anticipated to come from increased domestic consumption according to a supply norm of 240 liters per capita daily. Taking into account development controls on population density and buildable area laid out in the development plan and control rules of 1991, the Chitale Committee conducted a wardwise population projection, concluding that almost the entirety of additional water demand in the future would come from the suburbs; demand in the city, the committee reasoned, had reached saturation point. The Chitale Committee report was presented to the government of Maharashtra in 1994, and in 1999 the Water Supply Planning Department of the Municipal Corporation finalized its new Master Plan for Water Supply (1999) for source development, storage, transmission, and distribution based on the committee's projections. The 1999 plan detailed works that would account for urban development until 2021, at which point a new plan would be drawn up.

Urban development in Mumbai over the subsequent years, however, would diverge starkly from the projections of the Chitale Committee report, leading to patterns of water demand that differed dramatically from what was projected by the 1999 Master Plan for Water Supply. These deviations, moreover, are described by department engineers as being altogether different from the kinds of challenges that water supply planners faced in earlier decades, when the population simply grew faster than expected (aided by the contradictions of de-densification policy) and long construction delays forced engineers to improvise hydraulic solutions.[11] In recent decades tweaking the development planning rules has itself become a distinct and primary modality of urban development. The Municipal Engineers Association (2008) cites such activities as the most significant "hurdles" facing the department:

1   The frequent change in government policy regarding floor space index, transfer of development rights, no development zone and coastal regulation zone.
2   The haphazard growth of the city.
3   The random and concentrated developments at fag end of supply or at elevated terrains create huge problems in water distribution management.

These "hurdles" are connected to the peculiar way that the idea of "the market" was operationalized in the new development plan. The policy changes have not simply redirected the patterns of urban development away from those projected by the Chitale Committee report but have changed the logic of urban development and planning in ways that have had profound hydraulic implications.

Out of Thin Air: Solving the Land Puzzle

While city planners in the 1960s may have been right that Greater Bombay "experiences no difficulty of land requirements," many of the tracts zoned in 1967 for public use (low-income housing or civic amenities) turned out to be a challenge to acquire. Steep rises in land prices throughout the 1970s meant that actual market rates far outstripped official land prices, according to which dispossessed landowners were to be compensated (Phatak 2007: 45),[12] and reluctant landowners found myriad ways to evade giving up their lands. The passing of the Urban Land Ceiling Regulation Act (ULCRA) in 1976, for instance, while formally designed to prevent monopoly landholding in cities and to free up land for public amenities, in practice provided all sorts of ways for landowners to avoid losing their property.[13] One common loophole, popular among the largest landholders, involved placing large tracts of land into trusts, which were exempt from ULCRA if the trusts could show they were engaged in "philanthropic" works.[14] Another common strategy involved selling lands to developers and builders; according to one estimate, approximately 70 percent of all land that might have been acquired under ULCRA was subdivided and sold to property developers. If these sales were not explicitly *authorized* under the LAA and ULCRA, they were nonetheless *normalized* by state authorities, who granted new builder-owners "consequent authority" over the lands thus transferred (Nainan 2012: 105). In this way ULCRA worked in contravention to its stated mandate (to acquire lands for social purposes) and instead froze vast tracts of land in the city while creating a brisk business in the granting of exceptions (Narayanan 2003: 198).[15]

While ULCRA thus created all sorts of loopholes by which landowners of zoned plots could avoid parting with their properties, city planners encountered an additional obstacle to acquiring land for public purposes: many of these plots were found to be already "encumbered" by low-income residential neighborhoods. While in theory planners zoned public amenities only on lands listed as *un*encumbered at the time of the land-use survey, it is widely (and indeed officially) acknowledged that such inspections did not always take place (Joseph 1996: 311). So while some neighborhoods may very well have been built *after* the sanctioning of the development plan—a result of clever collaborations between landowners and local political leaders whereby the latter consolidated an electoral constituency and the former preserved his landholdings—it was, in practice, not possible to establish when any particular neighborhood had actually been built.[16] As a result while the sanctioning of the plan in 1967 designated structures on amenity-zoned lands officially as "encroachments," in practice there existed myriad combinations of tenancy arrangements shoring up residents' rights to stay put. Vote-empowered tenants partnered with the various political parties, particularly the regionalist-populist Shiv Sena Party, in advancing residency claims within Mumbai's complex, multilayered, and often contradictory policy framework.

With city authorities thus unable or unwilling to acquire land, Bombay's development plan remained largely on paper. Municipal planners, to whom these problems had rapidly become apparent, thus initiated the preparation of a revised development plan in 1977. Yet when the draft of the new plan was released for public deliberation in 1983, objections again poured in; of the 7,700 plots slated to be acquired for public purposes (amenities and infrastructures), formal objections regarding 3,800 were promptly submitted to the Planning Authority offices of the Municipal Corporation. The following years witnessed intense public debate, lobbying, negotiation, and compromise among the various stakeholders—city planners, political parties, landowners, developers, environmentalists, and residents—the period that coincided with national-level liberalizing economic reforms.

When the government of India announced the liberalizing reforms comprising the country's New National Economic Policy in 1991, Mumbai's boosters saw in "the market" a solution to these perennial challenges to land acquisition for planning purposes. As part of an effort to enlist the private sector in Bombay's transformation into another Singapore (later Shanghai), the government of Maharashtra approved a new set of development control rules in March 1991 that sought to put market mechanisms to work in carrying out various urban development projects: slum redevelopment, repair of dilapidated buildings, construction of roads and public facilities. The new development plan and development control rules involved dramatic changes in land use zoning to facilitate the anticipated shifts in the city's economy: any remaining industries were to be moved outside the city, with the freed-up areas to be developed with service-sector infrastructure and commercial real estate. Popular neighborhoods and "slums," meanwhile, were to be either removed to the urban periphery or redeveloped vertically (to open up land for commercial development) under the newly announced Slum Redevelopment Scheme, a new policy tool that diverged dramatically from existing approaches to low-income housing by proposing to use primarily private-sector resources. By compensating builders and landowners not *monetarily* but rather with *development rights*, the authors of the new development control rules hoped to simultaneously incentivize participation by landowners and developers—who had been so resistant to land acquisition for public purposes—while transforming the city at little or no cost to the state government. The new planning tools generated considerable enthusiasm in the private sector while instantiating a peculiar modality of development in which carefully designed, "market-responsive" policy loopholes facilitated reconfigurations of built space in accordance with a fast-paced, flexible accumulation ethic that characterized contemporary Mumbai.

To understand the dynamics shaping contemporary Mumbai, it is worth spending a little time to understand how these policy tools and loopholes work. Beginning with the 1967 development control rules, the amount of permissible development in various parts of Bombay was regulated by a limitation of the buildable area on a given plot, known as the floor space index. With an eye toward decongesting the downtown areas, in 1967 the FSI for the Island City was set at 1.0 (with the much higher ratio of 4.5 permitted in the new financial district at Nariman Point), while that of the suburbs was set at 0.5. While these official limits changed only slightly with the new rules in 1991 (the FSI in the Island City was raised to 1.33 while that of the suburbs was raised to 1),[17] the 1991 development control rules were peppered with officially sanctioned loopholes in the mechanisms of "incentive FSI" and "transferrable development rights" (TDR). While the 1967 development plan was supposed to be implemented primarily by means of land acquisition through eminent domain, buried in the development plan rules was an innovative alternative to monetary compensation for the construction of new roads zoned in the plan: landowners voluntarily transferring zoned parcels to the authorities would be compensated not in cash but in *development rights*; a landowner could use forfeited rights to buildable space on his remaining holdings, thereby allowing him to build above the FSI limits for the now smaller plot. With the passage of the 1991 development control rules, this incentive mechanism—whereby development rights on a forfeited piece of land can be used in another location as TDR—was dramatically expanded, producing multiple loopholes through which development could occur far above the FSI limits set by the development control rules.

The 1991 development control rules offered a few different ways for a builder or landowner to generate the rights to build in contravention to density laws and FSI limits given in the development plan and rules. Through "incentive FSI" builders are granted additional development rights in exchange for carrying out development on behalf of the public sector. First, as in 1967, if the landowner constructs on his land a piece of road that is zoned in the development plan for a road, then he receives "Road TDR"—building rights equivalent to one-fourth the square footage of the piece of land sacrificed for the road. Notably since Road TDR simply shifts the *location* of building rights, the actual *quantity* of built space stays constant after the transfer. (Since they are considered two-dimensional, roads do not consume any FSI.) This is not the case, however, for the other kinds of TDR that have been allowed by the new development control rules, which, as the urban planner and former chief of the Maharashtra Metropolitan Regional Development Authority V. K. Phatak (2007: 47) notes, is "the first time development rights were brought out of thin air, not related to land in any fixed proportion." Second, development rights can be generated under the provision for "Reservation TDR," whereby an owner of a piece of land that has been zoned in the development plan for "public purpose" can construct the planned facility (e.g., library, school, or hospital), and then hand it over to the municipality in exchange for TDR equivalent to the square footage of the facility he has provided. In the event that development rights cannot be used on site—for example, if the freed-up land is already zoned for some public purpose—the rules provide for the transfer of development rights. TDR allows builders to use development rights generated as compensation for land surrendered for some other public purpose elsewhere in the city as well as to buy and sell those same rights in an open market.

To incentivize private-sector involvement in the new Slum Redevelopment Program the new development control rules granted private-sector developers of tenement-style slum redevelopment housing extra development rights—*above* the FSI limits set by the development control rules—as a kind of housing cross-subsidy. Compensating builders with development rights, it was reasoned, would make tenements available at little or no cost to the state government. The program was to work in the following way: Wherever possible, slums were to be redeveloped on site, with an increased FSI 2.5 for slums (regular FSI in 1991 was 1 in the suburbs and 1.5 in the Island City), thereby allowing for the reconstruction of slum housing as high-rise tenement buildings and freeing up land for commercial development. Slum dwellers were then to purchase—at a subsidized price—180-square-feet rooms. Cooperative housing societies of residents were to be granted thirty-year leases on their buildings and would be prohibited from selling their rooms for ten years. With the remaining open space and extra building rights, builders would be free to develop the remaining land for commercial sale.

The slum redevelopment paradigm in Maharashtra mirrored the central government's 1991 draft National Housing Policy, which is notable for its silence on existing policy tools for housing the urban working classes (e.g., housing constructed by the Maharashtra Housing and Area Development Authority for "economically weaker sections" on ULCRA-acquired lands or regularization of tenancy rights and infrastructure upgrading as per the provisions of the Maharashtra Revenue Code of 1966 or Slum Act of 1971). The new scheme, as well as the new development control rules of which slum redevelopment was a part, was a culmination of a longer-term shift in housing policy that had begun with the Fifth Five-Year Plan (1975–80), when the central government in Delhi reconceived the state's role in the provision of low-income housing from direct provider to "facilitator" and "enabler" (World Bank 2005). The year 1991 should therefore not be understood as a single watershed moment but rather as a particularly potent manifestation of a longer-term, quieter shift toward market-led development that began in the 1970s.[18]

The 1991 Slum Redevelopment Program, however, led to the construction of only a tiny fraction of the hoped-for number of tenements. While the program's widely discussed failure has been attributed to a number of factors, the incoming Shiv Sena administration in 1995 focused its attention on two: the profit cap of 25 percent that curtailed the market-incentive mechanism and the 1985 cutoff date for eligibility that excluded many city neighborhoods from eligibility—and profitability.[19] When Shiv Sena christened its new Slum *Rehabilitation* Scheme in 1995, the removal of the profit ceiling allowed for potentially unlimited profitability in the business of demolishing, and rebuilding slum neighborhoods while changing the cutoff date to include *all* slums in existence as of January 1, 1995, dramatically increased the number of potentially eligible neighborhoods. The basic idea was to demolish and rebuild all of the city's slums as high-rise tenements using market incentives.[20]

Indeed the 1991 development control rules did not initially provide for the issuing of TDR certificates for slum redevelopment housing. But with the scope of slum redevelopment so dramatically expanded with the new Slum Rehabilitation Scheme in 1995—with *all* document-wielding residents now eligible for rehousing—it quickly became evident that the incentive FSI allowed by the 1991 development control rules would be insufficient to accommodate both resettlement tenements as well as commercial space sufficient to attract buy-in from the builders. Thus in 1997 an amendment was made to the development control rules, dramatically increasing the FSI allowed for slum redevelopment and concomitant free-sale component projects. The FSI for slum rehabilitation plots is (at the time of writing) among the highest in the city; for example, the FSI might be set at 1.0 or 1.33 for a particular plot, but if that plot is perchance found to be occupied by slums, then the developer can use a much higher FSI of 4 (3 in the suburbs).

Similar exceptions to zoning and FSI rules exist for the redevelopment of older, dilapidated buildings in the Island City, where FSIS regularly reach 6 or 7, depending on the specifics of the plot. "Cessed buildings"—dilapidated structures in the Island City that have been taken over by the state for purposes of reconstruction—can be rebuilt by the landlord or builder, who rehouses the tenants on site and then can make use of the buildable area equivalent to 50 percent of the redevelopment construction for use on site. Since the FSI used to rehabilitate these older, densely packed structures already tends to exceed the Island City limit of 1.33, with the additional TDR these redevelopment constructions in the downtown areas of Mumbai regularly exceed 6. As one builder told me, in practice "there is no limit."[21]

In 1997 an additional amendment to the development control rules allowed that if for one reason or another the development rights could not all be used on site at even these much higher FSI limits, then builders could be compensated with TDRS. This might be the case, for instance, if part of a site is reserved on the development plan for another public purpose; then the builder would not be able to assert his right to the construction of free-sale components in situ. In this case the builder could construct whatever civic amenity is zoned in the development plan and then collect both Slum TDR (for constructing the rehabilitation tenements) and Reservation TDR (for constructing the school or hospital), which he could then use in some other area of the city.

There are other, sneakier ways that builders can arrange to earn development rights as TDR rather than as on-site FSI—which is preferable when the TDR-generating site is on low-value land. For instance, one builder affiliate explained that sometimes in slum redevelopment projects he intentionally builds space-inefficient rehabilitation tenement buildings by loading the buildings with "concessions" such as extra-wide corridors and staircases that do not consume any FSI and are extremely cheap to build but earn the builder valuable equivalent development rights. In this way the builder dramatically increases the quantity of free-sale rights earned from the project while shrinking the available on-site area in which the commercial buildings might be constructed since the wide and multiple corridors in the Slum Rehabilitation buildings take up so much room. Thus the builder uses up the space within the allowable FSI of 4 (3 in the suburbs) but without exhausting his compensation development rights. Builders then receive the balance as TDR, which they use at a much greater rate of profit in higher-value areas of the city.

In another common practice, in the event that the population density of the existing slum is not high enough to produce development rights that will utilize the full capacity of the allowable on-site FSI for slum redevelopment, the list of families to be rehoused can be augmented. This can be done through official procedure with the approval of the Maharashtra Housing and Area Development Authority, to whom the keys for the additional rooms are to be turned over for use at some future time to rehouse "project-affected people" displaced by one or another urban development or infrastructure project. In general, however, builders find a way, as one representative put it, to transfer the flats "to their own people." This is accomplished rather conventionally by employing a real estate agent to find retail homebuyers, whose names are then added to the list of eligible families using spurious documents, with a portion of the proceeds making their way to the officials at the Slum Rehabilitation Authority. Meanwhile, in their free-sale buildings developers frequently load up FSI-free concessional spaces, in turn selling this additional space at a premium while encouraging buyers to quietly amalgamate extra-large balconies and flowerbeds later on. This increases the square footage of free-sale space, a larger proportion of which can now *not* be used on site due to FSI restrictions and therefore generates TDR. While the development control rules were amended in 2012 to rein in this irregular use of concessions (the so-called flowerbed problem), concessional spaces are still free of FSI in slum rehabilitation and other redevelopment buildings. Although the closing of the flowerbed loophole has paralyzed commercial real estate projects all over the city that are no longer financially viable (our municipal commissioner is "too good," one developer groaned; this time "he's *really* closed the loopholes!"), redevelopment remains highly profitable—by some accounts the *only* profitable kind of development in Mumbai at the time of writing.

All TDR, in other words, are not created equal; slum TDR is by far the most valuable. While the development control rules allow TDR to be bought and sold on the open market, one builder-affiliate explained that it is often more cost-effective to generate the rights by redeveloping slums: in 2010 one square foot of slum rehabilitation housing cost around Rs 1,100 to construct (Rs 1,400 in 2014), while a square foot of a free-sale building cost Rs 1,700 (Rs 1,800 up to twelve stories in 2014; Rs 2,300 over twelve stories). The market price of TDR in 2010 stood at Rs 3,000 per square foot, for a savings of Rs 200 for each square foot of space constructed using TDR generated from slum redevelopment. Additionally slum-generated TDR can be used even in so-called off-limits corridors—areas of the city where construction would otherwise be restricted.

The market in TDR sits at the heart of the Mumbai makeover plan, enabling the freeing up of land for large-scale urban redevelopment and infrastructural megaprojects by facilitating the removal and rehousing of the city's working classes. Slum clearance is such an integral part of the work of the Maharashtra Metropolitan Regional Development Authority (MMRDA)—the implementing agency for the many large-scale infrastructural projects associated with the state government's *Vision Mumbai*, world-class city initiative—that in order to streamline projects the government of Maharashtra in 1993 granted the MMRDA all the powers of the Slum Rehabilitation Authority. In order to re-house these families (and to earn valuable Slum TDR) developers can propose (or sometimes bid on MMRDA contracts) to rehouse a certain number of "proj-ect-affected people." Officially speaking, and particularly if projects involve World Bank funds, which come with rigid resettlement policy guidelines, the new tenements are supposed to be in as close proximity as possible to the originating area. In practice, however, people displaced from MMRDA projects find themselves in far-flung reaches of the city where large tracts of open land are available at minimal cost: in the marshlands on the urban periphery, in toxic brownfield sites, and frequently in infrastructurally disconnected areas zoned on the development plan for some (or sometimes no) other purpose. The legality of rehousing people in these sites is unclear; an officer of the Slum Rehabilitation Authority (SRA) explained that the state-level Department of the Environment "relaxes" its regular requirement of an environmental im-pact assessment for SRA projects;[22] an engineer affiliated with that department, needless to say, insisted that no such "relaxation" provision could possibly be found to exist "anywhere on paper."

The magic of the market in geographically flexible TDRs has given rise to a fever of slum rehabilitation–related construction in the city, with builders clam-bering to secure the requisite 70 percent agreement among "eligible" residents of slum neighborhoods on desirable lands (while the media reports regularly on allegations of fraud and malfeasance in slum rehabilitation).[23] Meanwhile whole townships of resettlement construction are blooming on the lowest-value lands on the urban edges, areas that are often inaccessible by public transportation, are devoid of schools or hospitals, and face severe hydrological challenges. Much of this construction, moreover, is done on speculation, in anticipation of *future* displacements by the MMRDA's infrastructure-related projects. The eastern suburb of Mahul in the M-East Ward, for example, a highly-toxic in-dustrial site that is a stone's throw from two petroleum refineries, an ammonia factory, and a chemical fertilizer plant, has since 2004 become home to more than seventy-five thousand people who have been displaced by the MMRDA's infrastructure projects.[24] The resettlement site, known as Vashi Nakka, is severely wanting in access to public transportation, cutting off already struggling working-class families from their income sources. It was also somehow constructed at an elevation higher than that of the water department's service reservoir, from which it is fed by gravity. The colony (a medium-size city, really) thus suffers severe and debilitating water shortages that the water department is, at the time of writing, still trying to address. Yet the well-known struggles of Vashi Nakka residents—issues that have been exhaustively documented by a World Bank–funded study (World Bank 2008)—notably have not precluded ongoing construction of resettlement housing in this clearly inappropriate location. As of 2010 Mahul alone contained more than nine thousand recently constructed but still empty rooms, built space sufficient to accommodate forty-five thousand hypothetical project-affected persons.

When I asked an officer at the Slum Rehabilitation Authority why these hundred or so buildings in Mahul were empty, he responded, "No [project-affected people] are willing to go there." Indeed since people displaced by World Bank–funded projects (as many of Mumbai's infrastructure projects are) must follow protocols for "participatory" displacement and resettlement, families are generally given a choice among a few different resettlement sites; Mahul's remote, polluted location and poor civic amenities render it a particularly bad choice.[25] Nonetheless the officer, a young man named Shinde, explained that their office was considering yet another proposal for additional resettlement housing in Mahul. "We haven't decided if we need it or not," he added. If displaced persons were refusing to live in the available empty tenements, I asked, why would the MMRDA need more? He responded that they might need them "in the future" (figure 2.1).

Shinde explained how the process works: The builder submits a proposal for a particular configuration of buildings (the architect's rendering) on a particular plot of land to the MMRDA, whose SRA officers assess whether "PAP housing" (housing for project-affected people) is needed in that area. If the project is granted this "locational clearance," the builder can proceed to construct the tenements in exchange for SRA-issued TDR. In light of the extent of planned and ongoing infrastructural upgrading that Mumbai's makeover entails, developers have little difficulty convincing SRA staff that "in the future" there may be a demand for housing for displaced people; Shinde had joined the MMRDA's SRA office only a few months earlier and was unfamiliar with the location of the proposed tenements in Mahul or the infrastructural challenges

FIGURE 2.1. Slum redevelopment buildings on industrially zoned lands in M-East, 2009. Photo by author.

of that particular site. Indeed "locational clearance" is granted by the SRA *be-fore* the Municipal Corporation is consulted about the availability of water or other civic amenities; it is "up to the builder," one senior SRA officer said, to secure the requisite no-objection certificates from the various offices of the BMC.

The ongoing construction of slum redevelopment housing thus can be said to bear very little relationship to anything that might be understood as "planning" in the conventional sense of guiding and providing for a projected and desirable future. Rather it is a modality of urban development impelled by the dual imperatives of immediate profit and expediency. The clustering of redevelopment housing in the highly polluted and infrastructurally impoverished location of Mahul in the M-East Ward is a function not only of the exceptions that such development enables—the "relaxing" (ignoring) of environmental protection rules, the increase in on-site FSI irrespective of supporting infrastructure, and the generation of TDRs for use in prime areas of the city—but of a peculiarity of the development control rules: TDR generated in the suburbs can be used only *north* of the location in which it was generated. This provision is based on the (overly simplified) assumption that, because Mumbai's real estate values tend to be highest the farther south in the city you go, an incentive to build farther north would work to decongest the downtown area. Since most TDR cannot be used in the Island City,[26] builders must use their TDR to extend the heights of buildings in suburban areas. An unintended effect of this rule is that the M-East Ward, which is at the southernmost edge of the suburbs, receives an overwhelming amount of Mumbai's slum redevelopment housing, the TDR for the building of which is used to build higher-value property in wealthier suburbs farther north in the city.

Displacement and rehousing is an ongoing process in M-East Ward, with slums bulldozed periodically, buildings erected at breakneck speed, and transit camps filled, emptied, and refilled.[27] And the exigencies of providing water to Mumbai's rapidly changing built space means that water engineers are impelled to make water appear in places not anticipated by the department's own planning trajectories, while attending to the very real temporal, geographical, and political imperatives to maintain pressure in the pipes. As the department's supply planners complain in the 2009 White Paper, such dynamics have "forced [the engineers] to take makeshift water supply arrangement, smaller water zones, curtailed supply hours and . . . inconvenient water supply timings" (Municipal Corporation of Greater Mumbai 2009: 7). Accommodating the proliferation of shiny high-rise towers, the seas of slum rehabilitation housing in far-flung areas, the luxury hotels, and five-star (sometimes aqueous-themed) residences boasting swimming pools and promising continuous water supply has resulted in constantly changing, often unreliable, and little understood hydrologies.

THREE

"YOU CAN'T STOP DEVELOPMENT"

Hydraulic Shambles

In May 2009 the Maharashtra Coastal Zone Management Authority (MCZMA) cleared a proposal, put forth by the Ministry of Urban Development on behalf one of the city's largest property developers, to change the land-use designation on the site of a defunct textile mill in the Island City (zoned in the 1991 development plan partly for industrial use and partly as public recreation ground) in order to make way for a five-star hotel. According to the minutes of the MCZMA meeting, the urban development secretary argued that violating the zoning laws to allow for the hotel might be in contravention of the *letter* of the law but would adhere to the *spirit* of the costal regulations (which are intended to protect the fragile environment) since building a luxury hotel on the site would prevent "encroachment" on the land by the urban poor. "The impact of [slum encroachment] on Coastal Ecosystem [*sic*] will be significantly more adverse than the planned development," the secretary reasoned. Besides, he added, McKinsey and Company's (2003) *Vision Mumbai: Transforming Mumbai into a World Class City* clearly states that, as India's commercial capital, Mumbai needs more high-end hotel rooms (MCZMA 2009).[1] Apparently convinced by this argument, MCZMA approved the rezoning but limited the buildable area according to the 1991 development control rules, with an FSI limit of 1.33. The rezoning of this eighteen-acre (72,593m²) site for high-end residential development presented somewhat of a challenge for the water supply planners, who had configured water infrastructure according to the 1991 development plan and control rules; nonetheless the hotel project might still have been manageable with an FSI limit of 1.33. In the following months, however, a series of negotiations with the Urban Development Ministry would see the FSI for the inner-city coastal plot raised to an astounding 10; in 2009 the site was approved for a 103-story, water-guzzling five-star colossus.

In response to the developer's request for a no-objection certificate from the water department (required by the Building Approvals Department before the awarding of a commencement certificate to the builder), the BMC's chief hydraulic engineer sent a memo to the developers stating in no uncertain terms that the "present capacity of network to supply additional water is Nil." The communications between the developer and the water department indicate that the hotel's anticipated water demand was 1.58 million liters per day (mld); while much of that demand was to be accommodated by nonmunicipal sources (groundwater, wastewater recycling, rainwater harvesting), the developer requested 0.5 mld from the BMC, which amounts to more than 0.01 percent of the daily water supplied to the entire city of Mumbai. The water department informed the developers that this water could be made available only upon completion of two major water supply projects for source augmentation and conveyance.[2] Unfazed by the department's assertion that there would simply be no water available in the near future, the developer expressed little doubt that the requested water would be provided. There would be no problem, one representative assured me, "because this is a developed city."

This series of exchanges reveals a paradox at the heart of Mumbai's world-class transformation. From the perspective of the builder proposing a 103-story residential building in a no-development zone, being a world-class city means that water for "high-end" constructions will be provided—somehow—notwithstanding water supply planning dictates or the material constraints of hydrology. A similar idea was advanced by the urban development secretary when he cited *Vision Mumbai* to justify the use of additional FSI in a no-development zone: as "the commercial capital" Mumbai is in urgent need of additional hotel space, and planning regulations should be flexible, responsive to the market and to the investment-attracting imperative rather than to the limits set by the development plan and control rules. A particular conception of Mumbai as the "commercial capital" is thus served up as an argument for *overlooking* development regulations that would guide and control the city's economic and physical growth in the longer term. Here, tweaking the development plan and control regulations is justified not in order to *transform* Mumbai into a world-class city over time but to *perform* Mumbai as an already world-class city. In contemporary Mumbai "world class" is an image that is performed and signaled in the present through spectacular feats of construction, where the dictates and materialities of planning itself are dismissed as vestiges of an outmoded, pre-world-class temporality.

Water department engineers blame Mumbai's world-class-city boosters for wreaking havoc on municipal water distribution—for creating hydraulic "chaos." The way market logic was operationalized in the city's liberalization-era development control rules has rendered infinitely malleable the regulative tools of the development plan: land use zoning, density rules, and FSI. The creation of a market in urban development rights has unbundled the regulatory regime governing the built space of the city from that of its water infrastructures. During the period of research the clumsiness of this urban development ballet was nowhere more apparent than in the pages of the daily print media, where, nestled comfortably among the stories blaming water tanker "mafias" for the dry taps of Mumbai's respectable residents, highly theatrical street protests of water shortage in the city's working-class neighborhoods (particularly during the run-up to an election), or high-profile visits by Delhi politicians to water-starved slums,[3] appeared a steady stream of full-page glossy images seemingly from another universe—or at least another city. While the municipal authorities announced citywide water cuts of up to 30 percent during the spring and summer of 2009, developers of high-end real estate boasted Jacuzzis, swimming pools (both in clubhouses and on private terraces), manicured "waterscapes" replete with waterfalls and "meandering streams"—veritable "islands of luxury" right here in Mumbai (figure 3.1). How do Mumbai's swelling ranks of gated communities, office towers, five-star hotels, and leisure complexes fill their swimming pools, water their gardens, and run their washing machines? While the human body can suffer long spells without adequate parking, ventilation, schools, or even hospitals, water is a more time-sensitive affair, access to which must be produced, in some way or another, every single day. How is water access accomplished? How, given the material and political constraints of the water distribution network, do luxury developments make good on their material and infrastructural promises? And what material implications might these interventions have for areas of the city to which such developments are invisibly but inextricably interconnected? The marketized city has two sides: a side *generating* development rights and a side *using* development rights. This chapter brings together material from both sides, drawing on accounts from two research sites that have a multidimensional relationship: they are located a

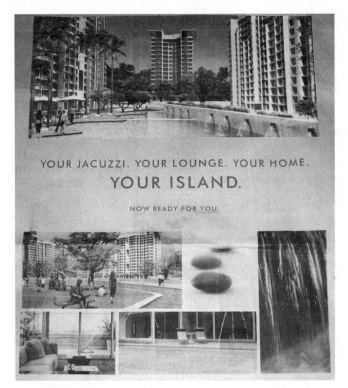

FIGURE 3.1. World-class islands. Source: *Times of India*, May 2009.

YOUR JACUZZI. YOUR LOUNGE. YOUR HOME.
YOUR ISLAND.
NOW READY FOR YOU.

stone's throw from one another in Mumbai's M-East Ward; one was produced using TDR generated by the other; and they are hydrologically linked, fed by the same below-ground water distribution main.

Watering TDR-Generating Development

The first decade of the twenty-first century presented the M-East water department's thinly stretched staff with a new challenge: approximately 200,000 project-affected people displaced by Mumbai's makeover-inspired binge of urban redevelopment and upgrading initiatives were shifted into resettlement tenements in the M-East Ward.[4] Indeed an overwhelming amount of the city's resettlement housing for the hundreds of thousands of people displaced by urban renewal and infrastructure projects has been (and continues to be) constructed in M-East. There are two significant factors contributing to this concentration of what are increasingly referred to in the city as "vertical slums": first, M-East has some of the cheapest real estate in Mumbai, a likely result of the neighborhood's proximity to the noxious Deonar Dump and municipal slaughterhouse, affording the area famously bad air and foul odors, as well as both physical and ritual pollution;[5] second, M-East is conveniently located at the southernmost tip of the Mumbai Suburban District, which allows TDR generated there tremendous flexibility regarding where it is used.

Since this massive transfer in population was made possible by a series of changes to the development control rules and land use zoning, the increased water demand was not anticipated by the water department's 1999 Master Plan for Water Supply. In this context ward-level engineers have had to scramble to allocate the ward's existing resources; the results have been mixed. Two of the largest resettlements—the sixty-nine-building strong Lallubhai Compound (with homes for at least fifty thousand people) and the similarly large Indian Oil Compound—were built between 2003 and 2005 only a few hundred meters from the severely hydrologically challenged neighborhood of Shivajinagar-Bainganwadi.[6] An October 2003 letter from the water department's Planning and Research Section addressed to the deputy municipal commissioner (Special Engineering) was unambiguous about the lack of infrastructural capacity to support these two projects:

> A huge SRA development is coming near Tata Nagar Govandi [Lallubhai Compound]. The [development plan] roads abutting to the SRA plot are not yet developed and there is no water main in close vicinity.[7] Further, the entire locality is slum and presently having short supply problems. . . . Water supply can be granted only after water supply to Mumbai is augmented and water supply network is strengthened. A huge SRA development is coming near Lotus Colony [Indian Oil Compound]. The demand of proposed SRA is about 3.82 [mld]. This plot is abutting to GM Link Road. The locality falls in Shivajinagar and Bainganwadi zone and facing acute short supply. . . . Such a huge demand cannot be fed from an existing network. Considering the huge development coming up in entire Mumbai and particularly in Eastern Suburbs, it will not be possible to release water supply till . . . December 2007 and [until] network is strengthened wherever necessary. The water supply situation in these wards is already critical and any additional load will create precarious water supply condition.

In light of the limitations posed by the existing water supply network, the water department granted the MMRDA its no-objection certificate for the projects on the condition that "water supply can be made available only after December 2007 subject to augmentation of water supply to Mumbai & laying & commissioning of adequate size of water mains."

Notwithstanding the water department's unambiguous assertion that water could not be supplied until 2007, displaced families were shifted into Lallubhai and Indian Oil beginning in 2004. The engineer recalled, "The [MMRDA] said, 'We'll lay the main, just give the water.' I told them, 'I *have* no water!' And they said, 'Just give us twenty liters for drinking;[8] we'll make borewells for other water.'" Indeed the approved plans for Lallubhai put demand for BMC water at 20 lpcd; water for flushing and bathing were to be provided by borewell, for which separate rooftop tanks on each of Lallubhai's buildings were constructed. Lallubhai Compound, however, is situated on marshy, reclaimed industrial land; needless to say, when the builders attempted to dig wells, they hit the swamp. The engineer sighed, "[The MMRDA] laid the mains, but then after, of course there was no water for borewells—it's a brackish area! So then MMRDA came back to me and said, 'Come on, give us forty-five liters, we've already started moving people in.'"

In order to facilitate water supply to the Lallubhai and Indian Oil resettlement tenements, the MMRDA constructed a new outlet main from the local service reservoir. The new main is not actually an outlet main, however, because it does not attach to the local service reservoir, Trombay High-Level Reservoir. Construction of a new outlet main would have been extremely time-intensive (not to mention costly), thereby defeating the just-in-time quality of this infrastructural intervention. Instead the main begins with a cross-connection with Trombay High-Level Reservoir's *existing* outlets. The MMRDA's new pipe, in other words, is a *redistributing* main, channeling water from the existing Gowandi Outlet to the resettlement sites. Yet while the pipe constructed by the MMRDA in 2004 provided for the redistribution of water *within* the Trombay High-Level Reservoir's zone, it was not until 2007 that additional water supply actually reached the reservoir itself to accommodate the area's hundreds of thousands of new residents.[9]

Lallubhai's water troubles, as this story demonstrates, began from the temporal disjunctures of marketized planning. The land on which Lallubhai is constructed is zoned in both the 1967 and the 1991 development plan for industrial use (which, as the Chitale [1999] Committee report makes clear, was predicted to pose no additional water demand on the distribution system) rather than for fifty thousand new residents. But despite the official procedure requiring the agreement (or at least no objection) of the water department for any new construction, Mumbai's boosters in the state government (the MMRDA, the SRA, the Ministry of Urban Development, and the municipal commissioner) disregarded the water department's clearly stated inability to provide water to the project and began allotting families at least two years before the water department could make adequate bulk supplies available in the local service reservoir. As one senior engineer bitterly recalled, the MMRDA knew that once they moved people in, the department would *have* to find a way to provide water: "Otherwise the corporators would scream and the public would be at our doorstep."

Lallubhai was one of a handful of such sites constructed and allotted between 1999 and 2006 in the M-East Ward, where, by some estimates, the residential population grew by 50 percent in seven years. In the meantime engineers, residents, and various political actors have scrambled and improvised ad hoc water-access arrangements, whose complex hydrologies would continue to impact infrastructural configurations even after more water became available to Trombay High-Level Reservoir—on schedule—in 2007. As a result, as of 2010 water access in Lallubhai tenements remained a hotly contested issue. Some buildings get significantly more water than others, due to proximity to feeder mains of course, but probably also due to a trend of installing submersible suction pumps inside tanks. (One of the area's elected municipal councilors proudly bragged that he had instructed his constituents to install booster pumps: "If the municipality won't give water, then people will have to take it for themselves.") Inside the buildings water flows are equally puzzling. Neighboring rooms produce water of dramatically different pressures and out of varying numbers of pipes. (Some can get water only out of one of the three or four taps, while others have full pressure in three or even four.) Meanwhile allotment irregularities have somehow allowed a handful of families to be put into rooms intended as housing society offices; these tiny spaces have only a single tap. At water time, accusations (and sometimes fists) fly as residents accuse housing society leaders of making extra keys to the rooftop so that favored residents can open valves to their homes after everyone has gone to sleep. (Buildings have rooftop valves that allow for a measure of control over which rooms on which floors are supplied; some top-floor rooms have their own valves, which are always the object of suspicion.)

In particularly dry times some full buildings with well-organized and politically connected housing societies manage to arrange for the occasional municipal water tanker; the very best manage to have new pipes laid to augment their supply, thereby further lowering water pressures to buildings downstream on the distribution main. In less fortunate buildings, however, the vagaries of the allotment process have left many rooms empty. Since buildings must have at least 70 percent of rooms allotted before they are permitted to register as cooperative housing societies—a procedure that affords both legal legitimacy and access to builder-deposited funds of Rs 20,000 per family intended to help with building maintenance fees—half-full buildings as well as those with large percentages of renting tenants (discussed below) have limited access to these more comprehensive modes of securing additional water supplies. Meanwhile the below-ground tanks of some entirely empty buildings overflow when the water is released after midnight, with entrepreneurial types sometimes collecting cash in exchange for "allowing" nocturnal residents to lower their buckets into the depths.[10]

Lallubhai residents for whom water is scarce sometimes jostle with the bike-and-can crowd to fill pots of water from pipes enhanced by suction pumps in adjacent neighborhoods. Those with too much pride to go "back to the slum" for water can have cans delivered—for Rs 10 or 15 each (over two hundred times the municipal rate).[11] In 2008 a local elected official installed eight hand-pump borewells near buildings in his area (Lallubhai straddles two municipal electoral districts), but only a few have ever functioned: one produces water so salty that laundry soap will not lather; another produces water with an oily film (it is an industrial area, after all); two others simply fell apart from excessive use after a few months; a fourth dried up. The other three produce brackish but relatively clear water that residents collect in pots and haul up flights of stairs for use in flushing toilets. During the driest and hottest summer days before the rain comes, a growing contingent of women makes the twenty-minute trek to the other side of the railway tracks, where residents of a former fishing village allow them to wash clothes using water from an open freshwater well.

Not surprisingly, many of Lallubhai's allotted families have sold or rented out their houses and moved away, invariably citing water trouble as a motivating factor.[12] Lallubhai is thus home to a brisk business in real estate brokering; commissions are so fantastic that one fellow from a neighboring area, a man named Rashid, subcontracted out his local water-selling business in the nearby slum so he could enter the Lallubhai brokering business. The exodus of allotment recipients from Lallubhai is creating very real challenges for the ones left behind: new renters or owners cannot become housing society members since SRA's resettlement policy prohibits selling or renting flats until ten years from the date of shifting. As a result many renters do not pay their maintenance bills at all, placing extra financial strain on remaining residents, who then have their electricity cut periodically for nonpayment of bills (and then are unable to pump their water to the rooftop tank for distribution). These residents must either arrange for a pilfered power supply to run the building's water pump or collect water by the bucket from the ground-level sump. A handful of residents on the lower floors have rigged individual hoses that run out their windows into the ground-level tanks, from which they suck water up to their rooms using individual suction pumps (mostly run on pilfered power). Residents, social scientists, politicians, and water department staff thus refer to Mumbai's slum resettlement buildings as "vertical slums." Rashid describes the situation:

> [The authorities] want to chase us off, that's why they don't give us water. Half of the rooms [in Lallubhai] have already been sold or rented because people don't want to live here—there's no water and it's in the middle of nowhere. . . . I used to live at Mahalaxmi![13] They don't want us to be happy here, they want us to sell and get out of here. Then, after ten years, when this place is transferred to the owners, it will be so bad that no one will want to stay here. Then the builders will just pay a little bit of money to buy out any remaining legal people so they can knock down the buildings and construct expensive, taller towers. The FSI will probably be higher by then anyway.

From the outset Lallubhai has experienced a process of water-mediated devaluation—"slumification"—that threatens to render the housing colony obsolete even before all the buildings are allotted. Indeed, as Rashid prophesied, in ten years some builder will probably manage to bring Lallubhai itself under slum redevelopment.

Upstream on the Pipe: Using Transferrable Development Rights

While Lallubhai residents complain of inadequate water supply, department engineers maintain that since 2007 they have been supplying 45 lpcd to Lallubhai. The BMC's official water supply norms, a senior engineer explained, dictate that "planned constructions including SRA" should in theory receive 135 lpcd. In practice, however, "SRA buildings are generally given 90 lpcd, but in case the SRA has come up in an area where there is acute shortage of water, they are given 45 lpcd." While 45 lpcd is a paltry amount, even *that* figure is vehemently disputed by many residents, who claim that their taps produce even less. My research in a handful of buildings found that some buildings receive significantly more water than others. Aggregate consumption, however, reveals very little about how much water comes out of the tap in any particular flat. With varying amounts of effort, time, and money expended, the fifty or so Lallubhai families in four buildings that I regularly visited between 2008 and 2010 were able to access anywhere from 100 to 200 liters per family per day (that is, between 20 and 40 liters per person) of municipal water. Given the newly laid outlet to convey water directly from the reservoir to the resettlement colonies,

TABLE 3.1. Zone-Wise Water Supply Estimates

Zone	Population (as of 2001)	Supply (in million liters per day)	Per capita daily supply
Island City	3,300,000	1,170	355
Eastern Suburbs	4,200,000	890	212
Western Suburbs	6,200,000	1,318	212
Total	13,600,000	3,378	248

The White Paper itself does not calculate the daily per-capita supply estimates; I have generated these numbers myself using population and zone-wise supply estimates given in the White Paper (Municipal Corporation of Greater Mumbai 2009).

why was water in Lallubhai *still* so scarce after the increased inflow to Trombay High-Level Reservoir in 2007?

The water department's 2009 White Paper (Municipal Corporation of Greater Mumbai 2009) gives the zone-wise water supply estimates shown in table 3.1.[14] While these estimates include not only residential but also industrial and commercial consumption (much of the city's industrial demand is clustered in M-East), even taking into account an estimated 20 percent leakage loss, adequate water supply (enough to supply not only the bare minimum 45 lpcd but the practical norm of 90—if not the real norm of 135) should, it seems, be available. Why is more water not reaching Lallubhai? To address this mystery, it is helpful to search a little upstream on the pipe; when it comes to water supply, how much water flows where and to whom is intimately related to the various and multiple forces acting on the pipes themselves.

The outlet main constructed by the MMRDA to feed Lallubhai and Indian Oil travels north from the reservoir, following the path of the older Gowandi Outlet toward the railway tracks.[15] Just before the tracks, the new main, which the water department refers to alternatively as "the 800" or the "GRP,"[16] is joined with this branch of the Gowandi Outlet (which has a diameter of approximately the same size, 760mm) just before the latter ducks under the railway tracks. The GRP then reappears on the northern side of the tracks, branching off once again from the Gowandi Outlet, and then forking into two lines. One line heads north, bypassing a new pumping station and storage tank, to boost the water mains along the highway, including a newly laid twenty-four-inch-diameter (600 mm) pipe that heads westward along the highway toward the sixty-one buildings of Indian Oil slum resettlement compound. The other branch of the GRP makes a sharp right just on the north side of the railway tracks, heading directly to Lallubhai.

An engineer named Mistry explained that although the GRP follows the same path as the similar size Gowandi Outlet between the Trombay High-Level Reservoir and the railway tracks, it was necessary to construct a separate line because the Gowandi Outlet branch that runs parallel to the GRP from reservoir to railway is the supply main for the area south of the tracks. If Lallubhai's and Indian Oil's water were to travel between the reservoir and the railway tracks through the existing Gowandi Outlet (rather than through the new GRP), in other words, most of the water would be dissipated into distribution mains south of the tracks, leaving insufficient water pressure in the pipes feeding the enormous new resettlement colonies on the northern side. It was for this reason that the MMRDA had to construct the separate outlet from the reservoir to the tracks, the parameters of which were formulated to ensure a certain pressure precisely at the point at which the GRP branches out toward Lallubhai and Indian Oil on the north side of the tracks.

The GRP is a market-driven hydraulic intervention itself, not envisioned as part of the 1999 water supply plan but rather constructed just in time to meet the changing topography of the world-class city. Yet notwithstanding the immediacy of this intervention, the period of construction was long enough for the GRP itself to become the site of a further intervention, when an enormous plot of land zoned for industry along the path of the GRP on the southern side of the tracks was suddenly rezoned for residential development.[17] Through the use of large amounts of slum-generated TDR—112,000 square feet of which was generated by the construction of Lallubhai Compound itself—this former bicycle manufacturing plant is now home to the gated residential community of Nestor's Palace (figure 3.2).

Upon entering the grounds of Nestor's Palace, the visitor is greeted by a large poster inviting her to "enjoy the flavor of Greco-Roman living." Each of Nestor's nine towers has been given a Greco-Romanesque name (some of which are water-themed, such as Atlantis); indeed the development's theme has a distinctly aqueous sensibility, replete with two large swimming pools. The first of the towers, built in 2005 (while the second phase of Lallubhai was still under construction), was even designed with bathtubs in each of its luxury apartments. Since the BMC Act actually prohibits the installation of bathtubs in private homes (since one bath uses up to 200 liters of water),[18] an anonymous complaint in 2006 led to the redesigning of the remaining develop-

FIGURE 3.2.
Nestor's Palace,
foregrounded
by a slum
neighborhood.
Photo by
author.

ments without bathtubs. It is, however, as a Nestor sales representative named Prakash explained, possible for bathtub-desiring homeowners to arrange for the installation of tubs later on, as long as they secure the permission of the housing society's other members (individual flats in Nestor's Palace do not have water meters but pay monthly dues to the society as part of a flat fee inclusive of property taxes and maintenance—water, electricity, security guards). Bathtubs, Prakash assured me, are not beyond the water supply capacity of Nestor's Palace, which "guarantees 100 percent" that there will be municipal water in the taps, twenty-four hours a day. In any case, he shrugged, most of Nestor's residents are not partial to baths, perhaps preferring to indulge their Greco-Roman fantasies in Nestor's swimming pools.

Nestor's swimming pools may or may not be filled with municipal water; the compound also contains a number of freshwater wells. While much of the territory of Mumbai is reclaimed land (notably the land on which Lallubhai and Indian Oil slum resettlement colonies are situated), Nestor's site, while zoned for industrial use since the 1964 development plan, was long used as agricultural land by the residents of area *gaonthans* (agricultural villages). According to the contractors, during the construction period there was no need to arrange for groundwater supplies to be brought in by tanker truck (the principal means by which water for construction purposes is accessed in Mumbai) since the on-site surface wells produced more than sufficient quantities of water.[19] For residential purposes, however, the wells remain unused.[20] "The people living here don't want to use well water," Prakash told me, "so we have BMC water."

Notwithstanding Nestor's disinterest in and professed lack of need for the abundant freshwater resources underfoot, the compound has been constructed with a large rainwater-harvesting facility, which, since 2002, is a requirement for all new constructions in Mumbai.[21] During one of my visits, the contractor pointed out a large below-ground concrete tank that he identified as a rainwater-harvesting facility; rainwater collected in the tank is to be used for gardening purposes. Since the water levels in the area's surface wells were already quite high on the eve of the rainy season, the requirement to harvest extra water in the ground seemed somewhat silly. The contractor agreed: since there is so much green space in the area (not only on the grounds of Nestor's Palace but in the adjacent village lands, some of which are still in use for agricultural purpose), the groundwater level quickly reaches the surface during the rainy season, turning Nestor's manicured lawns into marshy swamp. The rainwater-harvesting tank thus actually functions as a drainage system, with perforated underground pipes directing excess groundwater into the tank, from where it is pumped into the sewer.[22]

In other words, Nestor's Palace claims to use municipal water not only for its residents' drinking and cooking purposes but also for its washing machines, dishwashers, showers, and scattering of bathtubs. (Toilets are plumbed with recycled wastewater; each building has its own gray-water recycling plant for this purpose.) One (unaffiliated) contractor guessed this amounted to at least 225 lpcd.[23] While Nestor's Palace is of course in a different water supply timing zone from the resettlement colonies north of the railway tracks (even though they are located at upstream and downstream points on the same pipe, they are not supplied during the same zonal timing), the relationship between the two connections is more than metaphorical since the two developments share a water source at the Trombay High-Level Reservoir. Given that Nestor's Palace was constructed at the same time as the massive slum resettlement townships less than a kilometer away[24]—constructions to which only 20 and 40 lpcd were given—how did Nestor manage to arrange for such abundant supply when so little was available in the Trombay Reservoir for the resettlement tenements such a short distance away?

Sources both inside the water department and in the private sector explained to me the means by which additional water supply is arranged for new high-end (world-class) constructions. I posed the question to a ward-level engineer named Kailash, who responded, "It's easy. What the builders do is hire a licensed plumber to figure out the numbers. See, the size of the connection is determined by a formula, and if you just play a little with the numbers—the pressure in the pipes or the timings of the valves—then the formula will say that they need a bigger connection."

To provide water to Nestor's Palace, arrangements were made for a connection from the existing Gowandi Outlet. The cross-connection, which is opened by the ward staff's valve operators during their daily rounds, boosts water pressure in the Gowandi Outlet at a point just upstream of Nestor's connection. At the same time that the cross-connection is opened, a second valve is closed on the boosted main a little way downstream. A ward-level engineer, responding to my query about the nature and purpose of these two valves, explained that closing the second valve effectively traps the water, so that it is directed to a particular area. He moved his hand in circles above the unmarked space on my map where Nestor's Palace is situated: by opening and closing these valves, he explained, "we supply to this area." In this way the world-class development of Nestor's Palace is infrastructurally configured to "guarantee 100 percent" that the taps will be pressurized twenty-four hours every day.[25]

You Can't Stop Development!

While it is tempting to dismiss Nestor's hydraulic fortune as simply a cash-lubricated phenomenon, there are more interesting dynamics at play. When I asked Kailash whether the kinds of interventions made for world-class developments like Nestor's Palace can have adverse effects on water flows and pressures elsewhere in the ward, he grew agitated, answering firmly (and switching to English), "You can't stop development!" As a justification for an intervention to provide water to a world-class construction, Kailash's words are remarkable: "development" is described as something that is already here, a force unleashed at some point in the past that is now unfolding according to its own internal laws in a sort of manifest destiny that cannot possibly be stopped by any present intervention. At the same time, "development" is an ineluctable *future* toward which the city is headed, a project in which Kailash finds that his own expertise and present actions are—for better or for worse—enlisted. This is a similar use of the English word *development* by the earlier-mentioned property developer who was distinctly unfazed when informed by the water department that the network capacity to supply his 103-story luxury hotel upcoming in a no-development zone was "nil." The man assured me that of course the water would be provided: "There will be no problem. This is a developed city." With the "developed" character of Mumbai evidenced by already existing features of the built landscape, it seems, present-time actions to actually *produce* the world-class city need not be constrained by linear time—or by the materialities of water pipes and flows.[26]

Water department engineers, for their part, describe their position with a sense of helplessness and growing frustration. At the ward-level an engineer named Sheth explained that his job had become a little like the children's game of Kho Kho, which works somewhat like the American game of tag: one team chases the other for a fixed amount of time, tagging "out" members of the other team; then the tables are turned and the chasers become the chased. Sheth said that, similarly, when an area needs water, he must find a way to tweak the system—manipulate a valve, commission or decommission a water main, make a cross-connection—all the while trying not to compromise water flows and water pressures in other areas. But inevitably another area soon complains of shortage, and he must reconfigure the arrangement to accommodate this new demand. At some point the first party's taps go dry again and the configuration is again adjusted. So it goes. Another ward-level engineer confided that when an arrangement for a water connection to a new property is made, the department generally reaches an understanding with the builder that "full water" can be guaranteed only for a few months; beyond that, "anything can happen."

And indeed, in the spring of 2009 I met the secretary of an elite housing society called Guruprasad that had recently taken to hiring private tanker trucks to deposit 10,000-liter loads of municipal water on a biweekly basis into the society's underground sump. The secretary explained that until sometime in 2007 they used to receive plenty of water twice a day, for an hour or so in the morning and evening. Since the construction of Nestor's Palace across the street, however, the evening water supply had stopped and the daytime flows had decreased in pressure. Yet soon after Guruprasad's water tanker deliveries began, the groundskeeping staff of Nestor's Palace approached Guruprasad's watchmen to inquire how Nestor's might also arrange for water by private tanker. While water supply to the compound had been regular for a few months, the storage tank had recently begun to see significantly less water than before. The challenges faced by Nestor's water pipes went beyond the hydraulic, threatening to impact the world-class image—and thus the market value—of the not yet complete project. If the idea of the world-class city is intimately (if only implicitly) intertwined with an assumption of continuous, uninterrupted infrastructural connectivity, then in the context of increasing infrastructural volatilities produced by the world-class city building project itself, the normalization of continuous flow must be understood as a significant political achievement, one that requires continuous production and maintenance. That is, rather than be surprised at water shortages in "posh buildings," we might ask why anyone is surprised by such infrastructural disruption.

FOUR

"IT WAS LIKE THAT FROM THE BEGINNING"
Becoming a Slum

The Wrong Ward to Study

When Mumbai's hydraulic engineers talk about the city's water problems, they almost invariably make a reference to the city's slums, where over half of the city's population is said to reside.[1] More specifically mention is often made of a neighborhood known as Shivajinagar-Bainganwadi in the M-East Ward, which the city's water engineers describe as the embodiment of the challenges they face in supplying water to the city. "M-East Ward is not representative of our work in Mumbai," one senior water department engineer named Sharma said. "The problem is Shivajinagar. It's a slum area, an illegal area. It's not in the development plan—it's not planned! Legal structures are only those for which a plan has been submitted. But they've occupied illegally; they just keep on constructing illegally and then they steal water with illegal water connections." I had, Sharma insisted, picked "the wrong ward to study." The hydrologically challenged neighborhood of Shivajinagar-Bainganwadi is a counterpoint to the legal, planned spaces of the city, spaces that are said to reflect the rational designs of planners and experts rather than the haphazard, hazy legalities of the slum.

Sharma's identification of Mumbai's slums as the cause and embodiment of the city's water problems reflects a newly emergent and highly mobile discursive trend not only in India but within the international aid and development community at a global level.[2] Recent years have witnessed enormous amounts of attention (and donor funding) directed toward "slums" and the problems they are held to embody: overcrowding, poverty, lack of sanitation and clean water, and the various illnesses that thrive in such conditions. The United Nations' oft-cited *Global Report on Human Settlements 2003: Challenge of the Slums* predicts that, in the coming years, the vast majority of the world's population growth will take place in cities of the Global South, where it will be absorbed by and have its water needs met in the varied terrain of habitation, employment, legality, and sociality of the urban slum (113).[3] Development industry experts have converged on a theory that posits slums as the product of population growth that outstrips cities' abilities to plan for city dwellers' housing and infrastructural needs. "The failure of governments to do this in the past, the United Nations 2009 *Global Report on Human Settlements* proclaims, has resulted in close to 1 billion slum dwellers worldwide." Planning, the *Report* thus asserts, "will have to play a significant role in providing alternatives to the formation of new slums, given the anticipated doubling of the urban population over the next generation" (13). The notion that slums arise from lack of planning and must therefore be prevented or upgraded using planning-related tools has become a veritable battle cry as lending institutions, consultant experts, politicians, activists, and businesspeople from all over the political spectrum seek to facilitate, ameliorate, or profit from the trials and transformations of the southern world's burgeoning slums.

As we saw in chapters 2 and 3, Mumbai has received significant amounts of such attention. Since the Maharashtra government's approval of McKinsey and Company's (2003) *Vision Mumbai* report, displacement and rehousing has become a regular occurrence in Mumbai, with slums periodically bulldozed to make way for office towers and mega-infrastructure projects. Displaced families who can prove that they and their house meet a cutoff date for eligibility are rehoused in densely packed clusters of tenement-style apartment blocks that are sprouting up in the marshlands on the city's periphery, while those who cannot meet the cutoff date find themselves homeless. In partnership with the international development community, the city's boosters are thus engaged in a full-fledged effort to plan, bulldoze, and build their way to a world-class, slum-free Mumbai.

The set of theoretical oppositions on which the Mumbai makeover project hinges—planned versus unplanned, legal versus illegal, world-class versus

FIGURE 4.1. Gridded layout of Shivajinagar-Bainganwadi. Google Earth.
Image © 2014 DigitalGlobe.

slum—is, however, perhaps not as sound as it seems. Indeed the policy framework that would fix the city's infrastructural woes by supplanting slums with
planned housing blocks relies on an undertheorized notion of the slum as
the counterpoint to a planned, formal city and as an always already existing
place that is plagued by infrastructural problems (e.g., unavailability of water)
due to its status as unplanned or informal or illegal. In the hydrologically dystopic neighborhood of Shivajinagar-Bainganwadi, however, the notion that
water problems stem from the neighborhood's slummy, unplanned, and illegal
character is complicated by historical reality: the neighborhood *was* planned.
A cursory glance at satellite imagery reveals the gridded pattern of the neighborhood, which was laid out in the 1970s as a municipal housing colony
(figure 4.1). Shivajinagar-Bainganwadi complicates conventional dichotomiza-
tions of urban terrain as planned and unplanned, not-slum and slum, formal
and informal, and presents a puzzle: Why is this municipal housing colony
considered a slum? And how did municipal water supply to a government
colony become illegal? The neighborhood's transformation from planned municipal colony to illegal slum, this chapter shows, was facilitated by the politically mediated deterioration and criminalization of its water infrastructure in
the context of liberalization-era policy shifts that have produced Shivajinagar-
Bainganwadi's informality and illegality as a discursive *effect*. Shivajinagar-

Bainganwadi's water problems do not stem from the neighborhood's ontologically prior status as a slum; rather the neighborhood's reimagining as a slum has been mediated by the liberalization-era politics that have come to infuse the neighborhood's water pipes.

Of Plans and Slums

Notwithstanding Shivajinagar-Bainganwadi's reputation as "a slum area, an illegal area," the neighborhood is not, formally speaking, a slum, nor are its residents living there illegally. Accounting for Shivajinagar-Bainganwadi's reputation thus necessitates a brief exploration of the conceptual and legal history of slums in Mumbai. Notably there is nothing in any legal definition of *slum* that associates this category of settlement in contemporary Mumbai either with informality, planning, or lack thereof. Another legal category, "encroachment" (which has to do with unauthorized occupation of land or violation of zoning laws), comes closer to this notion. But as is commonly known in Mumbai, many five-star hotels and luxury housing complexes in the city are technically encroachments, and no one confuses these structures with slums. Slums, it seems, are something else, something that does not conflate with informality, illegality, or lack of planning. Legally speaking the 1971 Maharashtra Slum Areas (Improvement, Clearance and Redevelopment) Act (hereafter the Slum Act) allows to be "declared" a slum "any area [that] is or may be a source of danger to the health, safety or convenience of the public of that area or of its neighborhood, by reason of the area having inadequate or no basic amenities, or being insanitary, squalid, overcrowded or otherwise." Yet despite the formal definition, the word *slum* is commonly used in contemporary Mumbai somewhat interchangeably with terms like *encroachment* and *illegal area*. A senior water engineer reasoned that "the problem [with M-East Ward] is the illegal encroachments; the politicians and ministers protect all these slums. M-East Ward is a mess because the whole staff is preoccupied by Shivajinagar." This statement is striking not only for the equivalency it posits between encroachment and slum but in identifying the municipal housing colony of Shivajinagar with *both* of these concepts. This taken-for-granted conceptual conflation of encroachment and slum in Mumbai is a relatively recent phenomenon that has occurred in conjunction with the liberalizing economic reforms and concomitant housing policy shifts since the late 1980s and early 1990s. In order to understand this shift—and then to understand how this new meaning of slum has come to characterize Shivajinagar-Bainganwadi—we must explore the historical and legal interrelationship between the politics of master planning and of slum policy in Bombay, tracing the origins of the municipal housing colony Shivajinagar-Bainganwadi to the intersection during the Emergency years in the 1970s of these theoretically separate but practically intertwined logics.

While plans and slums are *legally* unrelated in a formal sense, the history of planning in Bombay is intimately related to that of slums, or more specifically with the practice of slum clearance. The completion of Bombay's first regional development plan in 1967 brought into being a set of macro-level planning tools (land use zoning and development control rules) to be used in controlling population densities. While the new zoning regulations permitted light industry (textile mills) largely to remain where they were in the Island City of Bombay, newly implemented density regulations meant that the industrial labor force would have to be moved. The municipality carried out resettlement efforts with little success in the years following the release of the 1967 development plan; for the most part the decade saw little in the way of large-scale demolition. Most attempts to remove working-class neighborhoods to the suburbs were defeated by the persistence, perseverance, and political savvy of the urban working classes; after any demolition, people simply rebuilt their homes, and overwhelmed and outnumbered municipal officials were often inclined and politically pressured to accept cash in exchange for turning a blind eye. In addition the 1966 Maharashtra Land Revenue Code established the means by which plan-violating encroachments could be legalized through a process termed *regularization*.[4] With the passing of the Maharashtra Slum Act in 1971, criteria were specified according to which a neighborhood could be declared a slum and thus become eligible for various improvement schemes. The declaration of a neighborhood as a slum, it must be noted, did not function to adjudicate legal from illegal land uses but rather to facilitate the provision of services—water, roads, sewerage— to underserviced neighborhoods. The years following the release of the development plan are thus remembered somewhat fondly by present-day Mumbai's housing activists and historians as a time during which incrementally built popular neighborhoods were treated as something of a housing solution and official efforts focused primarily on upgrading and service provision, facilitated by political processes of negotiation, compromise, and stealth.

"We Were Still Filling in the Swamps with Garbage"

Curiously the swampy northernmost section of Trombay Island, where the enormous municipal housing colony of Shivajinagar-Bainganwadi would come into being in the 1970s, was not actually zoned for residential use in Bombay's first master plan of 1964. In fact it is not zoned at all; on the land use plan the area is represented by a grayish expanse labeled simply "marshy land" (Correa, Mehta, and Patel 1965). Why so soon after the drawing up and approval of the city's first master plan did the area come to be used—in contravention to the development plan—for *residential* purposes? One answer seems to lie in contradictions internal to the plan itself. While the land use plan designates the area as marsh, the *Report on the Development Plan* (Government of Maharashtra 1964) describes it rather differently: as a garbage dump. At the time the development plan was approved, the land in question (which at the turn of the twentieth century was identified as a sufficiently remote site to receive the city's trash) had already received over sixty years' worth of Bombay's refuse. The 1964 *Report on the Development Plan*, however, is vague about the current and future status of the dumping site; in places it describes Deonar not as a dump at all but as a "reclamation," the 1,500 tons of garbage delivered daily "intended for reclaiming low-lying lands at Deonar." At the same time, however, the *Report* suggests that Deonar's days as a dump might be numbered. With much of the neighborhood zoned for industrial use, the *Report* suggests that "it might not be possible for the Corporation to use Deonar as a dumping ground" for much longer (107). The *Report* thus suggests contradictory designations and gestures toward multiple possible futures for the area that would come to be known as Shivajinagar-Bainganwadi, which is simultaneously zoned as marshland, referred to as reclamation, and discussed as having an industrial future. The development plan appears less like a guide to the future shape of the city than a reflection of unresolved battles over urban land use.

None of the plan's designations for Deonar (swamp, reclamation, industrial site) accurately predicted—nor apparently posed an obstacle for—the dump's transformation into a *residential* development just a few years later. In 1968 (only a year after the government of Maharashtra sanctioned the development plan) the BMC granted a lease to the Tata Power Company (whose services were under government contract) to house its workers on a strip of land on the western edge of the dumping ground, sandwiched between a tributary of Thane Creek and the dump. Within a few years (around 1971), when the construction of a bridge displaced a few hundred families from a central neighborhood of Bombay, the municipality directed the displaced families to rebuild their homes adjacent to the Tata Power colony.[5] This steadily growing neighborhood came to be known as "Lotus Colony" when a large number of Konkan (Maharashtrian) Muslims were displaced from a downtown area called Lotus, a neighborhood that was home to long-established Marathi-speaking Muslim communities of tailors and *zari* workers,[6] cloth merchants and traders. The arrival of the Lotus settlers changed the character of the neighborhood considerably;

as one longtime resident told me, "Those people were Maharashtrian Muslims from Bombay side, and many of them had worked for a time in the Gulf—so they had businesses in town and lots of contacts." Leveraging these networks, many Lotus families used their allotments to set up workshops rather than residences. Soon the area began to attract migrants from all over India, particularly Muslims from north India and West Bengal, who came to work in the tiny manufacturing spaces that began to flourish in what would become a thriving industrial and residential neighborhood with a distinctly Muslim character. The open-endedness of Deonar's future in the 1960s and 1970s is evidenced by its multiple designations in the development plan as well as by the creation of Lotus Colony. The future of the neighborhood was undecided, full of possibility, and a multiplicity of actors (the dump, the swamp, large and small industry, scrap traders, fishermen, farmers, and real estate developers) were busily staking claims.

When Prime Minister Indira Gandhi famously suspended the Constitution by declaring a national State of Emergency in 1975, the government of Maharashtra and the Bombay Municipal Corporation—both under the control of Indira's Indian National Congress Party—unleashed a two-pronged effort to modernize the city and render it more governable. On the one hand the newly constituted Maharashtra Housing and Area Development Authority carried out a mammoth work of surveying and enumerating 1,680 neighborhoods deemed by authorities to violate the zoning or density norms set in the 1967 development plan.[7] Meanwhile, in January 1976, residents of those areas (an estimated 2.8 million people, 47 percent of Bombay's population) were photographed in front of their homes and issued "photopass" documents that associated particular families with particular structures; photopass-holding families were to be afforded "some kind of security of tenure" (Government of Maharashtra 1976) as well as a guarantee of compensation in the event of demolition. And indeed concurrent with the survey and issuing of photopasses, the Emergency-empowered Bombay municipal authorities—in a move that contemporary observers consider largely opportunistic—unleashed a series of "extremely brutal" demolition sprees in areas that were standing in the way of infrastructure development and urban upgrading projects: roads, bridges, a tidier downtown, a fancier financial district (Mahadevia and Narayanan 1999). It was these Emergency-era demolitions that resulted in the creation of the enormous municipal housing colony of Shivajinagar on the swampy edge of the Deonar dumping ground in 1976.

My inquiry into the historical geography of Shivajinagar-Bainganwadi was inspired by a curious disjuncture between the neighborhood's reputation as a largely illegal, haphazardly constructed, unplanned area and its physical form: a grid of roughly equally spaced and sized plots of land, clearly suggesting the hand of state planners. While municipal officials readily conceded that the area was a planned municipal colony, any visual representation or written report on the planning of the neighborhood has proven elusive.[8] By way of explanation, an engineer in the BMC's Survey Department suggested that perhaps Shivaji-nagar "didn't happen according to any plan; it just filled in, slowly slowly, over time." I responded that he must be right, but certainly that could not have been the *plan*! He offered that in those days, good plans were not made for resettle-ment colonies; there may not have been a plan. I pleaded that there must have been one; after all, the neighborhood is a grid. *Someone* must have drawn it out on paper first, at least so that the water department could put in all the pipes.[9] A laborer standing nearby, familiar with the neighborhood, nodded his agreement with my assessment. "Yes," he said, "there must be a plan, it was clearly planned." This sentiment was echoed by a senior engineer from the water department who remembered the planning and laying out of the municipal pipelines for Shivaji-nagar in the late 1970s. After I recounted my protracted hunt for the plan, the en-gineer firmly responded, "The maintenance department has it—they *must* have it! But they won't give it to you, you have to understand. They want to say now that it was like that from the beginning. If you have the plan, you can fix the date when it came up; they don't want you to be able to do that." The engineer's insis-tence that the planned history of Shivajinagar had been deliberately obscured is compelling less for its plausibility than for its insight that the planned history of Shivajinagar is inconveniently at odds with the way that the neighborhood is now popularly and legally treated: as an illegal slum.[10]

Notwithstanding present-day characterizations of Shivajinagar-Bainganwadi as a slum, the Emergency-era resettlement policy by which the colony was es-tablished articulates quite a different idea. A slim pamphlet published by the government of Maharashtra on the heels of the 1976 photopass survey clarifies that, in the event that tracts of land should urgently be needed "for some other public purpose," the state government would relocate photopass-holding fami-lies to "some other places where they will be provided with playgrounds and other amenities *in order to ensure that a new slum is not created*" (Govern-ment of Maharashtra 1976: 13; emphasis added). And indeed Shivajinagar-Bainganwadi—far from a slum—was born with significant infrastructural investments. The area was laid out in two phases, Shivajinagar 1 and Shivajinagar 2 (now known as Shivajinagar and Bainganwadi), with fourteen roads and at least ninety-four blocks (known as plots), each with eight lanes, or *chawls*. Each chawl was designed to be allotted to sixteen families (eight on each side of the lane), each outfitted with a toilet block and four shared water taps (known as standpipes), two on either end of the toilet block. The BMC provided the land, water lines, and toilets, but homes were to be built by each family itself, as one NGO puts it, "as per their means": either *pucca* (out of concrete and brick) or *katcha* (out of cloth and bamboo poles and whatever materials were readily available).[11] The BMC declined to formally lease the land to settlers; instead the residents of each ten-by-fifteen ground-level space each pay a small amount (originally Rs 25 rupees; these days Rs 100, a little over $2 in 2009) each month to the Municipal Corporation as "compensation" for occupying the Corporation's land and as payment for the supposed provision of civic amenities.

While the neighborhood filled up in waves over three decades, much of Shivajinagar was settled during the neighborhood clearances of the Emergency years, when the Corporation took advantage of its special powers to forcibly acquire land for use in accordance with the 1967 development plan. Among the first arrivals were residents of a long-established community of lower-caste Maharashtrians in the downtown area of Churchgate, adjacent to the Maharashtra government's administrative headquarters (or Mantralaya), where many residents worked. Others came from areas that were demolished in a wave of urban development and infrastructure projects, including those in the now posh areas on the western sea face, and in the city's present-day financial district at Nariman Point. The second phase of Shivajinagar—now known as Bainganwadi ("eggplant field"), after the vegetables that were displaced to make way for the neighborhood—was similarly settled during the late 1970s through a process of demolition, resettlement, and migration. The shifting of the city's slaughterhouse from the western suburb of Bandra into the M-East Ward (in accordance with the 1967 development plan) brought a large contingent of butchers, who were given allotments in Bandra Plot on the eastern side of Bainganwadi; when a municipal bus depot was constructed on the southeast corner of Bainganwadi, the municipal employees staffing the depot were given housing allotments in the nearby BEST Plot;[12] a large swath of working-class housing was cleared in Deonar itself to make way for a new bridge that would facilitate road accessibility to the planned slaughterhouse; other neighborhoods were moved for reasons that have been lost to history. "I don't know why they tore us down," said a shop owner named Rajesh. "Why do they ever move slums? Just to move them! Maybe there was something in the development plan. . . . But they didn't build anything, there's just *jhopadpatti* there now."[13]

Whether or not there ever existed a formal plan for the municipal housing colony of Shivajinagar-Bainganwadi itself, the development plan of 1967 suggests that with the ongoing "reclamation" in Deonar, this expanse would in the future cease to be "marshy land," though what would replace the marsh was not yet decided. Shivajinagar-Bainganwadi's creation during the Emergency years, however, occurred while this garbage-mediated swamp-to-land transformation was far from complete. I spoke with a retired municipal employee named Quereshi who had worked as a bulldozer technician throughout the period of reclamation. Quereshi explained that, until 1984, there was a train line that departed from a garbage depot, just south of where Shivajinagar-Bainganwadi now sits. The entire area north of the depot was filled in with sacks of garbage until 1984, when the garbage train was decommissioned and the tracks removed. "If you dig down anywhere in this neighborhood, you'll find those sacks. We just filled [the swampy areas] and then extended the track," he explained. "Then when that part was filled, we undid the bolts of the track and moved it again."

While the municipality filled up the land with people west to east across the expanse of open land, the swampy sections in the middle of what is now Shivajinagar-Bainganwadi—where Quereshi and his colleagues were at work dumping sacks of garbage—had to be skipped over. These middle areas, in other words, were not laid out with streets and pipes. But there was some "good land" to the east that used to be a vegetable garden. "[The municipal authorities] filled up the area with people," Quereshi explained, "while we were still filling in the swamps with garbage." A closer look at the satellite image reveals a curious series of deviations in the gridded pattern of the neighborhood (figure 4.2); in a central section of Shivajinagar the roofs of houses are organized in a diagonal pattern, suggesting orientation toward the garbage railway, which, as Quereshi told me, moved a number of times as it made its way across the neighborhood's swampy midsection. As Quereshi and his colleagues dumped and bulldozed, enterprising settlers constructed homes on the newly created land, an area that came to be known as Saibaba Nagar. One longtime Saibaba Nagar resident described it to me: "There was a big lake. When you look on the map now it looks like plots, but that's not how people settled, not in a line. They settled where there was land: first a hut here, then a hut there."

From 1976 until 1984 the area that Quereshi and his colleagues were filling in with garbage was gradually transformed from an open expanse of water ("a big lake") into an official plot inside the municipal colony. While the lake region was thus not laid out with roads and municipal water pipes in the lattice framework characterizing the rest of the neighborhood, by 1984 any confusion over whether Saibaba Nagar was land or water had been resolved. In a proposal presented to the Development Plan Department, which was then in the process of finalizing the 1984 development plan, the Municipal Corporation's Slum

FIGURE 4.2. Detail of Saibaba Nagar's diagonally oriented roofs. Google Earth. Image © 2014 DigitalGlobe.

Improvement Cell proposed the former lake as a possible site for a municipal school. On the 1984 plan that was finally accepted, however, the area in question is simply depicted as a somewhat larger plot. The incremental settlement and eventual regularization of the neighborhood (accomplished so seamlessly in this case, with the simple assigning of a number to the new, oddly shaped plot) demonstrate how historically inscribed contestations over land constitute a politics of claims making that interfaces with and often precedes dynamics of master planning.[14] Indeed the 1984 development plan seems more an interpretation and coding of a particular claim rather than as a guide to future development.

Dry Pipes

A great many families who were allotted plots in Shivajinagar-Bainganwadi never actually settled there. Their reasons were relatively straightforward: first, many of the displaced families had long-standing social and business networks elsewhere in the city to which they simply returned; second, living next to the city's dumping ground was apparently not a pleasant experience. Accounts of the neighborhood's early days are vivid: the smell from the dump was horrific, and the neighborhood was nothing more than a swampy jungle full of garbage where mosquitoes swarmed. Not surprisingly, many people left in the early years (if they came at all), selling, renting, or simply abandoning their plots of land and going to live with relatives in more salubrious parts of the city or back to parts of the city where they had lived for generations, where they had jobs, relatives, schools, and hospitals. Also, despite the presence of legal water pipes, getting water to come out of the taps soon proved to be something of a challenge.

The neighborhood's earliest settlers—in the southernmost plots closest to the feeder main—report that once upon a time (in the late 1970s) there was water in the pipes. In the early years each plot's four standpipes were fully pressurized for up to six hours every morning. But this abundance was fleeting; the duration of supply became shorter, and within a few years many standpipes, particularly those farther back from the feeder main on the highway, started to go dry. By the early 1980s, residents report, many of the municipally supplied standpipes had been completely abandoned. A woman named Usha recalled, "That's when we started running around with pots to find water." While women balancing vessels on their heads roamed Shivajinagar-Bainganwadi's lanes, their sons, husbands, and brothers ventured farther outside the neighborhood. Waking at dawn to hang big blue plastic cans from the frames of sturdy steel bicycles, they set off sleepily into the vast industrial landscape to compete for road space with fertilizer trucks and oil tankers while keeping an eye out for water.

The drying up of the housing colony's pipes in the 1980s can be attributed to at least three factors. First, according to the water supply planners, Shivajinagar-Bainganwadi posed challenges from the outset. After the Municipal Corporation approved the development plan in 1967, the water department drew up its *own* Master Plan for Water Supply, a plan for the following two decades that used the development plan's projected population estimates to calculate present and future spatially distributed water demand. Based on these predictions, water supply planners drew up plans for augmentation of aggregate storage and collection capacity and for a network of service reservoirs across the city, from which local areas would be supplied. With the Emergency planning in 1976 of Shivajinagar-Bainganwadi, however, the water department scrambled to ration its supplies (the area that would become Shivajinagar-Bainganwadi was not actually zoned for residential use in the 1967 plan), laying additional lines from the service reservoir that had just been constructed to provide water to the slaughterhouse and other industries zoned in the 1967 development plan for M-Ward. The drying up of the pipes in the 1980s thus resulted not from any *lack* of planning but from the heavy-handed efforts to implement the development plan itself—efforts that, somewhat ironically, disregarded the very plan the municipality had served up to justify those same efforts in the city center. It would not be until 1984, with the commissioning of an additional service reservoir, that the water department would be able to provide water sufficient for the planned colony. But by then another factor had already intervened.

While Shivajinagar-Bainganwadi residents took to climbing on and off of bikes and huffing forty-liter cans around the neighborhood, as early as the late 1970s migrants as well as displaced families from other parts of the city began to settle in the vast, marshy terrains outside the gridded area. While large-scale abandonment of allotted plots meant that there was plenty of available space in the "planned" areas of Shivajinagar-Bainganwadi, there was little incentive for people to move there: there was little water, no housing, and, because the plots were registered in the names of allotted families, no more security from eviction than there would be in an unplanned neighborhood. One of the area's earliest and most populous settlements is Kamla Raman Nagar, which is situated on the swampy area to the southeast of the Bainganwadi plots and was settled in the late 1970s, before most of Bainganwadi's plots were allocated. A quick survey reveals the appeal of this neighborhood, which is conveniently located close to the main road and the bus stop. Until the early 1990s there was a large freshwater pond that provided a free and convenient source of water for bathing and for washing clothes. (No one drank this water.) And Kamla Raman Nagar had a final, less visible advantage: the neighborhood is sandwiched between two large water mains, one along the highway just to the south of Kamla Raman Nagar, which fed a number of fertilizer industries in the area, and another along the main road at the south edge of Shivajinagar-Bainganwadi, where the distribution mains for Bainganwadi are laid.

While Kamla Raman Nagar had clear advantages over Bainganwadi, it had the disadvantage of being unauthorized; despite proximity to large water mains (the whereabouts of which were never much of a secret), there were no municipal water connections. Neighborhood leaders thus arranged for a handful of municipal water connections from the pipes feeding Bainganwadi-Shivajinagar in order to provide water to the growing numbers of residents. A neighborhood leader recalled, "I led a protest march and we went to the ward office. The engineer backed down and agreed to give us seven connections. . . . Once we had a few, then it was easy to arrange for more." Needless to say, all of the water that was going to Kamla Raman Nagar was not going to Bainganwadi. Thirsty Shivajinagar-Bainganwadi residents sought ↙ turn the tables of their losing water battle (they were downstream on the water main from

Kamla Raman Nagar) by installing hand pumps on their connections, which saw decreasing pressures and shortening hours of supply; connections without hand pumps simply went dry. Soon, in a tit-for-tat escalation of the water pressure wars, everyone began to install increasingly powerful motors on their drying-up pipes, attempting to suck with ever-increasing strength a little more of the water their way. Since water taps in Shivajinagar-Bainganwadi produced water at lower and lower pressures for a shorter and shorter time, fewer and fewer families could fill their vessels from a single tap. This inspired some residents in the still wet southernmost plots to approach the ward office of the water department to apply for individual water taps. The steadily increasing number of individual connections may have provided short periods of relief, but the proliferation of taps ultimately exacerbated the problem by further reducing the already low water pressure.

Throughout the 1980s neighborhoods like Kamla Raman Nagar emerged all along the northern and eastern edges of Shivajinagar-Bainganwadi through a variety of processes and arrangements that index a lively politics of housing possibility and infrastructural provisioning during these years.[15] By the late 1980s, for instance, in line with the improvement-oriented conception of slum that prevailed before liberalization, the water department laid a new water main to Kamla Raman Nagar directly from the feeder main on the highway, thereby providing a municipal water supply while relieving demand on the distribution mains in Shivajinagar-Bainganwadi.[16] Indeed while Shivajinagar-Bainganwadi and the surrounding areas presented significant challenges for the water department, these challenges were treated as *hydraulic* rather than *legal* problems.

Slum Redevelopment and the
Birth of the "Illegal" Water Connection

In 1988 the government of India formulated a new National Housing Policy, which aimed to meet the country's rising shelter needs through dramatically expanded involvement of the private sector, financial markets, and NGOs. First articulated in Maharashtra by the Congress government's chief minister Sharad Pawar, "slum redevelopment," as chapter 2 shows, was at the center of the broader plan to transform Bombay into India's financial capital and global service center: slums were to be either removed to the urban periphery or redeveloped vertically (to open up land for commercial development) under the 1991 Slum Redevelopment Scheme. This approach to slums thus presented a sharp contrast with that of the previous decades (although eerily reminiscent of the

Emergency-era demolitions that created Shivajinagar-Bainganwadi) that had centered on upgrading and improved service provision through regularization and declaration.[17] These changes have severely constrained the water department's ability to carry out water supply planning activities, as evidenced by the case of Shivajinagar-Bainganwadi. Indeed the advent of slum redevelopment in 1991 sidelined policies based on the formal definition of a slum as an underserved neighborhood eligible for infrastructural-upgrading programs. This presented an increasingly acute problem throughout the 1990s for the growing neighborhoods on the periphery of Shivajinagar-Bainganwadi, which were not fitted with below-ground water mains. Until the early 1990s residents of these far-flung neighborhoods regularly pooled their resources and applied for municipal water connections to be laid to the closest possible pressurized main inside Shivajinagar-Bainganwadi. As populations grew, however, distribution mains in Shivajinagar-Bainganwadi dried up and residents were left with little choice but to get on bikes and buy water by the can—which in 2011 cost anywhere from Rs 3 to Rs 5 for forty liters, around seventy-five times the municipal rate. Every morning sees a mobilization of astounding dimensions in the neighborhoods of and around Shivajinagar-Bainganwadi, where people often bypass the long lines to venture farther and farther afield looking for water.

In order to provide water to the hordes of roaming bikes, entrepreneurs in well-positioned (high-pressure) spots in Shivajinagar-Bainganwadi have arranged for *many* connections and in recent years have sought to increase the duration and pressure in the connections through a clever (if bizarre) technology. After the water department's laborers have fit a new connection to the municipal pipeline, private plumbers remove the fittings (which enter the pipe only to a depth of a half inch) and instead insert lengths of pipe all the way to the bottom of the water main. This allows the pipe, which is attached to a suction pump, to access water even when the pipes are not pressurized. These days, brokers and plumbers tell me, there is not a single productive pipe in Shivajinagar-Bainganwadi without a "vertical piece," as the technology is known. Needless to say, stuffing the water mains with vertical one-inch sections of pipe has only worsened water pressures farther downstream; during the eighteen months that I researched in the neighborhood, micro-innovations continued apace. In 2010 the neighborhood witnessed another plumbing innovation whereby a rubber hose is attached to the end of the vertical piece, which is then laid along the floor of the pipe, where it can catch every last dribble. As of 2012 even the best-placed connections could not hope for water in the absence of strong suction pumps. The pumps are illegal, of course, effectively criminalizing the entire neighborhood, including the Shivajinagar police station, which has a pump on its own water connection.

Meanwhile those whose connections have dried up have continued to receive water bills regularly. (Meters are nowhere to be seen. The newer ones are quickly stolen—and are thus infrequently installed—and many of the older ones have sunk underground, beneath layers of paving and repaving as the neighborhood struggles to keep from sinking into the marsh.) When these people eventually go to the water department to inquire about getting a new connection, they are told that they must first pay thousands of rupees in delinquent water bills (for water they never received of course; in the absence of functioning meters, bills are simply drawn up according to estimates calculated according to supply norms) before such a request can be considered. These families then have a few options: some have pooled their resources and paid exorbitant fees to have connections "transferred" further upstream on the distribution main, laying out the costs of steel piping and fitting themselves, and then offsetting the costs by letting their neighbors use water on the connections for a fee. The transfer can happen in one of two ways: "legally" or "illegally." The transfer can be done "legally" by paying a fee to a broker (brokers tell me they use much of this to pay "speed money" to overworked water department staff), who then arranges for the new connection to be officially documented and thus followed by regular and legitimizing bills. But the fickleness and unpredictability of the water grid (even if a transfer is done "legally" there is no guarantee that the new connection will produce water, either now or in the future) are such that many families minimize their financial risk by opting for the cheaper, "illegal" transfer. The broker-negotiated payments are less, but the family does not receive documentation in the form of a regular bill; there is thus a risk that a connection that is transferred without documentation could be cut in a municipal raid.

Indeed, about once per week, the M-East ward water department staff engages in a ritual cutting of "illegal" connections in Shivajinagar-Bainganwadi—a task that involves randomly selecting a pipe or responding to an often politically motivated complaint, following the pipe to its home, and then asking the homeowner to produce documentation of the pipe's authenticity: a water bill for the pipe in question (one that bears an address near enough to the particular pipe to be plausibly related to the pipe) and identity documents (usually a photopass or ration card) bearing that same name and address. While the fate of illegally transferred connections is generally bleak, in practice even most of the legal connections are vulnerable to being proclaimed illegal since there is frequently a lack of correspondence between the names on water bills and the identity documents of those living in the homes to which the bills are sent. This lack of correspondence can be explained largely by a government circular issued in March 1996 by the newly elected Shiv Sena government of Maharashtra, according to which residents of "unauthorized structures" that do not preexist the 1995 cutoff date cannot be supplied municipal water connections.[18] In order to examine the means by which cutoff-date politics infuse the landscape of water access in Shivajinagar-Bainganwadi, it is necessary to briefly attend to the shifts in slum and housing policy and ideology that have characterized liberalization-era Mumbai.

The Cutoff Date

The Shiv Sena swept the Maharashtra Legislative Assembly polls in 1995 on a promise to provide free houses to Bombay's estimated 4 million "slum dwellers," elaborating on the already existing housing policy shift that had been advanced in conjunction with (and in the spirit of) the national-level liberalizing reforms and "world-class city" idea. Shiv Sena's rise to power in Bombay must be understood in light of broader political dynamics characterizing liberalization-era India. Scholars of Indian politics have noted a curious paradox in India's political landscape: while political discourse continues (as it has since the 1960s) to be dominated by populist politics articulated through local and regional caste identities,[19] the increased presence of lower-caste elected officials and government employees has, curiously, not led to the implementation of macro-level policies to further a pro-poor agenda nor translated into significant concrete gains for socially and economically marginalized people. While a populist discourse of social justice infuses the language of contemporary Indian politics, the implementation of liberalizing reforms in the early 1990s essentially removed macro-level economic issues from the political agenda altogether (Yadav 1999). This marriage of populist identity politics with economic liberalization formed the backdrop to the rise of India's Hindu Nationalist Bharatiya Janata Party (BJP) in the 1980s and 1990s.[20] Scholars of the movement's rise have detailed how the BJP leadership consolidated a base of support among the middle and lower classes by mobilizing a unifying conception of Indian national identity based on Hinduness, or *Hindutva*, thereby playing on widespread anxieties produced by increasing political and social fragmentation, while dodging the intractable conflicts over liberalization that had contributed to the electoral defeats of the previous administration.[21]

The city of Bombay has a particularly interesting place in this story, as the epicenter of India's encounter with the global has been presided over by the exclusionary, ethnonationalist Shiv Sena party. Founded in 1966 as a "sons of the soil" movement, Shiv Sena leaders decried the fact that despite Bombay's rebirth in the 1960s as the capital of Maharashtra, since the mid-nineteenth century the city's economic and political scene had been dominated by non-Maharashtrians. Sena leaders found enemies in successive waves of migrants to the city; in the 1960s South Indians were held responsible for unemployment among Maharashtrian youth, as were the political left and trade unionists of textile workers through the 1980s. When Shiv Sena formed an alliance with the BJP in the 1980s, Muslims from North India became the target, accused of harboring sympathies with Pakistan and posing a security threat. In the 1990s Shiv Sena won control of both the state government of Maharashtra and the renamed city of Mumbai, riding to power on an ideology that fused chauvinistic, populist celebration of the Marathi-speaking "common man" with a flashy, consumption-oriented ethic of urban "actionism" (Hansen 2001: 53) that summoned disaffected young Marathi speakers of the lower-middle classes to reclaim India's premier city as their own and to increase their share in the spoils of urban, capitalist modernity. The slum policy innovations of 1995 (the removal of the profit cap on slum redevelopment and the extension of the cutoff date to bring all existing slums under the ambit of redevelopment) provided a way for state authorities to capitalize on the populist political climate and the aspirational fantasies of the urban poor by promising free housing for the masses, while also unlocking possibilities for property developers (whose role in campaign finance is hardly a secret in Mumbai) to realize fabulous real estate surpluses.[22] The Slum Redevelopment Scheme was thus greeted enthusiastically not only by builders, for whom it promised boundless profits, but also by the city's slum-dwelling masses, for whom new flats in high-rise buildings promised an improved standard of living and suggested that they too could capitalize on the city's real estate boom.

The somewhat contradictory marriage of private accumulation with populist justice that infuses contemporary Mumbai's policy approach to slums is mediated by the cutoff date, which functions as the currency of inclusion in the fantasy of fortune that has captivated contemporary Mumbai as well as the medium through which the everyday violences and dispossessions that characterize actually existing world-class city making are legitimated. Indeed in order to legitimize a policy that detractors were quick to note might encourage additional migration to the city, party leaders promised to prevent any new encroachments by excluding post-1995 neighborhoods from the Slum

Rehabilitation Scheme and by disallowing the provision of civic amenities to areas that did not meet the 1995 cutoff date. It was in this spirit that, in 1996, the government of Maharashtra issued the circular prohibiting water supply to illegal (i.e., post-1995) neighborhoods; by refusing water connections, the Shiv Sena administration sought to stem the flow of migrants to the city—the rallying cry upon which the party's electoral successes had hinged. The cutoff date thus enables an enormously lucrative real estate industry through the mechanism of slum redevelopment, while simultaneously producing the very conditions that are served up to justify slum redevelopment interventions in the first place: illegality and dysfunctional infrastructure. The legal/illegal binary on which the legitimacy of world-class city making is premised is produced through the everyday performances of enforcing the cutoff date.

Becoming Illegal

Beginning with the 1991 Slum Redevelopment Scheme, slum policy in Mumbai has become effectively synonymous with demolition, with eligibility for rehousing in high-rise tenement buildings enmeshed with the legality-mediating vagaries of the cutoff date and its attendant army of proofs: photopasses, ration cards, and electoral lists. One effect of this shift has been the conceptual conflation of the previously distinct concepts of slum and encroachment. As already noted, the legal categories are formally distinct in Mumbai; the former is defined (rather fuzzily) by poor quality of housing or civic amenities, and the latter by lack of conformity to various land-use and zoning laws. According to earlier slum-upgrading policies, identifying a neighborhood as a slum made it eligible for programs to redress its lack of civic amenities with civic infrastructure and upgrading schemes.[23]

In order to be eligible for inclusion in a Slum Rehabilitation Scheme, each household must provide proof that it meets the 1995 cutoff date. The 1971 Slum Act, however, is unclear on whether the eligibility requirements for rehousing in the event of demolition apply to *families* or to *structures*—an ambiguity that in the preliberalization years may have allowed for a measure of flexibility in the administration of slum policies, the subjects of which were whole neighborhoods rather than individual residences.[24] With the shift in slum policy from infrastructure provisioning to demolition and resettlement, however, each eligible family occupying each home in a particular area has come to represent a fixed amount of redevelopment housing, in exchange for the building of which a builder is compensated with equivalent free-sale development rights. The process of sorting the eligible from the ineligible has thus become wrapped up with the high-stakes business of generating development rights.

While the photopass is the clearest and most secure form of documentation, a great many households in Shivajinagar-Bainganwadi and the surrounding areas, including many whose homes preexist the 1995 cutoff date, do not have photopasses. Some of the families surveyed in the 1976 slum census reported that they did not receive photopasses until decades later (if at all), while since 1976 there have been only two half-hearted and largely ineffectual efforts to issue photopasses—once in 1985 and another in 1990. Without photopasses families whose neighborhoods are slated for demolition under a redevelopment project have been compelled to produce other kinds of proof: they must prove residence in the city since 1995 (evidenced by having their name included in the 1995 electoral list); they must demonstrate that they are the current, official residents of the structure in question (i.e., with ration cards, utility bills, birth certificates). Since the housing market in Mumbai's popular neighborhoods is extremely liquid, it is quite common for pre-1995 structures to have changed hands in the interim years. There has thus come into being an unofficial practice of having lawyers draw up sale documents that are shored up with court affidavits.[25] Whether or not such documents—or any particular combination of those just described—are accepted as adequate proof seems to be determined more by politically mediated negotiations than hard-and-fast evidence.

When the government of Maharashtra issued the circular in 1996 requiring that anyone applying for a water connection from the Municipal Corporation must provide proof that they meet the 1995 cutoff date, they pulled issues of water access deep into the heart of the city's most volatile, complex, and high-stakes political issues. Previously the water department did not often concern itself with adjudicating legal from illegal connections.[26] As one senior retired engineer explained to me, since the Municipal Corporation Act of 1888 (Section 92a) gives the Corporation the right to sell piped water as a "movable property," the water department is entitled to provide a water supply to whoever agrees to pay for it. Sometime in the 1960s, the engineer recalled, the water department decided that the BMC Act gave the water department the right to sell water even to residents of unauthorized structures (encroachments). Reflecting this practice, the Municipal Corporation's preliberalization Water Charges Rules include an Appendix E that outlines "conditions governing the supply of water through standpipes to unauthorized hutments and structures."[27] The conceptual shift in the meaning of *slum* that has taken place in the past two decades—the conflation of slum with lack of authorization or planning—is reflected in a little-noted but important change in the Municipal Corporation's Water Charges Rules that took place during these years. Notably the earlier versions of Appendix E (from 1981, 1983, 1985, and 1987) made no mention of water supply to slums, presumably because prior to 1991 the whole business of declaring slums was wrapped up with a host of national- and state-level initiatives that had defined the concept in the first place, largely in order to provide civic amenities to underserved urban areas. (Furthermore, as one retired senior engineer explained, since the BMC Act does not even recognize the category slum, there was no need or grounds for special rules governing water supply to them.) In 1994, however, the heading of Appendix E was altered to read "Conditions governing water supply to slum areas," and the old title, "Conditions governing the supply of water through standpost connection to unauthorized hutments and structures," was made into a subheading. This new wording suggests that "unauthorized hutment or structure" might simply be a *clarification* of the meaning of *slum*. This kind of understanding is reflected in the description of Shivajinagar articulated by the engineer cited at the beginning of this chapter: "[Shivajinagar] is a slum area, an illegal area. It's not in the development plan—it's not planned!" I asked another senior water engineer, who was in the department at the time of the change in Appendix E in the early 1990s, to explain this curious linguistic shift. He responded, "You are right; 'slum' and 'unauthorized structure' are not the same. The department has used these words without bothering to go into the details. . . . I too never read my rule book so meticulously." The discursive shift in the meaning of *slum* has been accomplished so completely that the distinction from "unauthorized" area is dismissed as "details."

Since both the gridded areas of Shivajinagar-Bainganwadi and a majority of the settlements that came up around it clearly preexist the 1995 cutoff date, there should be no way to deny legal water supply to the area, which in any case one would presume to already *have* water connections (and thus would not need to apply for *new* connections). But the unpredictability of the grid has given rise to an increasing demand for additional connections as well as the transfers of older, now dry connections to points upstream on the water mains. In applying for a new connection or for a connection transfer, however, applicants bump up against the vagaries of the cutoff date rule. This presents a problem for a vast number of Shivajinagar-Bainganwadi residents who are not the original allotted persons; most have either purchased the homes from someone claiming to be the rightful owner or are renting from someone who may or may not have the structure registered in his or her name.[28]

While it is at least formally possible (if practically both expensive and extremely time consuming) for newer homeowners in Shivajinagar-Bainganwadi (although not for renting tenants) to have their homes registered in their names,[29] this is not the case for older (pre-1995) declared slums like Kamla Raman Nagar. The Maharashtra Slum Act does not recognize any sale or transfer of a structure among residents at all, meaning that even if a structure is thirty years old and its residents have lived in the city since independence, the residents are often unable to acquire documentary proof of address.[30] Thus even legal broker-negotiated water connection transfers are often constructed using spurious documents.[31] The water department's official list of connections thus might contain a relatively accurate picture of the locations of billed connections, but during a municipal raid, if the name on the bill does not match the identity proof of a structure's resident (as is often the case), even these legal connections are dubbed unauthorized and summarily cut.

Further complicating the situation, the homes and shops in the neighborhoods on the periphery of Shivajinagar-Bainganwadi do not have precise addresses; the ration cards and photopasses held by some longtime residents of these neighborhoods simply give the names of the members of a given household alongside the name of the neighborhood—"Rafiq Nagar," for instance, or "Kamla Raman Nagar." This lack of precision makes it harder for the water department to prove that a particular ration card is associated with a particular pipe in a particular location (which may or may not be adjacent to the actual residence of a ration card holder), while simultaneously rendering it impossible for cardholders to assert that it *is*. Ultimately the ability to prove that a water connection is authorized or unauthorized has more to do with networks of power and politics than with hydraulics or law. Indeed the municipal actions that I observed during my time in Mumbai—during which department staff use a handsaw to slice through insufficiently proven connections and plug the open ends with wooden stoppers—revealed that the sorting of legal from illegal pipes is largely a political process (figure 4.3). Pipes that have been declared illegal, for example, can be reestablished as legal later on by leveraging various kinds of networks and resources. As one engineer explained, "You've seen how we do it—we just go out and cut. Then we reconnect the ones that can prove they are legal. So maybe we disconnect twenty illegal connections and then five people come back and apply for reconnection." Whether and whose connections are cut is underpinned not by any adjudicating of legal from illegal connections but rather by local networks of power, knowledge, authority, and complaints of which the ritual connection cutting is simply one expression.

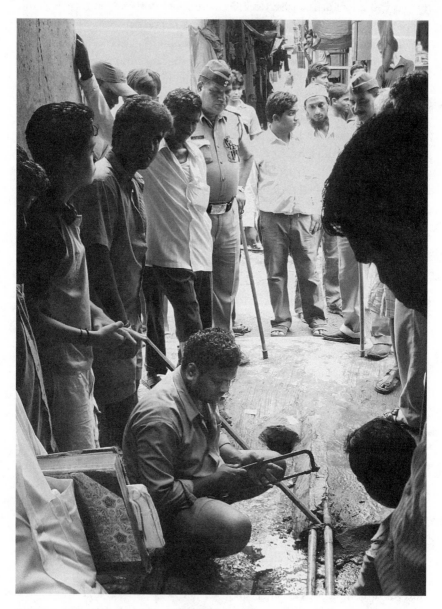

FIGURE 4.3. Cutting connections. Photo by author.

From Illegal Water Connections to Criminal Slum

Families in Shivajinagar-Bainganwadi and the surrounding neighborhoods that are not prepared to pay for a transfer (legal or illegal) generally access water in one of two ways. If they are fortunate enough to live close enough to someone with a well-placed connection and a powerful pump, they can buy water *time* on someone's connection, paid a month in advance. In 2010 ten minutes (about two hundred liters of water) cost around Rs 300, which amounts to approximately twenty times the municipal water rate (for slum areas) of Rs 2.5 for one thousand liters. If the family is not well located, then they walk or get on the bike and purchase water by the can.

On top of the expense of buying water by the can (which is both costly and time consuming) the practice is criminalized. The M-East water department staff conducts periodic raids to hunt for illegal connections and to confiscate suction pumps, bicycles, and even water vessels. Yet as the staff is well-versed in the somewhat slippery hydropolitics underpinning issues of legality, the raids take on something of a ritualistic quality. One day in 2010, for instance, I overheard a local engineer advising a resident in a far-flung neighborhood who had complained that her pipe has no water pressure. The engineer responded by asking whether she had a booster pump on the pipe, which she did. The engineer explained, "Living as far away as you do from the main, you will need at least *two* motors to produce water." He suggested a location for the second pump. The woman, nodding suspiciously, responded, "If you say so, sir." The engineer then added with a good-natured chuckle, "Then, of course, I'll have to come some day and take your motors"—a line that produced laughter all around.

A final option, and one that is increasingly exercised by frustrated Shivaji-nagar-Bainganwadi residents, is to sell or rent out the house and move to a place where getting water is less of a challenge. Indeed the daily struggles for water and resulting deteriorating quality of life have driven many longtime residents out of the neighborhood, which is increasingly populated by recently migrated renters, mostly Muslims from the north Indian states of Bihar and Uttar Pradesh but also a scattering from West Bengal, whose native language, Bengali, has inspired the widespread rumor (which has now become a generally held belief) that the neighborhood is a hideout for antinational Bangladeshi terrorists. The assumption that Bengali speakers are Bangladeshi nationals is puzzling since Bengali is formally recognized as an Indian language by the government of India and is the official language of the Indian state of West Bengal. I sought explanation for the rumor from a local NGO that has been active in the neighborhood for nearly thirty years. The director of the organization, which specializes in helping families apply for identity documents like ration cards and photopasses, explained that in the mid-1980s a handful of Bangladeshi refugees settled in the area since it was "a thriving Muslim settlement." She estimated that there are perhaps only a few hundred such families living in the neighborhood today, most of the people being Indian-born. "People say it's a Bangladeshi area, but it's not."[32] Moreover, she pointed out, "India has signed the UN convention stating that Indian-born children of refugees will be citizens, but because of political reasons, the officials will not give them the papers." Without identity papers, of course, Bengali-speaking residents cannot prove that they meet the 1995 cutoff date for legal water connections—not that legal connections would be very helpful anyway, given the lack of pressure in the pipes. The bizarre notion that Shivajinagar-Bainganwadi is populated by foreigners and terrorists permeates popular understandings and political approaches to the neighborhood.[33] One senior water engineer described how, in 2003, after hearing water shortage complaints from local politicians, the additional municipal commissioner threatened, "Don't give them a single extra drop of water or I'll have you transferred to a bad post. I've been [to Shivajinagar]. They're all Bangladeshis."

The infrastructural deficiencies of this neighborhood (as well as its proximity to the noxious Deonar dump, which now towers an astounding nine stories over the neighborhood) make Shivajinagar-Bainganwadi one of the cheapest residential rental markets in the inner suburbs.[34] In a city where low-cost rental housing has been decimated by rent control laws that have frozen rents since the 1940s, the rental stock in Shivajinagar-Bainganwadi is very much in demand. Yet the deleterious environment, the constant police presence (the criminalization of the neighborhood has led to an increased presence of police, who reportedly collect regular payoffs from the neighborhood's water vendors), and the regular water department raids (which frequently result in violent skirmishes) have made Shivajinagar-Bainganwadi one of the most notorious neighborhoods in Mumbai. An often sensationalist media regularly reports on the shadowy activities of residents, sometimes said to have connections to international terrorist groups, as well as of a so-called water mafia in the area that is said to "steal" water from the neighborhood pipes and is held to be somehow responsible for periodic water shortages across the city.[35] It is no surprise, therefore, that longtime Shivajinagar-Bainganwadi residents are fleeing the neighborhood, which is described as an increasingly unlivable slum.

While the municipal housing colony of Shivajinagar has been referred to for years as a slum, the force of this utterance took on a performative valance when, in the spring of 2010, the entire neighborhood (including the surrounding areas of Kamla Raman Nagar and Rafiq Nagar) was surveyed by a prospective developer in anticipation of a slum rehabilitation project. Shivajinagar-Bainganwadi's identity as "a slum area, an illegal area," now targeted for redevelopment policy intervention is of course paradoxical since illegal (i.e., post-1995) households are not actually *eligible* for inclusion in redevelopment schemes. This contradiction is reflected in the popular conflation of the notions of slum and illegal area or encroachment in contemporary Mumbai—evidenced, for instance, in the changes made to Appendix E of the Water Charges Rules. Given this paradox, what might it mean when Shivajinagar-Bainganwadi is referred to by the media, politicians, water engineers, and residents themselves as a slum? And what, moreover, does Shivajinagar-Bainganwadi's newfound identity as an illegal slum suggest about the project of world-class city building in Mumbai?

To answer these questions, it is helpful to briefly consider the complex nature of the verb *to mean*, which is often used to posit a relation of equivalence between a word and the phenomenon it professes to represent but which might also indicate a relationship of *intention*—that is, with an orientation toward the *future*, as in "What do you *mean* to do with that saw and wooden stopper?" "Well, I *mean* to cut your illegal water connection."[36] It is this latter, future-oriented usage that might be helpful in thinking about the meaning of *slum* in contemporary Mumbai, where the concept is used in popular parlance to refer to almost anything that looks like it could stand to be redeveloped— anything, that is, that does not conform to a world-class aesthetic.[37] From a market perspective, in other words, *slum* describes built forms that economically underutilize the lands that they occupy. In world-class-era Mumbai, the "verticalization" (Rao 2006) of the city's built space has thus recast a huge variety of urban forms as inefficient and obsolete: fishing and agricultural villages that have been annexed by the city; working-class housing on industrial estates; municipal colonies like Shivajinagar-Bainganwadi. Built space that does not conform to Mumbai's world-class aesthetic thus enters the surveyor's gaze as slum for the purpose of redevelopment.

The vagueness of the concept slum in contemporary Mumbai reflects a similar ambiguity in how the term is used in international development circles. The United Nations (2003) *Challenge of the Slums* report, for instance, admits to an incongruity between identifying a slum and operationalizing the concept for policy purposes. Indeed although general understandings of slum abound, measurable and usable definitions are elusive.[38] In an effort to forge a more quantifiable understanding of slum—a concept targeted by so much contemporary development policy thinking and aid money—the United Nations (2000: 7d) has come up with various indicators that can be used to adjudicate whether a neighborhood can be *counted* as a slum for survey and redevelopment purposes: availability of water, access to sanitation, overcrowding, quality of house construction materials, security of tenure.[39] ("If you're missing just *one* of these criteria," a senior United Nations officer explained during a 2011 lecture that I attended in Mumbai, "then you're a slum and must be *counted* as such for the statistics.") The meaning of *slum*, in other words, is given by the actions involved in surveying and mapping *potential* slums, with the survey itself producing a neighborhood's identity *as a slum*, thereby rendering the area eligible for policy intervention.

The conceptual conflation of the formally distinct concepts of slum and encroachment—a blurring that mirrors (and is likely borrowed from) the policy expertise of the global development industry—has obscured infrastructural possibilities inhering in earlier meanings of the term. Whereas in earlier years the water distribution network was systematically extended in order to water neighborhoods like Kamla Raman Nagar, this hydraulic possibility has been occluded by the new survey-enabled politics of slum, wherein structures or residents identified as eligible for rehousing are converted into equivalent and tradable units of market-valued development rights. The hydraulic effects of this material-discursive shift in the meaning of slum have been dramatic. The proliferation of suction pumps, the ongoing innovation in microtechnologies of access (like the "vertical piece" and the rubber hose attachment), and the constant transferring of connections upstream on the distribution mains have produced geographies of water pressure that defy any possible logic of hydrology; by increasing the *velocity* at which water flows through the mains, the proliferation of suction pumps actually *decreases* pressure in the pipes and curtails the distance into the neighborhood up to which water reaches. Department engineers are thus constantly redrawing distribution zones (and changing water timings in shrinking zones) by adjusting and readjusting valve openings and timings, implementing shorter and often inconvenient water timings in an attempt to compensate for (or at least keep up with) the changes produced by ongoing, piecemeal interventions in the network.

In a second, related effect of the discursive shift in the meaning of slum, the deterioration of Shivajinagar-Bainganwadi's water infrastructures has recast the municipal housing colony as informal and illegal.[40] Since households unable to prove that they (and their homes) meet the 1995 cutoff date are cast as illegal encroachers on the city, the local water department largely occupies itself not with fixing and improving the distribution network but rather with public, ritualistic performances of the legal-illegal divide. Meanwhile regular media reports on water department raids against the so-called water mafia said to operate in Shivajinagar-Bainganwadi function as spectacular public affirmations of the neighborhood's illegality. By pulling issues of water access into the murky politics of cutoff dates, the populist-profiteering politics of slum rehabilitation have produced the neighborhood's illegality and informality as discursive *effects*, occluding the neighborhood's history and legal status and recasting it as ripe for redevelopment.

When I asked M-East Ward's colony officer for clarification of Shivajinagar-Bainganwadi's formal slum status he responded, "Shivajinagar is not a slum . . . but it will be *treated as a slum*." While officials at the Office of the District Collector conceded that Shivajinagar-Bainganwadi is in fact a municipal colony, the neighborhood is considered a slum because it was surveyed in the 1999 "slum census," carried out by the Congress administration in conjunction with an electoral promise to shift the cutoff date to 2000.[41] When I asked how the surveyors decided which neighborhoods to include in the slum census, the colony officer responded, "We surveyed illegal areas."[42] Although Shivajinagar-Bainganwadi is not an illegal area, he concluded that it was probably included in the survey because, well, it *seems* like a slum.

The Irreducible Materiality of Infrastructure

When the Congress Party swept the 2004 Maharashtra Legislative Assembly elections on a promise to shift the cutoff date for slum rehabilitation eligibility from 1995 to 2000, the party leadership presumably hoped to please property developers (who would be gifted a windfall of potential slums to redevelop and thus development rights to earn) and to update the populist mandate. The promise met with predictable fury from opposition leaders, who accused Congress of pandering to Muslim and north Indian vote banks in slums, but a stronger and quite unexpected critique emerged from the ranks of elite civil society. In 2006 the residential welfare organization Janhit Manch filed a public interest litigation case against the government of Maharashtra, arguing that the Slum Rehabilitation Scheme was destroying their neighborhood, a posh area in the western suburbs. An overwhelming amount of the transferrable development rights generated by the frenzy of slum redevelopment in the city, they argued, had been utilized in their area, where residential property values are among the highest in the city. The proliferation of construction violated the FSI limits specified in the development control rules of 1991, Janhit Manch maintained, and had produced population densities and configurations of built space that made a mockery of the carrying capacity of available infrastructures, resulting in traffic-choked streets and sputtering water taps. The extension of the cutoff date to 2000 would only worsen this problem, thereby violating their rights as property owners. The Bombay High Court, convinced by these arguments, ruled in favor of preserving the cutoff date of 1995.

The Congress-led government of Maharashtra appealed the ruling to the Supreme Court, but in the meantime the 1995 cutoff date came to seem increasingly arbitrary because the electoral mandate of the Congress government was wrapped up in the promise to change the cutoff date and also because a number of slum rehabilitation projects were actually implemented using the year 2000 as the date. (Among these were slum rehabilitation projects carried out in conjunction with infrastructure-upgrading initiatives using World Bank funding, since Bank-funded projects have their own rules for eligibility that do not map neatly onto those of the Slum Rehabilitation Authority.) Local political leaders increasingly railed against projects that exclude households whose proofs fall between 1995 and 2000. With the cutoff date thus in limbo, attempts to adjudicate legal from illegal neighborhoods, buildings, people, and pipes have become ever more farcical, increasingly plagued by accusations of corruption and malfeasance.[43]

Shivajinagar-Bainganwadi's infrastructurally mediated, survey-enabled reimagining as a slum recalls scholarly debates about the relationship between knowledge and power.[44] Theorists have characterized knowledge-production technologies like surveys as governmental techniques to manage unruly populations—tools that render people and places legible and thereby amenable to governmental intervention.[45] Yet Shivajinagar-Bainganwadi's (and Mumbai's) story does not end here, with globally empowered discursive frameworks and capital-backed builders enlisting people and their homes into a hegemonic politics of world-class city making by reconceptualizing them by means of the governmentalizing technologies of survey as equivalent units of development rights. The 2010 slum survey was only one of a number of such surveys in Shivajinagar-Bainganwadi. At the time of writing, none of the innumerable schemes to redevelop Shivajinagar-Bainganwadi (in whole or in part) shows any sign of coming to fruition. A young man named Santosh, whose family owns five homes in Kamla Raman Nagar, described at least two other, smaller surveys in his neighborhood. In 2009 Santosh's family had signed on with a small-scale slum redevelopment scheme involving only a few hundred structures—a scheme that had subsequently fallen through. "Some local people and politicians got together and offered to make [the project] happen for some builder—to collect the signatures from all of us." Santosh laughed. "They took a lot of money from the builder to broker the deal . . . but then there was so much infighting that in the end the people who had collected our signatures chased off the builder and just pocketed the money."

Slum redevelopment in Shivajinagar-Bainganwadi has come increasingly to seem like a builder's fantasy. "Oh, *that* won't happen," laughed a youth-wing party leader named Imran, waving his hand dismissively at my question about the 2010 developer's survey in Shivajinagar-Bainganwadi. I met Imran in his breezy, marble-floored office at the far-flung edge of Bainganwadi after learning about a remarkable project with which he and his party office were affiliated: an enormous masjid and madrassa being planned on the adjacent block, designed to rise to an astounding (and legally wooly) height of seven stories, towering over the sea of surrounding low-rise structures.[46] Imran himself was impeccable, his embroidered button-down shining an impossible, blinding white on this dusty edge of the dusty city. He apologized for his lack of English; he grew up poor in Bainganwadi, he explained, and lack of English was the only thing thing holding him back. "If only I knew English I could do so much!" I worried aloud about what might happen to their planned masjid and madrassa should the area come under a slum redevelopment scheme. Imran at first looked puzzled, then chuckled good-naturedly at my naïve concern. "Oh, *that* won't happen," he reassured me. It's true, builders have their eye on the area, he explained, "but builders don't have all the power."

FIVE

"NO HYDRAULICS ARE POSSIBLE"

Brokering Water Knowledge

We now use the country itself, as its own map, and I assure you it does nearly as well.
—LEWIS CARROLL, "The Man in the Moon," *Sylvie and Bruno Concluded*

One steamy afternoon in June 2009, while I was hiding from the midday, premonsoon swelter under the windy heat of my ceiling fan, my phone rang. "Hello, madam!" announced the booming voice of Mr. Korelekar, the assistant engineer of the M-East water department.[1] Korelekar, who is a part-time stage actor, tends to lend a theatrical air to his dealings. His call came as a confusing if pleasant surprise. In the nine months that I had known him, getting in touch with Korelekar had always been something of an endurance test of patience and persistence; this was the first time *he* had called *me*. "Madam," Korelekar began, haltingly, "do you remember *that map*?" Yes, I certainly remembered that map—how could I forget? I had spent months tracking it down after catching a glimpse of it in Korelekar's office one day in January 2009—a hand-drawn, colorful tangle of lines and numbers, created, I was told, by a handful of ward-level engineers for their own use. After my initial sighting I had pleaded with Korelekar relentlessly to let me see the map again, after it somehow disappeared from the wall where I had noticed it, and to allow me to make a photocopy of it. "Yes yes, madam, anytime" was his refrain, but somehow "anytime" never seemed to arrive, and at some point the map was proclaimed missing. After some months I managed—through a sympathetic subengineer—to get my hands on the map (which was eventually found in a desk drawer) and to make a photocopy. I had had this copy of the map in my possession for approximately a month when Korelekar's call came that June afternoon. Yes, sir, I replied, it's here on my wall. "Madam," he continued, "do you think I might *borrow* that map?" The original copy, he explained, had gone missing again, and they were in urgent need of it. Certainly, sir, when shall I bring it by the office? "We're outside your house, madam," came Korelekar's insistent reply. I looked out my window, and sure enough, a compact Maruti with tinted windows was idling outside the gate. I peeled the tape off my wall (removing with it not-insignificant portions of wall paint), rolled my map into a neat tube, and, securing it with a rubber band, skipped down the stairs, feeling light and happy that for once I was able to be useful to the engineers who were so tolerant (if not always entirely forthcoming) in the face of my endless questions and requests. As I approached the car, a darkened backseat window lowered halfway. As a gust of frigid air wafted out of the air-conditioned space inside, I glimpsed four engineers squeezed into the backseat: Korelekar, his boss (the deputy hydraulic engineer), one of M-East's subengineers, and another man whom I did not recognize. I slid the map through the open window, and Korelekar thanked me, the dark pane of glass rising as the car sped off. It would be another month before I managed to reappropriate my map.

The hand-drawn map so coveted by Korelekar is, of course, not the only existing representation of the water supply and distribution mains in M-East. The department's official procedure for documenting expansion and change in the distribution system, as explained in chapter 1, is to draw them onto Mumbai's development plan sheets, the blueprint copies of which I had been able to acquire with relative ease during the initial months of my research. As that chapter showed, perhaps the most significant legacy of a two-decades long series of debates, experiments, and speculations over increasing use of private-sector actors and market logics in Mumbai's water distribution system has been the dismantling of the water department's informational infrastructures. This chapter shows how, in this context, infrastructural knowledge itself has become a crucial and elusive resource, yet one that cannot be described in economistic terms as scarce. Indeed the fragmentation of informational infrastructures has not resulted in *less* knowledge but rather in the profusion and diversification of sites of knowledge production, circulation, and use, and thereby (and perhaps most important) in the redistribution of control over infrastructural resources. Knowledge about things like pipe locations, water pressures, and timings and operations of valves—as well as the webs of power and influence that animate these volatile flows, appearances, and disappearances of water—inhabits a landscape of rumor, stealth, and speculation. The everyday risks of water shortage that infuse the city's hydraulic landscapes across class lines are managed and mitigated by the forging and maintenance of elaborate knowledge-exchange networks.

Working without Maps

The disbanding of the water department's survey section has meant not only that many new pipes are unmarked, but that the department has lost track of the location of many older pipes due to changes in the above-ground built space of the city. The scale of the development plan sheets means that planned roads are depicted simply as lines; depictions of water mains that were constructed along these actual or hypothetical roads (water lines have been laid along "development plan roads" that were never built) show only the path of the road along which a water line has been laid, without any indication of the main's precise location along the road. For many years personal memory compensated for this informational deficit; any question regarding the whereabouts of a particular main could usually be answered by asking around the department until someone who remembered the main could describe its precise location. As the city has grown, however, many of its roads have been widened. The speed at which the market-animated, above-ground face of the city is changing often outpaces and supersedes the department's informal information-sharing mechanisms. Gupta declared, "We don't know which side [of the road] got expanded!" A good-humored engineer named Gurav related to me the following story:

> A few years back, we were trying to find a trunk main that was laid in 1976, and we simply couldn't find it. The problem was that on our maps, the landmark was a post office gate, which had been moved. We dug and dug, day and night, for four days. We called up the fellow who was recorded as having supervised the laying of the main—he was retired of course, but we were desperate. We just wanted to ask if he remembered where it was, but he got defensive, thinking we were accusing him of not having laid it at all. He insisted, "I laid it! I laid it!" But we didn't doubt he had laid it, because water was coming into the areas fed by the main; we simply couldn't *find* it. Finally, one of the workers pointed to a fellow, a drunken homeless fellow who was sleeping in a culvert a little ways off. The worker said, "That man is always here, he probably knows where it is." I was desperate—I'd have asked a donkey if there was one there to

ask!—so we approached this fellow and woke him up. He said, "Come, I'll show you." He took us to within a few feet of the main. We asked him how he knew where it was, and he told us that he used to work in the water department—he was a valve operator. We asked him, "Why didn't you come and tell us?? You've been here watching us for days as we dig up the whole street!" He said, "I was having a good time watching you. Besides, you didn't ask me."

Upgrading roads with concrete and widening them has thus placed additional obstacles on accessing knowledge about underground networks of flow, rendering obsolete plans and maps of road networks that are simultaneously (and paradoxically) outdated and not yet achieved and setting up a physical barrier to regular surveillance and maintenance, which requires extraordinary mobilizations of labor, time, and equipment to overcome.[2]

I had the opportunity to observe such a mobilization in July 2009 when I accompanied a crew from the M-East water department to investigate a complaint about water leakage from underground; local residents had reported that water was overflowing from under the edge of a newly paved road in the Deonar municipal housing colony.[3] The following account, excerpted from my field notes, gives a sense of some of the ways that obstacles are managed by department staff in the field:

When we arrive at the spot where the leakage had been reported, we are greeted by a man holding a long metal pipe with a metal cup on the end. Introducing himself as the "sounding man," he explains to me that he had been there the previous night to "listen" for the leak:[4] "It's easier to hear at night," he tells me, because there is less traffic. It must be a sewage leak, he says, because "it doesn't sound like a water pipe." Pipes have a certain kind of sound, he explains, whereas sewage leak sounds are indistinguishable from the sounds made by other below-ground water flows; since the municipal colony is built on reclaimed swampland, the sounding rod picks up all manner of subterranean sloshing.[5] Suddenly, as we are talking—as if on cue—a flood of water emerges from the edge of the road and flows into the street. The sounding man reaches down and scoops up a handful of water, bringing it near his face; he smells it and pronounces: "Sewage." I ask, "Are you sure?" He shakes his head, "No, I don't know." But what do you think? "Sewage," he tells me, "because it smells like sewage and because it doesn't sound like a water pipe. Although . . . to be honest, with the traffic it's impossible to hear much."

I ask Kore, the junior engineer who has been dispatched to oversee the leak-detection mission, if the sudden flood might be the result of the opening of a nearby valve; perhaps the area's water supply hours had just begun? He shakes his head, explaining that "surges like this can happen anytime; if there's airlock or something, suddenly there can be a rush of water." I ask the engineer whether there is a sewage pipe below this stretch of road and he shrugs. "Is there another kind of pipe here? A water pipe?" Shrugs again. Confused about how to interpret the shrugs (Kore often insisted on speaking to me in Marathi, which I do not speak; perhaps, I thought, he had not understood my question, which I had posed in Hindi), I pointed to a valve on the opposite side of the roundabout. "There's a water main passing around that side," I say. "Is there one over here too?" He shrugs again, saying (in Hindi this time— mercifully), "There are some new pipes over there, but we don't know about old ones." I ask, "Is it marked on some map? Perhaps there is a map showing the path of the pipe from the Deonar Municipal Pumping Station to the various sections of the colony?"[6] The shrugging continues: "No one knows." Unconvinced, I approach the senior-most of the M-East labor crew—a man named Gani—asking him to explain to me how it is possible that no one seems to know what is below the road—"Don't you guys know? The engineers are transferred every few years, but you have been here in M-East for so long!" Gani shakes his head apologeti-cally: "I've been here twenty years," he tells me, "and even I don't know."

Whatever the origins of the fluid, the ground would have to be opened. The five members of our M-East labor crew begin digging, using shovels and pickaxes to carve a two-foot-deep trench out of the shoulder of the concrete road. The liquid, however, continues to flow into the trench, out from underneath the road; after an hour the engineer phones the Main-tenance Department to request road-breaking equipment.

We wait. It starts to rain, gently at first, but soon the darkened sky is emp-tying itself freely upon us; it's monsoon season, after all. Our crew disperses into various bits of shelter: into teashops, doorways, and a tiny Ganesh temple. The clerk behind the counter of the chemist shop under whose aw-ning I had taken cover announces (unprompted) that the leakage is from a sewage line. An hour passes and the rain slows, but we are still waiting for the road-breaking equipment and crew. Two hours later (around noon), an enormous gray truck pulls up producing a huge air compressor, two jackhammers, and fifteen additional flip-flop-clad workers.

[a few hours later]

When the jack hammerers have completed their work the excavated area is brimming with water. Gani smiles when I ask him what they have found: "We've found a well!" Gani inserts a long bamboo pole—at least 15 feet long—into the watery depths to assess the depth of the "well" but still cannot reach bottom. One of the flip-flop crew lets escape a giggle; a nearby group of laborers erupts with laughter. I watch in disbelief as cars, trucks and motorbikes breeze by along the smooth concrete newness that suddenly looks to be supported by nothing more than an open expanse of water below. Kore calls Korelekar and receives instructions to have the crew pump out some of the water out of the "well." Gani explains to me: once they reduce the water level, they will open a valve from a nearby feeder main. If the water level in the well rises, they know that the leak is from a water pipe.

The road-breaking crew pulls a generator and a suction pump out of the truck, attaching the pump to a hose. One end of the hose is inserted into the well and the other is directed toward a storm water drain. After half an hour, Kore pokes again at his mobile phone. We all stand around the hole and within a half hour, the water has risen slightly. The engineer announces that it must be a water pipe leak. I ask, dumbly, "But where's the pipe?" No one knows. Now what? "We call Korelekar." He calls Korelekar, who's gone to a neighborhood on "rounds" with a municipal corporator. "He'll be here soon," Kore says. Two hours pass and the rain has returned; the well has quickly refilled to its original level—maybe because of the rain, maybe because of a pipe. After a bit of milling about and a somewhat contentious discussion with Kore,[7] the road-breaking crew packs up the air compressor, jackhammers, generator, and suction pumps. They all pile in the big gray truck and leave the five-member M-East crew in the rain, which is now falling in sheets. The crew disperses once again to their various scattered shelters to smoke, drink tea, and wait.

An hour later—around 5:00—a sub engineer from M-East (a friendly and unassuming fellow named Bhide with an easy smile and a ready humor) arrives to wait with us for Korelekar, joining me under the chemist shop awning. I ask him about the road: How is the water department supposed to do its work if they concretize the roads? Now you have to get road-breaking equipment every time you want to fix a pipe! Bhide tells me that before they pave the roads, the water department is instructed to shift all the utilities to the shoulder. "But when they built this road they must not have known about the old pipe," he tells me. "It must be very deep."

Just after 6:00 a jeep arrives. The back door swings open to produce an expansive golf umbrella that struggles open against the weight of the sky, followed by Korelekar and one of M-East's chaviwalas—a man named Balekar. They splash over to the well and watch while Gani again demonstrates the well's impressive depth with the bamboo pole for Korelekar's benefit. Korelekar tells Bhide that they will need to bring back the road-breaking crew with the generator and pump—they need to suck out all the water in order to see what is down there. But it's late now—almost dark—and the crew has gone home; the well will have to wait for tomorrow. The workers mark off the excavation with some orange fencing and we all retreat from the monsoon torrents.

The following day the maintenance team found and repaired an eighteen-inch water main, sunk more than fifteen feet under the newly paved road. One of the laborers, a man in his sixties named Barve, smiled as he told me, "I knew it was there all along. I kept saying it, but the [junior engineer] didn't listen to me." He told me that, finally, when they had sucked out all the water and were still unable to see any pipe, he had approached Korelekar and told him directly, "Sir, I worked on a pipe here many years ago." He explained to Korelekar that in the 1970s he had worked on an eighteen-inch pipe running along this stretch of road; in order to find it they would have to dig a little farther out into the center of the road. "We found the pipe. It was a few feet in front of the well," out where the edge of the road *used* to be, before widening and paving. The pipe was cracked and the water pouring out had excavated space around it, creating the "well." "We put a big clamp on it. Now it won't leak." I asked Barve whether he thought that the water main still fed some parts of distribution system or if it was capped. "Korelekar says it's capped," he replied, then slowly added, "but Korelekar doesn't know." I asked him to explain where the water came from: Where does this enormous water main connect to the distribution network, and where does it go? "Who knows? Ask the chaviwala."

The episode illustrates how the fragmentation of knowledge about the water distribution network shapes the everyday work of Mumbai's water department field staff and by extension influences hydraulic outcomes across the city. The field staff began their intervention with an attempt to identify the source of the water using a sounding rod. Yet since the colony is constructed on land reclaimed from tidal swamps (as is much of Mumbai), the sounding technology was unable to distinguish between the sounds of municipal water, piped sewage, and other kinds of subterranean flows and streams. The problem of deciphering liquid sounds was exacerbated, as the sounding man explained, by the noise of constant traffic, which, unlike only a few decades earlier, now rumbles all night long. So, unable to decipher the source of the overflowing liquid by sound, the staff resorted to opening up the ground to have a look— an exploration that served as much as an information-gathering mission as a leakage-repair effort. Yet this clearly well-institutionalized practice of opening up the ground to survey, maintain, police, or repair water mains is becoming increasingly difficult as more and more of Mumbai's epidermis is coated with the modernizing veneer of concrete.

Notably the staff commenced their exploration through sight and sound of the actually existing terrain rather than by consulting the water department's official plan or maps. Indeed the conspicuous absence of any form of map at the site is striking for what it reveals about engineers' lack of faith in (and perhaps also lack of access to) the department's official maps, which at the time of writing had not been updated in at least two (and more likely closer to three) decades. My repeated inquiries over the course of the day about the possibility of consulting a map earned me either helpless shrugs, dismissive hand waves, or confused looks. At one point, thinking that perhaps the engineers and field staff did not understand what I was asking, I drew a map in my notebook, indicating the positions of the feeder mains whose locations I had come to know, and asked various people to show me how the pipe for which we were searching was connected to the municipal grid. It quickly became apparent that no one present had seen any of the various maps or plans on which my own rendering was based. While the ward office has its own collection of maps and plan blueprints, I never once witnessed them being consulted.

Private Maps

The obsolescence of the official maps—coupled with fragmentation, dispersion, and personalization of knowledge about water pipes and flows—has led to the proliferation of what might be described as "private maps": renderings drawn up by ward-level staff (in collaboration with their most trusted laborers) largely for their own use. Korelekar's hand-drawn map, for instance, is not actually his own creation; rather it was drawn by a subengineer named Sheth sometime in 2005 or 2006, before Korelekar was transferred into M-East Ward. Sheth is older than Korelekar by at least a decade and has spent most of his career in Mumbai's eastern suburbs. The BMC Act requires that engineers be transferred every three years, but there are a number of loopholes that can facilitate longer tenures. As of 2008 Sheth had already been in M-East Ward for at least eight years. He was transferred to another posting (again in the eastern suburbs) shortly after my arrival in Mumbai, but he was frequently found in the M-East Ward water department office (as well as in various field sites in M-East), where his knowledge of the system made him indispensable. Without Sheth to act as interpreter, the hand-drawn map itself did not seem to provide much in the way of clarity. (At a certain place on the map, for instance, a line indicating a water main merges inexplicably with another depicting the edge of the railway track.) Yet while Sheth's knowledge of the distribution mains in M-East is extensive, his hand-drawn map makes no reference to the cracked pipe in Deonar Municipal Colony, the abandoning of which presumably predates his own experience-based knowledge of the ward.

Even had Sheth's map provided some clue about the cracked pipe, however, this information would not have been available to the junior engineers and laborers on site, since this private map is carefully guarded; the two private maps to which I was able to actually gain access are not available to seniors in the head office nor to lower-level staff in ward offices.[8] Whatever the information depicted on Korelekar's private map, the M-East labor crew would in any case have spent much of the day just as they did: waiting for the assistant engineer (who on that particular day happened to be on rounds with a local politician) rather than in attending to other work—making new connections, for instance, or repairing other leaky mains and valves. As it happened—given the map's silence regarding the cracked main in Deonar Municipal Colony— once the assistant engineer finally arrived on the scene, information about the source and location of the water was gathered by leveraging the intimate knowledge of subterranean flows from two of the ward's laborers. The chavi-wala knew that should there be a pipe under that stretch of road, it would have to be in some way connected to a particular feeder main. By briefly opening the valve on that main, he pressurized the water distribution network in the entire area and was thereby able to observe that the liquid, which rose in conjunction with the pressurization of the area's network, was indeed municipal water. When excavation failed to locate any pipe, a piece of information stored in the personal memory of an older laborer facilitated its discovery.

Just as the locations of water pipes are matters of rumor and speculation, the whereabouts and existence of maps depicting these locations are equally elusive; the handful about which I knew were discovered and acquired by chance, rumor, guesswork, and persistence. One afternoon I had gone to look at an old concrete water main near my house where, on the previous day, I had seen two boys fill some buckets. I had walked by the main hundreds of times without giving it much thought, but closer inspection revealed that it had a large crack that had persisted through repeated patching efforts. The boys must have been collecting water from this crack. I asked a man nearby, who introduced himself as the "landlord" of a series of small, ramshackle shops and shacks lining the highway, about the pipe; I was curious as to the extent of his knowledge and interest in this pipe, both of which proved extensive. Just as he was rehearsing for me his encyclopedic understanding of the directions and timings of flow not only out of this pipe but of all the outlet mains emerging from under the wall of the adjacent Atomic Research Center (inside of which the Trombay High-Level Reservoir is ensconced), a man approached us, a water department laborer who recognized me from my regular visits to the water tanker-filling yard. The worker, a man named Patel, was off-duty but had come over to see what I was doing. Confirming the landlord's account and knowing my interest in learning about the distribution network, Patel pulled me aside, out of earshot. "There's a map," he almost whispered, depicting the size and position of the inlets, outlets, and feeder mains fed by the Trombay High-Level Reservoir. He himself had once seen the map when visiting the reservoir while on duty. Asking me not to disclose the means by which I had come by this piece of information, he told me the name of an engineer who might know of the whereabouts of the map.

After a series of inquiries about the possible existence and location of this map, I found myself in the office of a zonal-level engineer named Kamat. He was not the man whose name Patel had given me, but a more senior engineer. Kamat invited me to sit and said that yes, there was a map, but it was only a *schematic* drawing and moreover depicted the mains only inside the boundaries of the Atomic Research Center, not throughout the whole ward. I insisted that I was told about another map, a representational map that showed the placement and size of mains and connections throughout M-East. He shook his head silently but did not ask how I had come to hear of such a map, thereby fueling my suspicion that he might be familiar with it. Kamat turned away from me, speaking in Marathi to another engineer in the room, hoping, it seems, that I might simply go away. After a half hour or so he turned to me again, asking, "What was it that you wanted to know?" I repeated that I was searching for the map of the inflows and outflows of Trombay High-Level Reservoir. Sighing, he asked, "But how would such a map help you?" I responded that I had no way of knowing if the map was helpful until I saw it. (My other motivation—simple curiosity as to whether such a map actually existed and, if so, to what extent and by whom it was known—did not seem like an answer that would get me very far.) Kamat turned away from me once more. Another fifteen minutes passed before I asked gently whether it might be possible for him to perhaps phone up to the reservoir to maybe ask about that map. Kamat responded,

"Which map?" I described again the map that I sought. Regarding me blankly, he lifted the phone receiver, poked at the dial, and spoke in Marathi. A few minutes later a young man arrived holding a big roll of paper, which, once unfurled, revealed itself as the map I sought. "I made it," Kamat told me, "about five years ago. So there are some things that are outdated now."

In the weeks after acquiring a copy of Kamat's map, I took to carrying it with me on my visits to the M-East Ward office so that I might record on it the things I learned. (The map had earned my respect once I noticed a red line representing the eighteen-inch main that we had searched for in Deonar Municipal Colony. I was fascinated by the inclusion of this mysterious and elusive piece of information on Kamat's map until I noticed that the old water main is also clearly marked on the blueprint copy of the department's official map, which dates from 1973.) On one occasion I pulled out the map in Korelekar's office in the presence of a junior engineer. During my conversation with Korelekar (who claimed he had never before seen the map) the junior engineer pored wide-eyed over the map, inching closer and hovering over it until eventually he had positioned his body in such a way that I could no longer see the map at all and had to ask him to please move back a little. He apologized, explaining that he had never seen a map of the water distribution network before. A similar sentiment was expressed by the water engineers in the maintenance section, who, upon seeing Kamat's map, pleaded with me for a copy of it. On another occasion, passing through the halls of the M-East Ward office with the rolled-up map in hand, I was approached by another junior engineer. "Madam," he began, "you know a lot of things, and so do I. Let's meet outside the office. Maybe we can help each other."[9]

Knowledge beyond Maps

In the absence of maps, official or private, how is knowledge about the water distribution system produced, circulated, and used? Given the accounts presented in previous chapters of hydrologies that do not have any clear place in the city's physical, legal, or institutional frameworks, even private maps need to be supplemented by other kinds of information if they are to be useful; the city's water infrastructures exceed the command or knowledge of any single individual. Getting water to come out of municipal pipes is an activity that requires continuous attention, a measure of stealth, and intimate knowledge of a complex and dynamic hydraulic, social, and political system. In Shivajinagar-Bainganwadi, for instance, the tangles of one-inch-diameter water pipes are simultaneously productive of visibility and obscurity—of legibility and stealth. While the jumble of pipes—a phenomenon referred to by department engineers

FIGURE 5.1. Spaghetti pipes. Photo by author.

as "spaghetti pipes"—makes it exceedingly difficult to pinpoint which pipe is connected to which house, individual households know precisely which pipe is theirs and can often track the path it follows to where it is connected on the distribution main (figure 5.1). When a connection stops producing water, individual owners walk the length of their connection, checking to see if their pipes have been stolen (steel piping has a high resale value) or whether their *connection* has been stolen—that is, whether the overland pipe has been cut at the source and affixed to another, the water diverted to some other (now undecipherable) end point. This practice is common not only in Shivajinagar-Bainganwadi, but in any area where the "spaghetti pipe" phenomenon prevails. To lessen the risk of theft, the owner of a new or transferred connection will often make payments not only to the plumber or broker who has negotiated the details of the transfer with the water department but also to a local person whose residence or office is near enough to the connection point on the water distribution main that he or his friends can monitor the comings and goings in the area; indeed water connection transfers are often managed by these self-described "social workers" themselves, who maintain working relations with particular plumbers and brokers.[10] In exchange for a fee (sometimes referred to as "bhai charges"),[11] the social worker will keep an eye on the new water connections, thereby preventing any political rivals who might be seeking to contest the authority of a local power-broker from cutting and reselling the water connection in question. By the same token, residents tell me, failure to pay bhai charges risks inspiring a social worker himself to sell the connection. It is this kind of intimate and place-based knowledge, born of experience and proximity, that shores up local political authority in the neighborhood.

Meanwhile residents of single chawls—neighbors and friends who share meals, holidays, and child care responsibilities—conceal from one another information about their water connections: where a pipe connects to the distribution main, the pressure and duration of water that the connection produces, the number of members that pay monthly fees for access to the pipe (as well as the amount of those fees), and the precise time at which the water begins and ceases to flow (a factor that can vary dramatically according to where the pipe is attached to the grid). In the chawl where much of my research attention in the neighborhood was focused, for instance, there were six water connections on a block with thirty-one residences,[12] each home to anywhere from two to eight people, for a total of 155 individuals. Each of the taps had a different configuration of ownership and access: one tap (Tap A) had been in existence for approximately a year at the time of research. Thirteen of the chawl's homes had pooled their resources and applied for the connection—the fittings and pipes and fees. Previously these thirteen homes had purchased "water time" from the owner of a second tap (Tap B), a neighboring family on the same block who, reflecting the significance of water in shaping relationships in this neighborhood, were known to chawl residents simply as "Paniwali" and "Paniwala" ("water woman" and "water man"). At some point during the year prior to research, however, thirteen of the residents, tired of paying monthly fees to Paniwali and Paniwala and willing to make an investment, calculated that if they were able to arrange for a connection to a high-pressure spot on the distribution main, they themselves would be able to rent out water time on that connection. The money earned from this new arrangement was collected periodically by the person under whose name the water department bill was sent and who used the funds to pay the bill. Any remaining money was divided evenly among the thirteen connection owners, who were thereby recouping their (not insignificant) initial layouts.

A third tap (Tap C) was the oldest connection on the block, dating from the 1980s. Fixed with a hand pump (the other five are fitted with electric pumps), it had not produced water with any modicum of reliability for nearly a decade. Sometimes, particularly after some change in the water supply timings or valve openings and closings, the tap would come back to life, as if "by magic," as such occurrences were jokingly described. For this reason chawl members did not immediately give up on the tap and request a transfer (which can be quite expensive) but simply supplemented their spotty tap with piecemeal purchases—

first by the can or pot from neighboring plots, but for the past few years from Paniwali and Paniwala (Tap B), who had decided to invest in a new connection as soon as they bought their house a few years earlier. When the neighbors tired of prepaying by the month, they approached the water department to see about transferring the hand-pump connection (Tap C) to another spot on the distribution grid. However, in the interim years their water bill had grown to astounding proportions; as of January 2009 the bill amounted to Rs. 29,991 (around $675). Thus the thirteen residents had opted to invest in a new connection (Tap A), abandoning the hand pump, which continued to produce water on a completely unpredictable basis.

Of the remaining seventeen homes, nine have continued to pay monthly fees to Paniwali and Paniwala, which allows them to use Tap B for either five or ten minutes of the (approximately) two hours each day that the pipe is pressurized. To use the tap, each family unfurls its own piece of plastic pipe, which is connected on one end to the tap, with the other end draped into storage vessels, usually a 200-liter barrel that is kept either on a small ledge outside the back door of some of the larger houses (those that span the entire width of the block to the narrow back lane behind the house, approximately twenty feet) or inside the house itself. Having lost thirteen customers, Paniwali and Paniwala have found new "members" (as those prepaying monthly water-time fees are known) from less hydrologically equipped chawls nearby. In recent years, as the grid has become increasingly volatile, the demand for reliable water providers has grown. So many people wanted to become paying members on Paniwali and Paniwala's connection that in the winter of 2009, the couple invested (with income earned from Tap B) in a second connection (Tap D), which they acquired by presenting documents from another house that they own a few lanes over.

Prepaying by the month to be a member of a certain tap, however, does not always guarantee a set number of minutes; the time windows within which water arrived and disappeared varied up to a half hour on either end of a two-hour window of "official supply timings" in this particular chawl. For those taps operating on the monthly prepay member system (Taps A, B, and D), there is a hierarchy of priority: Owners fill first, officially for a set amount of time but practically speaking some families manage to take more and some less. Next, members are given use of the tap. During weeks of relative stability in pressures and timings, a set order was implemented, while any change in the system would cause the system to be renegotiated. Finally, if water pressure still remained in the pipe after all the members had filled, then these tap owners sometimes allowed the bike-and-can customers to use the tap, charging anywhere from Rs 2 to Rs 5 to fill a forty-liter jerry can.[13]

Revenues earned from selling water by the can are significantly greater than what is earned from selling water time on the connection—a price that largely reflects the financial risks involved in supplying water in this way. Bikes and cans make it easy to identify connection owners who sell water (a practice that, as described in chapter 4, is criminalized); engineers explain that finding a water vendor is simply a matter of following the hordes of bikes. Those who sell water to bikes and cans thus run a significantly greater risk of having their motors taken during an early-morning raid, of being arrested, or of having their pipes labeled illegal and cut. By contrast, while the sale of water to monthly prepaying members is also criminalized, the practice is much less frequently targeted during raids since prepaying members (whose residences are in proximity to the connection on which they have purchased water time) are supplied by plastic hose—a medium of distribution that is visibly indistinguishable from how connection owners fill their *own* water storage containers. Owners' decisions to allocate time on their connections to either members or to bikes and cans is thus a calculation of risk and profit. For ten minutes of water time in the chawl I studied, a family pays approximately Rs 300 per month. If the owner were to allocate those ten minutes to selling water to bikes and cans, at Rs 2 per can (the lowest price I encountered over an eighteen-month period) and at the rate of 1.5 cans per minute (a conservative estimate; I have seen a high-pressure connection fill a can in fifteen seconds), a connection owner can collect Rs 900 per month for the same ten minutes, thereby tripling his revenue.[14]

Tap A's group of thirteen had rented out water time to six of the remaining eight residences and to a handful of families on an adjacent plot and almost never sold water to the bikes and cans. Most of these six residences, which are located along the narrow back lane, used to fill from a fifth tap (Tap E) that mysteriously dried up about a year ago. Since no one among the six residences knows where the connection is attached to the neighborhood's distribution system (all but one of the residences are occupied by renting tenants), they have not been able to trace the problem. The general suspicion, however, is that someone has either stolen or diverted their connection or removed and stolen their steel pipes.

The remaining two residences (in a house with a rental unit on the second floor) share a single, recently constructed tap (Tap E). The homeowner's husband, who has been working in Saudi Arabia for the past two decades, has sent home enough money for the family to afford their own private connection. When I asked the owner why she did not rent out unused water-time on her pipe to neighboring families who are much in need of a reliable water supply, she explained that "renting water time to outside members is illegal"—and besides, she cannot stand all the fighting over water so early in the morning; it upsets her stomach.[15]

During the months that I researched in this particular chawl, water-related disputes were a regular occurrence. Since the neighborhood's water infrastructure itself is constantly in flux—pressures in various taps rising and falling, water timings contracting and expanding, new connections appearing, old ones drying up and being reborn—the water distribution arrangements among residents are constantly being renegotiated: prices and time intervals vary month to month, renting tenants move in and out of the neighborhood, and vertical home additions are added, changing patterns of localized demand. These fluxes are responsive too to the periodic police and BMC actions: the illegal-connection-cutting drives, the early-morning raids on the selling of water to the bike-and-can crowd. Disputes in the chawl invariably involve accusations that one or another household had acquired extra water by furtive means or had resold water without sharing the revenues with a connection's owners. Stealth-related opportunities for individual households to acquire more water are tied up with the unpredictable nature of the distribution system, which both produces water-access opportunities (by allowing extra water to be acquired before anyone notices) and provides a ready excuse for any resulting shortfalls. (When later-filling members' timings are cut short, it is not easy to decipher where all the water went.) The physical configuration of the neighborhood, as well as the fact that water is supplied before sunrise, makes even *seeing* where the water is going at any given time something of a challenge. Since most families keep their water storage containers either inside their house (for safekeeping) or outside their back door, water hoses attached to the tap in the lane would disappear through a curtained doorway. Since time is water in this particular chawl, the order in which people fill their vessels is generally a function of efficiency and proximity; if a hose has traveled through the front door of one home to fill a barrel in the back alley, then the hose will simply be passed to the nearest and most convenient member afterward. If, however, that member is not yet ready—if the member has gone to use the toilet, has overslept, is attending to the breakfast of school-bound children or work-bound spouses, or has simply not kept track of the time and the hose—then the first member will often simply keep on filling more and more of his or her own vessels until someone notices and intervenes. At the dark and sleepy predawn hours of water supply most people are inside their home preparing tea and battling back uncooperative eyelids (as opposed to, say, policing the water tap with a stopwatch), so there is ample room for opportunism. Indeed during the period of research one of Tap A's thirteen owners regularly—and without detection—controlled the tap for upward of twenty minutes.

Another member family has an arrangement with the owner to fill a set number of cans for a relative, whose own chawl has no pressurized water connections. The relative would leave the Rs 2 per can with the family, who would pass this money on to the connection owner every morning. However, since the cans are filled inside the house—where the family's own storage barrel is located—this family would also sometimes fill one or two additional cans for outside parties without sharing the revenues. Such clandestine filling of cans is not always a premeditated act; opportunistic selling to a bike-riding passerby by prepaying members is not uncommon. These kinds of routine, opportunistic acts, while are of little financial or hydraulic significance, fuel an atmosphere of suspicion in the chawl, where grumblings occasionally erupt into full-blown shouting matches when a family does not manage to fill its vessels before the tap goes dry at the end of two (or so) hours.

Any Plan Will Be Ruined

While the M-East water department staff constantly made slight adjustments to the distribution system (by changing the timings or operations of valves, by enlarging or extending sections of the distribution network, etc.), the winter of 2008–9 saw two major changes in Shivajinagar-Bainganwadi's hydrology, the combination of which had significant, unintentional, and somewhat mystifying effects on the already enigmatic workings of the distribution network. First, in an effort to discourage the overt selling of water, the neighborhood's water timings were shifted from 4:30–6:30 a.m. to 6:30–8:30 a.m. Since the water timings of various zones are part of an elaborate choreography of pressures and timings, tied up with the need to maintain the reservoir at a minimal level to allow (at least theoretically) adequate pressure at the far ends of the distribution system, Shivajinagar-Bainganwadi's water-timing change happened in conjunction with another major innovation: the commissioning of an enormous new underground storage facility and pumping station with a capacity of 6 million liters just upstream of Shivajinagar-Bainganwadi. A senior engineer related the history of the pumping station, which was conceived sometime in 2002. The challenge in supplying Shivajinagar-Bainganwadi is that it is situated six kilometers from the reservoir; by the time the water reaches Shivajinagar-Bainganwadi, pressure in the pipe is too low. The Trombay High-Level Reservoir is supplied water from a 1,800 mm-diameter line that taps into the 2,300 mm trunk main feeding the Island City. From 4 to 10 a.m. every day, the valve supplying the reservoir is partially shut to allow for enough water to flow to the city's southernmost service reservoirs during the hours of peak demand. During these morning hours only a fraction of the regular pressure in the 1,800 mm inlet remains. (And much of that water is diverted before it ever reaches the reservoir in order to pressurize the pipes in Lotus Colony from 4 to 6 a.m.) Local politicians had repeatedly requested direct supply also to Shivajinagar-Bainganwadi during those hours, but the need to meet peak demand in the Island City precluded this possibility.[16]

By the same token, increasing the *duration* of Shivajinagar-Bainganwadi's supply timings was ruled out because it would dangerously lower reservoir levels during the nonsupply morning hours. Shivajinagar-Bainganwadi is supplied from the reservoir during the peak hours when the inlet pipe to the reservoir is not pressurized; should reservoir levels drop, areas of the M-East Ward supplied in the late morning (after Shivajinagar-Bainganwadi) would thus experience low (or no) pressures. By contrast, a local storage and pumping station for Shivajinagar-Bainganwadi could be filled at *any* supply time that the reservoir could sustain—after midnight, for instance; water could then be pumped to Shivajinagar-Bainganwadi at a more convenient and less-dark hour. In addition having a reservoir so close would (theoretically) allow water to be distributed at a much higher pressure; over the six-kilometer path from reservoir to tap, pressures are lost not only to friction but from what one engineer described as "so many tappings" watering the neighborhoods along the way. Augmented water pressures, it was hoped, would obviate the need for all the motorized suction pumps and would bring to life long-dry taps. Meanwhile changing the water supply timings to daylight hours would provide a strong disincentive for connection owners to sell water to the bike-and-can "illegals" living in the peripheral neighborhoods that are not fitted with pipes by increasing the risk (and thus the costs) of detection.

When the pumping station plan was put into action, however, things did not go quite as hoped. The pumping station itself was commissioned in late October 2008 but with so little fanfare that it went largely unnoticed. In the initial months Kamla Raman Nagar experienced a bonanza of water from its supply line from the highway, while water pipes in Shivajinagar-Bainganwadi did not see much change at all. (It was not until January 2009 that it became widely known in Shivajinagar-Bainganwadi that the long-anticipated pumping station was actually operational.) Seeking an explanation, I tracked down Sheth, the ward-level engineer who had created the hand-drawn map discussed earlier, in his new office in the Water Supply Construction Office of the Eastern Suburban Zone. If anyone understood what had happened in the wake of the pumping station's commissioning, I reasoned, it would be Sheth. I caught up with him in a tiny air-conditioned trailer not far from my home, a space he referred to as his "outpost."

The pumping station, Sheth explained, was originally proposed by the assistant engineer preceding Korelekar. Echoing the engineers in the supply planning offices, Sheth maintained that supply problems stemmed from the distance at which Shivajinagar-Bainganwadi is situated from Trombay High-Level Reservoir; by the time the water reached Shivajinagar-Bainganwadi pressure in the main has been depleted. (It is unclear how this conclusion was reached since there were no pressure meters anywhere in the area before the commissioning of the pumping station.) After the pumping station was constructed, two pressure meters were installed—one before water empties into the tank and another after it has been pumped out. The meter upstream of the pumping station currently measures around fifteen pounds. This number, Sheth conceded, cannot be retrospectively assumed to have been the pressure in that main before the pumping station was constructed since the pumping station itself, as department engineers pointed out, has a pressure-*reducing* effect on the areas just upstream of the tank. (The low-pressure tank downstream increases the *speed* of upstream water, thereby lowering *pressure*.) So while the pumping station probably increased pressure somewhat at the point immediately after the pumping station—where pressure readers now report pressure around forty pounds—there is no way to assess in any comprehensive way how significant the pressure increase has been since the commissioning of the pumping station.

In a technical oversight during the initial months of the pumping station's operation, Sheth explained, a crucial valve was left open (whether or not this oversight was intentional is a matter of some speculation among water department staff), causing water to flow in ways and directions unanticipated by the official plan. When the pumping station was commissioned, they had wanted to supply water to Shivajinagar-Bainganwadi not only from the pumping station but also directly from the feeder main itself. This was to be accomplished by leaving open the valve between the pumping station's inlet and outlet pipes (figure 5.2). The idea was that they would fill the pumping station from the reservoir between 4 and 6 a.m. Then they would close the inlet valve (A) to the pumping station and open the outlet valve (C). Since the inlet valve would remain pressurized until 8:30, Valve B, which connects the upstream and downstream sections of the feeder main, was also left open. When the pumping station was switched on, water would flow north toward Shivajinagar-Bainganwadi both from the pumping station and the reservoir.[17] When this

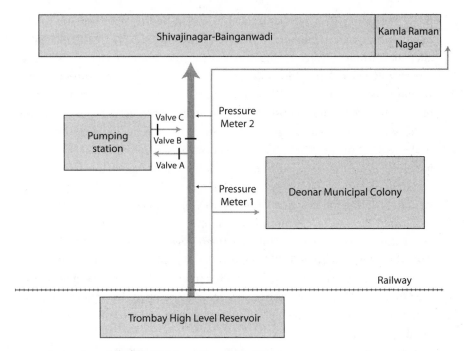

FIGURE 5.2. Pumping station. Created by author based on interviews with water department engineers.

plan was put into operation, however, pressures were so much higher at the point after the pumping station (pressure meter 2) than before the pumping station (pressure meter 1) that much of the water simply went the wrong way; instead of heading north toward Shivajinagar-Bainganwadi, water from the pumping station traveled south, pressurizing the twelve-inch-diameter main that feeds Kamla Raman Nagar. Thus for a few months—until someone figured out what was happening—Kamla Raman Nagar's pipes saw significant increases in water pressure (as did Deonar Municipal Colony, whose small storage tank is connected to the twelve-inch main).

With the opening of Valve B counteracting any increased pressure north of the pumping station, Shivajinagar-Bainganwadi's own pipes appear not to have been significantly affected (pressures being no lower than they had been before the pumping station). Once the water department realized what was happening, however, they closed Valve B. While this fixed the pressure problems at Meter 2, the closing of Valve B revealed an unintended consequence of the pumping station, which proceeded to wreak havoc on Kamla Raman Nagar's pipes: the twelve-inch pipe continued to be fed by the main heading to the pumping station, but pressure in the twelve-inch main decreased significantly after the closing of Valve B. The problem was the pumping station itself: the opening of Valve A to allow water to flow into the (low-pressure) pumping station tank had the unintended (and somehow unanticipated) consequence of speeding up the water upstream in the main (water under pressure flows more quickly toward lower-pressure areas), thereby reducing pressure in the feeder main at the point where it intersects with Kamla Raman Nagar's twelve-inch line. To fix this issue, Sheth explained, the department planned to make a cross-connection to Kamla Raman Nagar's main just north of the pumping station. Over the following two months the engineers constantly adjusted and readjusted the valves, attempting to convince water to flow to the intended destinations. Yet, somehow, Kamla Raman Nagar ended January with taps drier than they started. A local Congress Party–affiliated social worker named Sheikh whose water connection at his home on Bainganwadi periphery had seen dramatically lower pressures took to showing up at the pumping station at 5 every morning to wake up the staff (with tea) and to ensure they turned on the pumps correctly.

Since the change in the water supply timings—and in the wake of the commissioning of the new pumping station—not only Kamla Raman Nagar but much of the eastern half of Bainganwadi began to report shorter than usual supply. Even along the narrow road running parallel to the highway at the southern end of Shivajinagar, a quiet street that is home to the Shivajinagar police station called Church Lane, taps had suddenly and inexplicably dried up. Throughout the winter of 2009 complaints mounted and department engineers began to field an increasing number of requests for emergency supply by water tanker truck. Throughout the month of March the number of municipal water tankers delivered to Shivajinagar-Bainganwadi climbed steadily. Korelekar suspected some sort of hydraulic problem in the pipes. "There must be some kind of airlock," he explained. Because of the intermittent supply system, air can easily become trapped at certain points on the pipes; if the air is not released, it can block the flow of water, drying up taps downstream.[18] They would have to open the road to inspect the pipes directly.

I arrived in Bainganwadi one morning in March 2009 to check on the water and to hear about any changes. The rickshaw dropped me at the corner of the highway in order to avoid what appeared to be an enormous traffic jam. As I approached the intersection, I saw that the road had been opened. Earth-moving machinery stood idle next to a fifteen-foot mountain of dirt and muck, while a crowd of curious men and boys (and a handful of women) lined the opposite side of the ten-meter-long ditch that had been dug across the intersection. At the base of the pit two teenage boys were digging with picks, scooping dirt into buckets that other boys were hauling up with ropes and depositing on the pile. I recognized a scattering of engineers, but none from the M-East Ward. Spotting a young woman who appeared to be an engineer, I approached and introduced myself as a researcher. The woman, Sangeeta, proudly announced that she had just joined the construction wing of the water department as a junior engineer. It was refreshing to see a woman working out in the field, and I told her so; she smiled. "All the women stay in the office doing paperwork, but I get so bored in the office, I want to come into the field—to learn about the distribution system!" I asked her why they were digging up the road, and her face fell as she shook her head. "Even I don't really know. You'll have to ask one of the more senior engineers." I approached an engineer named Joshi, who told me that "water is not coming" in much of the area. They believed the problem on Church Road began where the thirty-inch main joins with the twelve-inch pipe below Church Road. They were digging up the valve to see what the problem might be, but they had not yet been able to locate it. (Overhearing us, a man looking to be well into his seventies pointed at the ground near the edge of the pit and proclaimed, "It's right down there.")

When I returned the next morning, the team of excavators had unearthed not a thirty-inch main, but two twelve-inch mains sunk over fifteen feet into the marshy ground, running north-south in the path where the thirty-inch main should have been (fig. 5.3). Meanwhile a nine-inch pipe headed west along Church Road. The Church Road main was not connected to a thirty-inch main but rather to one of these twelve-inch mains. Sangeeta was nowhere in sight (she later explained that she had been asked to stay in the office), so I approached Joshi again. He said the thirty-inch main must be buried very deep; they had dug down over fifteen feet but did not manage to find it. None of the engineers present had known about the twelve-inch mains ("We can't know what's there until we dig!"), but Joshi confirmed that they were both indeed operational, probably attached to one of the older mains somewhere by the slaughterhouse. Since the crew was unable to find the thirty-inch main, they were going to try to fix the airlock on Church Road's main by shifting the nine-inch pipe from one twelve-inch main to the other.

Within a few weeks it was evident that this intervention had failed to improve Church Road's water pressure. Speaking in his office, I asked Korelekar if they had any other ideas as to what might be causing the pressure problems

FIGURE 5.3. Searching for a main. Photo by author.

along Church Road and in Kamla Raman Nagar and eastern Bainganwadi. He sighed, repeating that the problems must be the result of an airlock. I asked him to explain; after all, the area of Kamla Raman Nagar experiencing dry taps is fed by a different distribution main than that supplying Bainganwadi (and since the time change in Bainganwadi, even the supply timings were different). Korelekar nodded. "Yes, it's true."

He suggested that the problem must be the local "water mafia," which uses suction pumps to steal water out of illegal connections that they then sell at a profit. Indeed department engineers often told me that it was the hundreds (if not thousands) of individual suction pumps that made any intervention futile; in this context, one exasperated senior supply planning engineer fumed, "no hydraulics are possible!" Korelekar expressed little surprise that the pumping station had not had the anticipated affect: "Any plan will be ruined."

In the winter of 2009 the ward-level engineers began a renewed series of early-morning raids, trawling the lanes in a small pickup and a police escort. Seeing a cluster of bikes and cans, the engineers would push their way through sleepy-eyed men waiting for water to seize motors attached to sellers' connections. Some vendors identified as "big sellers"—those with multiple connections—were taken down to the station and assessed steep fines.[19] One morning the engineers arrived in our chawl, appearing suddenly at the foot of the lane close to Paniwali's home. Paniwali quickly pulled the motor on her pipe inside her home, but it was too late—the engineers had already seen it. "They came into the house!" she told me afterward. "I didn't think they would come *inside* the house. They just reached in and took it! I paid five thousand rupees for that motor, and they just took it." Paniwali was angry. Hers was the only motor in the chawl that was taken that day; her daughter had skipped out the back door to alert her father, who was filling cans from their other connection a few lanes over, while Tap A's owners, who had encased their motor in concrete to avoid detection, simply shut off the power switch to silence the hum. (Tap E, obscured in the shadows of the narrow back lane, escaped notice.) Paniwali fumed, "The people on this block, they didn't say anything to defend us—we were just filling water for members! [Tap A's owners] are jealous of us because we have more money than they do. Why didn't they take [Tap A's] motors?" Paniwali's anger was directed at her neighbors for not standing up for her as much as for escaping her fate, but her husband's ire was reserved for the engineers themselves: "It's the BMC's fault that [the bike-and-can customers] have to come here to fill their cans. If they did their job properly these people wouldn't come here to buy water from us!" While he understood the BMC's reasoning—that all the motors and connections were preventing water from reaching farther downstream on the pipe, thereby rendering the pumping station futile—he insisted that until they provide piped water to peripheral areas, the bikes and cans will keep coming. By providing water to bikes and cans, Paniwala asserted, he is doing the BMC's work for them. In addition to blaming the neighbors and the engineers, both Paniwali and Paniwala reserved particular distain for the "big sellers" on the main road, particularly one fellow named Shah, whom they held responsible for bringing the BMC's attention to this block in the first place. "This is all his fault," Paniwali fumed. "He was selling so openly; he had four connections with two motors on each one. He was selling shamelessly! He is very immoral, he is not an honest person."

Paniwala told me (with some satisfaction) that they took Shah down to the station and held him all day. They took all of his motors and released him after a Rs 10,000 fine. "He made us all look bad, he was just selling so obviously, just trying to make money. It made us all look like we were immoral." Leaving Paniwali's, I went to hear the story from one of the owners of Tap A, a man named Suresh, but rather than tell me his story, he pressed me for the account I had heard from Paniwali: "Did she tell you what happened? What did she tell you?" I nodded silently, dodging his effort to procure any information about Paniwali's connections. Suresh continued, "Remember how noisy it used to be on the road? Now everyone is completely silent. No one turns on any lights, they just wait in the dark. Everyone is selling again—except Shah, he's scared. But now people are more careful."

Residents of Shivajinagar-Bainganwadi attributed the altered geographies of flow as much to the timing change as to the pumping station. The two connections belonging to Sheikh (the Congress Party worker who brought tea to the pumping station operators every morning) dried up completely. A few days after the timings had been changed, I visited him at his home. His water connection snaked overland approximately a third of a kilometer, from his home to a pressurized point on the distribution main. He had twenty members, each of whom prepaid him monthly fees for five minutes of water from his connection. Since the change in the timings three days earlier, Sheikh's tap had not produced a drop. Unable to supply water to his members—and thus at risk of losing his credibility as a reliable water provider and party worker—he had leveraged his party connections to the local corporator to arrange for regular visits by 10,000-liter municipal water tankers, from which he supplied water to his members. Sheikh was exasperated: "This pumping station has made everything worse. What's the point of the pumping station? The water was fine until the pumping station!" The elected officials from his party had called a meeting for that afternoon at the water department's head office; they would fix it, Sheikh said. For emphasis he pulled out his phone and dialed, informing me that he was calling one of the department's senior engineers. "Hello, sir! Sir, this is Sheikh calling. I tell you, this timing change has gone on for five days and since then there has been no water. So please do one thing—just send us our water the old way, early in the morning, and not through the pumping station. We haven't had any water since that tank was built. Just send us our water directly from Trombay High-Level Reservoir, okay?"

Sheikh was not alone in these sentiments, but his feelings were not universal across the neighborhood. In the chawl I was studying, Tap B sprang to

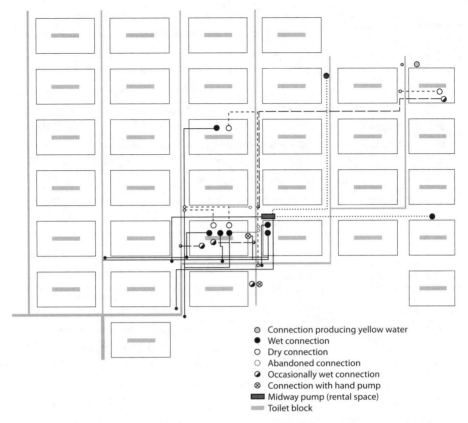

○ Connection producing yellow water
● Wet connection
○ Dry connection
☽ Abandoned connection
◑ Occasionally wet connection
⊗ Connection with hand pump
▬ Midway pump (rental space)
▨ Toilet block

FIGURE 5.4. Connections map. This map provides the details of one plot in Shivajinagar-Bainganwadi whose taps provide water of dramatically different quality and pressure. The dots depict the locations where each tap is connected to the distribution mains. The map gives a sense of the disparity between above- and below-ground geographies of access and gestures toward the politics that infuse these geographies. Created by author from interviews and observations.

life after the timings were changed, while one of Paniwali and Paniwala's connections somehow started drying up a full forty-five minutes before the other. (After a few weeks Paniwali paid Rs 7,000 to a broker to have the BMC transfer it to a spot adjacent to Tap A's connection, the location of which she had somehow deciphered.) One of the busiest water vendors in an adjacent plot suddenly saw all three of his taps go dry, while the pressure to Tap A's connection was suddenly so strong that one morning the rubber hose exploded off the metal tap under the force, soaking a uniformed schoolgirl as she walked by on her way to class. Younger children danced gleefully under the spontaneous fountain, while their parents tripped over one another trying to reattach the hose. Engineers expressed bafflement at the changes in the distribution network. Since the constant transferring of connections means that there is no longer any correlation between the position of a house and the location on the grid of that house's municipal water connection, it is exceedingly difficult for engineers to assess water pressure at various points around the neighborhood (see figure 5.4). When I asked the senior-most ward-level engineer whether he thought the pumping station had helped water pressures, he responded that he believed things had improved "in the middle area" but that he really had no way of knowing. The months following the change in supply timings only deepened these dynamics, as dry taps were followed by a flood of applications for transfers to alternative spots on the distribution main.

Class-Blind Hydrologies

These dynamics of rumor, stealth, and knowledge are not confined to popular neighborhoods and slums like Shivajinagar-Bainganwadi; speculating on the mysterious forces orchestrating the city's capricious hydrologies is a pastime that transcends class and community lines. In the middle-class housing society where I lived between 2008 and 2010, for example, our water was supplied from the municipality for just two hours per day, from 2 until 4 in the afternoon, during which time the water collected in the housing society's underground storage tank. Every evening the society's watchman switched on a pump that lifted the water from the underground sump to an elevated holding tank. From the elevated tank he would release the water during two half-hour intervals, once in the early morning and once in the evening, by opening a valve. The water would then flow from the elevated tank to each of the forty-eight buildings' separate underground sumps, from where it would be once again pumped up to storage tanks on the roofs of buildings. My landlord had an automatic sensor on our rooftop storage tank that would switch on the electric suction pump when water levels fell below a certain level in the tank; there was a similar sensor in our house's underground tank that would switch off the automatic pump if the water level in the underground tank fell short. So while the pipe feeding our society's tank was pressurized for only two hours a day, the taps in my kitchen and bathroom had relatively constant and consistent water pressure, available twenty-four hours a day.

This elaborate network of downward flow and upward pumping was rife with contention, as some houses invariably received less water than others; accusations and speculations were thus whispered over afternoon tea that certain houses had installed "online" pumps that were switched on when water from the community overhead tank was released. Whistle-blowing housewives were known to time their morning walks to coincide with the early-morning water release so that they could listen for online pumps. The information gathered from these water-policing missions was rarely used to confront the offending house (which in any case could simply be explained as the sound of the pump lifting water to a house's rooftop tank) but provided endless fodder for gossip and rumor among neighbors. On one occasion the society secretary collected information from each house's private water meter and compiled the numbers in a spreadsheet listing the house numbers, names of residents, and total monthly consumption (with stars next to the names of families whose meters were nonfunctioning). At the top of the spreadsheet was printed a message: "This is for the information of the members. Those whose meters are not functioning will be charged on last quarter's readings. The managing committee appeals to those members/residents whose meter readings are more than 30 [kiloliters] per month to use less water so that there is an equitable distribution of water and because the society is already receiving less water than usual quota from the BMC." When my house received the notice, my landlord looked over the list and pointed to the high level of consumption at the neighboring house. (The three residences in our house consumed a total ten kiloliters in February 2009; the neighboring home, with just one family, used forty-nine kiloliters.) "They have a motor online," she stated matter-of-factly. "They don't even have a borewell." Apparently the list was circulated in the hope that publicly shaming the offending online-motor users would lead them to abandon the practice. However, conversations with residents after the release of the notice revealed some skepticism that public shaming would be very effective as a water-disciplining strategy. By way of explanation, one longtime resident confided that in recent years increasing property values had resulted in higher rates of turnover in this long-established society, where many residents had lived since it was built in the 1970s. Recently, a retired physicist named Dixit explained, "Other types of people have moved in." A man described as being "in the construction business" drew particular disdain. "He only moved here for profit," so he did not respect the established rules and unwritten norms of the society. "He cuts down trees to make room to park his cars."[20] No subsequent list was distributed that would confirm or refute the circular's success, yet water supply to our own home remained consistently between ten and fifteen kiloliters per month for the duration of my stay, suggesting that no significant redistribution had occurred as a result of the circular.

A few weeks after the distribution of the circular, a member of the housing society noticed a steadily growing flood of water emerging from cracks in the center of the adjacent highway. Since the flood appeared every day at the same time that our society's underground sump was supplied, the society secretary surmised that our own water troubles stemmed from this mysterious flood—the water flowing down the highway was *our* water. Armed with this fragment of knowledge, the society sent a letter to the M-East Ward office, reporting leakage in the water main along the highway. After a few weeks the flood continued and the secretary had heard nothing from the ward. She was not surprised; somebody needed "to pursue" the case, she told me, to "physically go" to the ward to meet with the engineers. One society member, a retired engineering professor named Trivedi, volunteered for the task and went to see the deputy hydraulic engineer of the eastern suburbs to report the leakage. After spending the better part of the day waiting to meet the engineer, Trivedi came home rather exasperated, with the report that the flood of water along the highway had nothing to do with the water supply to our housing society, which is connected to a different branch of a distribution main upstream.[21] Moreover the deputy engineer had dismissed Trivedi's complaint that the society's water supply was running short; according to our water meter, we were receiving 200 lpcd for each household. Trivedi had pointed out to the engineer that for a household norm of five people, this amounted to only 40 lpcd—less than a third of the official supply norm for residential water supply. The engineer warned Trivedi not to push the issue; to do so would only bring trouble on the society. This had happened once before, the secretary told me, a few years back: after reduced pressure in the society's water connection had resulted in persistently lower levels in the underground tank, the society had arranged through a broker for an additional, metered water connection to be joined to a different distribution main. This solution had worked well for a few months, but when water pressures fell in this second main too, the acting secretary had filed another complaint. When an engineer came to investigate the problem, he told the secretary that, according to official figures, their water needs were being met by just the one connection; the original connection was cut. Since then a few people have had borewells dug for use in toilet flushing and cleaning. During the eighteen months that I lived in the society, at least three homes had dug borewells—an activity that was quickly proving to be equally fraught.[22] One resident confided that she suspected the new well dug for the house across the street had tapped the same underground stream feeding her own borewell; it was only a matter of time, she worried, before her own well dried up.

Given the unpredictability of the distribution system and the opacity of the department itself, how are the risks—the financial risks from investments in access methods that may or may not produce water and the risks of water shortage itself—managed? The uncertainties that infuse Mumbai's pipes are hedged with social and relational knowledge networks, through which fragments of rumor, memory, perception, and speculation are woven together to make judgments and shape action. How people make sense of the unpredictable and often violent whims of pipes and pressures reflects a keen sense of the fluid, dynamic quality of infrastructure and access. People place faith neither in the hard physicalities of steel and piping nor the moralistic legalities of right and entitlement. These things are neither stable nor enduring; they can become obsolete overnight, can vanish without a trace. To stay safe in this context one must keep up with the city—read the signs, interpret the rumors, and assess when and how to act as well as when to wait. Such constellations of knowledge, interpretation, and judgment hinge on the relational interactions that comprise everyday life in the city. Eyes and ears are constantly on alert for a fragment of knowledge or, more important, for an ally who might have access to reliable information.

Even actions based on seemingly solid information are fraught with risk. In winter 2009 I met a young family—Rookiya, her husband, Salim, and their infant daughter, Sonia—who had recently moved out of their rented home in the large neighborhood of Janata Nagar, a self-built neighborhood in the marshlands of Mankhurd, where they had lived since their marriage two years earlier. In Janata, Rookiya explained, getting water was always a struggle; there was no tap nearby. The closest taps were a ten-minute walk toward the highway, but the water there was expensive (Rs 3 per can) and came for only two hours in the night, from 8 to 10, and lines were so long that sometimes she would wait with her cans for two hours only to go home empty-handed. Following the lead of his neighbors and colleagues, Salim, who drives an auto rickshaw, had found a reliable and cheaper tap in the nearby neighborhood of Ganeshwadi, where a handful of residents had somehow managed to arrange for larger, two-inch-diameter water connections and where the neighborhood's location at the intersection of multiple water supply zones meant that water pressure was available from various suppliers throughout the day. Salim had been a regular Ganeshwadi customers for nearly a year, filling his auto rickshaw with cans and driving to Ganeshwadi during the slow-business midday hours, when he and Rookiya decided that they could save both time and money if they moved to this water-abundant neighborhood. When I spoke to Rookiya in her Ganeshwadi home, she laughed wryly at her own naïveté: "Everyone from Janata would come here for water, so we thought there was no water problem here. But now that we live here we only get water every few days, even though we prepay two hundred rupees per month. And even then, we just get one barrel. It's not enough." She explained that the paniwalas first give water to the people with bikes and cans, and only after to the people who actually live in the neighborhood. "They wake us up at any hour, even three in the morning, if the water is there and the bikes are gone." Lately she had been going to her sister's house in the slum resettlement tenements of Lallubhai to have a bath. A few times a week she hauled her family's laundry on foot to the far side of the railway tracks—a twenty-minute walk—to use the water from the open well at Deonar Village for washing clothes. For fresh drinking water, Salim sometimes took the rickshaw to another neighborhood; the local connection owners in Ganeshwadi sometimes refused to sell water by the can to local members. Rookiya sighed as she said, "Now we're thinking of moving somewhere else."

Rookiya and Salim believed that their mistake in moving to Ganeshwadi stemmed from the partial information on which they based their action. They had seen water with their own eyes, they experienced its reliability for months, but in their case the information they did *not* have—on the extent to which the area's water was made available to local residents—proved crucial. This time, Salim told me, they would only consider a neighborhood where they have family, or at least close friends, who have more thorough information on how to secure water access. While Salim thus assessed the situation in terms of more or less complete and accurate knowledge, his comment suggests a more subtle point: that to obtain and secure water access requires not just knowledge of water flows in a particular moment but reliance on relations of trust that will facilitate an *ongoing* flow of information about a constantly changing, uncontainable, inherently risky network.

Since water access is often produced by improvisational means (e.g., navigating cutoff-date theatrics or orchestrating the kinds of piecemeal interventions already discussed), arranging even for standard water access is fraught with risks stemming from informational uncertainties (Will the water actually come?) and financial hazards (Will this arrangement last long enough to recoup an investment?). Reliable water access thus hinges on access to relational and informational networks that allow for adaptation to the changing infrastructural and hydrological configurations. Back in Shivajinagar-Bainganwadi Tap A produced particularly strong water pressure—stronger than that of any other connection in the lane. Meanwhile Paniwali and Paniwala's second connection (Tap D) struggled to maintain even minimal pressures. Paniwali explained that a few months earlier Tap A also had decreased pressure and shortened supply duration, and she had sought a transfer to a different spot on the main. Meanwhile the nephew of Tap A's owner, who works as a laborer in the local ward office's maintenance department, made some inquiries among his friends and colleagues and arranged for the connection transfer to be made to a particularly high-pressure spot. For this reason Tap A had no further problems. When Paniwali's own second tap was made, however, no such careful attention was paid to the location of the connection since she had no personal contact inside the water department; the spot was selected by the ward staff, who assume no responsibility for subsequently depleted pressures. (In the words of one senior engineer, the department does not "entertain complaints of low pressure.") Paniwali suspected the department staff of intentionally making transfers to low-pressure spots so as to secure their own future earnings from informationally deprived customers like herself.

This kind of relational risk management and knowledge sharing is accomplished not only (or even primarily) through preexisting networks like kinship but is also established through the practice of sharing and exchanging information and favors. For example, when a staff member at Nestor's Palace approached the grounds crew of a neighboring housing society to inquire about hiring a water tanker, he not only sought out information but in doing so offered two crucial bits of knowledge: whatever was causing the shortage in the neighboring society was affecting other areas of the distribution main, and the shortage in the neighboring society was not *caused* by Nestor's Palace. Armed with this information, the housing society avoided what would have been a useless and costly procedure of digging up and replacing the stretch of pipe connecting their tank with the distribution main—which had been the recommendation of the ward-level engineer who had visited the site to investigate the shortage. Instead the secretary arranged for continued supply by tanker while they looked into other options.

Relations of reciprocity and interdependence underpinned the vast majority of water-related interventions that I observed during my research. In Lallubhai water supply was characterized by extraordinary variability from building to building. On hearing from multiple sources that one particular building had recently had their connection transferred to a point upstream on the water main, I approached the society chairman to inquire whether this was true and, if so, how it had been arranged. I met the secretary, a man named Shenoy, in his home on the seventh floor. Although the room was a standard-size Slum

Redevelopment Authority building—225 square feet—significant alterations had been done to give it a larger, breezier appearance: the concrete floors had been outfitted with luminous white marble; the walls shone with mirrors; the ceiling fan was fitted with graceful, curved golden branches tipped with globe-like lightbulbs. Shenoy's wife, Nandani, served me milky, sweet coffee with a side dish of spicy cashews while their son completed English exercises in preparation for a later meeting with a private tutor. This family was doing its best to preserve a middle-class lifestyle in spite of the locational and infrastructural challenges posed by relocation to Lallubhai.

Shenoy's family was allotted a home in Lallubhai after their home in a neighborhood called Indira Nagar was demolished in conjunction with an MMRDA road-improvement project. While Shenoy had owned that home for over two decades, he had not actually lived in Indira Nagar since before 2002, when he and his wife moved to Navi Mumbai in search of more abundant water supply and a larger living space in which to raise their sons. At the time their Indira Nagar house was surveyed for demolition, it was occupied by renting tenants. In order to claim their Lallubhai room, Shenoy rented out their much larger property in Navi Mumbai and moved to the SRA building; the tenants had since gone to live "in some other slum." When they first arrived in Lallubhai "there was nothing here—not even light fixtures," and their pipes produced only a trickle of water. Shenoy's brother, however, worked as a driver for a prominent politician whose party affiliation happened to be that of the local corporator representing Indira Nagar (which is also in M-East Ward). Through this party network Shenoy managed to contact the municipal corporator of his now demolished neighborhood, where Shenoy and Nandani were still on the electoral list. This corporator (who, incidentally, began his own political career as a "plumber," brokering water connections) arranged—in collaboration with the Lallubhai-area opposition party corporator—to make a formal request with the water department for an additional water supply connection to the building.[23] (The two corporators were affiliated with rival political parties, but had a long-standing acquaintance and a history of collaboration—a relationship that Shenoy attributes to their common roots in the M-East neighborhood of Chembur.) While Shenoy's building's water connection was formally processed as a "transfer," the old line was left intact in order to ensure sufficient supply; the meter was simply shifted over to the newer pipe.

Since the new connection was laid, water had not been a problem in his building. Pointing to the two 200-liter barrels in the kitchen, Nandani told me that they always keep one barrel full as a reserve supply in case of shortage, alternating which barrel is in use to keep the water fresh. The family used approximately one barrel of water every day for cleaning, flushing, and washing; for cooking and drinking, Nandani filled three large aluminum pots that she cleaned out every day. In all they go through about two hundred liters of water daily—about fifty liters per person for their family of four. They planned to stay in Lallubhai for the requisite ten-year period, after which they will sell their room at a profit and move back to their home in Navi Mumbai.

Shenoy's building's improved water supply was arranged through a network of information, kinship, and favors that involved Shenoy, his brother, his brother's employer, the employer's political party, two corporators of rival parties, a municipal engineer, and ward-level staff. Each of these actors provided a crucial bit of information, which was leveraged in configuring a solution to the building's water problem; none of the actors could have orchestrated the intervention on his own, and none could have foreseen what the final outcome would be. At each step along the way each actor drew upon his own informational and social resources in order to move the project toward an unknown resolution. Configuring pathways of knowledge, access, influence, and mediation is a regular social practice engaged in not only by the urban poor but also by industries, commercial businesses, luxury townships, and posh buildings.

Following a casual conversation with my neighbor, Mr. Gondalia, on the topic of knowledge brokers, he related the following story, which he had written up a few years earlier for the amusement of his colleagues at the Atomic Research Center, where he worked as a nuclear scientist:

My little tale refers to late June one year, when I had lived here over twenty years. I had to renew my driving license. My son had just turned eighteen, and I had promised that he should also get his.

We drove to the Regional Transport Office a few kilometers away, armed with ration card, birth certificate, money, a bottle of water, and all necessities. The clerk at the scraggy counter handed us blank forms and pointed to a little shed in the slums just behind where we could get photographed. It was a unique multi-utility shop run by a doctor. He issued medical certificates required by RTO [Regional Transport Office], and also wielded a Polaroid for instant photography, with free loan of uniform caps for three-wheeler drivers who never wore them on duty. He also personally maintained his touts' commission accounts.

We got my certificate of fitness to continue being a driver, and the photographs. However, the inspectors threw tantrums (as we had dared to go without an agent) and also threw the papers. However, we survived and on the third attempt managed to get the forms accepted. We found a quiet spot in the sultry shed, and stood waiting to be called for the next stage.

Soon a gent had joined us. He spoke good English. "Sir you want a new license?"—*No, renewal.*—"Baba's license?" *He has Learner's License.*—"Applying today?"—*Yes.*—"Want pen, sir?"—*No, I have.*—"Filling forms? They are in Marathi. . . ."—*Yes, we did that.*—"Photos sir?"—*We got them.*—"Photocopy of Ration card, Passport?"—*Got it.*—"Stapler?"—*It is here.*—"Gum?"—*I have it in my bag.* My answers were indeed truthful.

At this point the gent, rather agent, turned and gave a brief searching look. Politely he asked, "Where do you work, sir? BARC?" Proudly I replied in the affirmative. It was my turn now to ask. "Why did you ask if I am at BARC?"

Deadpan, he replied, "Sir, you made the application yourself. Didn't take an agent. You came ready with everything. You are educated people, and can do these things. Time you can afford, but have to save expenses."

While meant to be entertaining (and thus probably somewhat of a caricature), Gondalia's description of an encounter with an agent is revealing. First, the agent's comment that Gondalia and his son were able to navigate the state bureaucracy without an agent because they are "educated" reveals the important knowledge-bridging work of brokering. Because they are literate (in Hindi, English, and Marathi), the father-son pair was able to acquire information about the procedures for each application, were capable of reading and understanding the questions asked on the Marathi-language application forms, could fill out the forms themselves, and could arrange for the required number of photocopies of all the necessary documents. Would-be applicants who do *not* possess this knowledge—for instance, the estimated 33 percent of Mumbai's residents who do not know Marathi, or the 15 percent of adults who are officially illiterate in *any* language—would need to find a way to access the information. To do so, an applicant can either find a trusted friend or acquaintance who can bridge the informational gap, or, if no such knowledge-bridge is available (or known), the applicant can purchase the necessary information from an intermediary who is deemed to be reliable.

The incident that Gondalia describes, however, involves the rather straightforward matter of applying for a driver's license. The opacity of the water distribution system—in which water flows are hidden inside pipes that are buried underground; where the laws governing legal supply of water are in turns contradictory and vague and where the legal status of residents themselves is deeply political and constantly in flux; where standard procedures for providing metered municipal water supply are largely operationalized through improvisational practice; and where even the relatively standard activities and interventions are invariably carried out in stealth-infused ways that are subject to ongoing and continuous renegotiation and adjustment—renders water access somewhat more fraught with unknowns (and unknowables) than applying for a driver's license. The scope for brokering information is limitless.

While I was sitting in the office of a neighborhood-level political party worker in the popular neighborhood of Phule Nagar one afternoon, a man identifying himself as a "plumber" stopped by to collect money and documents from a group of households that wished to apply for a new connection. The plumber, a man in his midthirties named Sanju, is not actually licensed as a plumber. Officially speaking, the BMC Act stipulates that, when making a new connection, the municipal staff is required to extend the pipe to within five hundred feet of a dwelling; extension of water connections to the house itself is to be carried out by an officially licensed plumber. While there are at least twenty "plumbers" that frequent M-Ward, only three of them are actually licensed; the others work under the licenses of others, presenting photocopies of other plumbers' licenses when they make applications on behalf of customers. Sanju explained that there is simply more demand for the services of plumbers than the licenses can meet. The plumbers are "local men" who know about the distribution system in particular neighborhoods; each plumber specializes in a particular area, about which he has detailed knowledge. The engineers "know nothing about the network or the system. They have no idea. So we hand-draw maps of neighborhoods and propose to put a new or transferred connection here or there. If an engineer expresses any doubt about the proposal or the map, it's easy to convince him."

The kinds of services that Sanju provides are in demand by Mumbai's poor, "illegal," working-class, and slum-dwelling residents. In Gondalia's story the agent reflects that the man and his son choose to manage their business without hiring an agent because they can spare time but not cash. This observation gestures toward the socioeconomic shifts that are taking place in contemporary Mumbai: globally connected business and economic sectors such as banking and financial services, real estate, information technology and telecommunications generate salaries that place educated, often high-caste professional elites like Gondalia—who a generation ago were considered to be quite well-off—in a position perhaps more accurately described as simply middle class. (Despite his impeccable education and prestigious employment history, Gondalia and his wife navigate roads choked with chauffeured BMWs and Mercedes-Benz in their old Maruti 800.) Many of the salaried professionals (doctors, university professors, public sector engineers, and scientists) I encountered in Mumbai describe their own socioeconomic status in such relatively declining terms. When it comes to paying for knowledge brokers, as the agent's comment suggests, these highly educated, middle-class professionals will often attempt to use their own knowledge resources to avoid paying a broker. Regarding water-related works, however, the handful of such do-it-yourself efforts about which I heard were frustrated by the opacities of the system; even the most careful and systematic individuals who tried to do it themselves often eventually ended up hiring a broker. One housing society secretary was president of an engineering college. For many years, whenever his society had water problems, he would go to the ward office to manage the situation; the ward staff was particularly responsive to this fellow, another resident explained, in the hope that—in exchange for prompt attention to the society's problem—a son or daughter might find a friendly audience among the college admissions committee someday. This state of affairs continued for many years, and the society never had any persistent water trouble. Recently, however, the ward-level staff had not been as responsive to this fellow's requests. When repeated visits to the ward in 2009 failed to draw the desired attention, the society hired a broker who accomplished the desired connection transfer within a few days. Whereas older elites used to be able to leverage their own knowledge, social networks, and authority in such transactions, in recent years the demand for special, exceptional attention has grown such that brokering procedures (and prices) have become somewhat standardized.[24] These everyday experiences of broker-mediated transactions are intimately related to popular and political narratives about departmental corruption.

SIX

"GOOD DOESN'T MEAN YOU'RE HONEST"
Corruption

In February 2009 an angry crowd pushed its way into the office of Mr. Kore-lekar, the M-East Ward's assistant engineer.[1] The men were residents of Kamla Raman Nagar, demanding that the engineers stop targeting their neighbor-hood with early-morning raids and just give them back their water. "Where is that chaviwalla?" one of the men reportedly shouted, referring to the valve operator. "We'll teach him to turn off our water!" The comment was overheard by Balekar, the chaviwalla whose valve manipulations had pinpointed the mys-terious origins of the Deonar Municipal Colony leak in chapter 5, who had weathered the incident crouched behind a desk in an adjacent room. Follow-ing the incident he went into hiding, staying with relatives in another part of the city. I spoke with Balekar's family in their Shivajinagar home a few days later; his wife said that he was afraid for his life: "They were mentioning him by name. He's very upset and isn't speaking to anyone." The location of their home is well known among residents of Shivajinagar-Bainganwadi; sometimes people stop by and ask questions, or try to convince him to open or close this or that valve. After the February incident Balekar requested a transfer to another ward. Korelekar, however, convinced him to stay in M-East; Balekar's understanding of the workings of the distribution system was unsurpassed in the department, Korelekar explained,[2] and they could not afford to lose him. Instead he was assigned to a different shift rotation, during which he would not need to operate valves anywhere near Shivajinagar-Bainganwadi.

The spate of early-morning raids that had prompted the February incident, Korelekar explained, was inspired by the mysterious drying up of pipes in Shivajinagar-Bainganwadi discussed in chapter 5. Following the change in the water supply timings and the commissioning of the new pumping station, complaints of dry taps, shortened supply hours, and lower pressures had poured in from across Shivajinagar-Bainganwadi and the surrounding areas, and Korelekar had surmised that there must be "some kind of airlock." Since airlock is a problem that is invisible from above ground, and since dry taps are the only symptom of this hydraulic complication, it is an explanation that I frequently heard cited by engineers trying to appease angry neighborhood leaders; it is an entirely plausible explanation for almost any incidence of water shortage, both hard to dispute and completely without author or blame—the result of neither incompetence nor malfeasance, but a manifestation simply of the unruly pipes themselves.

Yet while the airlock explanation is difficult to refute, it is equally hard to prove. And indeed my conversations with area residents, plumbers, and neighborhood leaders revealed that airlock explanations were received with much skepticism; popular explanations offered very different theories of the shortage's origins. In the weeks prior to the February incident, rumors had circulated through the largely north Indian Muslim neighborhood of Kamla Raman Nagar that water supplies intended for their area had been intentionally diverted by corrupt department staff to the nearby area of Deonar Municipal Colony, just to the south. Most of the department engineers and laborers are Maharashtrian, it was said, and Deonar Municipal Colony, which houses primarily Maharashtrian government employees, was gifted this extra water out of ethnolinguistic preferential treatment. Besides, a neighborhood-level social worker reasoned, "everyone knows" that the chaviwalla keeps a key at home and sometimes uses it at odd hours.[3]

The February 2009 incident in Korelekar's office was precipitated, residents explained, by a department action early that morning, during which department engineers had seized a number of motors on water connections that were already struggling against the mysterious shortage. "Even *with* the motor the water is barely coming," one resident fumed, a young woman who had not been involved in the march on Korelekar's office but who expressed little doubt that the department engineers and laborers were to blame for the shortage. "They've closed the valve." Onlookers nodded their agreement. With this diagnosis, no matter who else may have been involved—no matter what kinds of favors or payments may have changed hands—any manipulation of the distribution system, it was reasoned, would necessarily have involved one of the ward's chaviwallas. Having worked the neighborhood's valves for nearly two decades, and being himself a resident of Shivajinagar-Bainganwadi, Balekar is widely known to have intimate knowledge of the area's pipes and valves. Moreover, residents were quick to point out, he himself is Maharashtrian. Balekar thus represented the most visible face of the "corrupt" operations that were credited for drying up the neighborhood's pipes.

The episode itself was not unusual. Attacks and threats of violence to municipal water engineers and department staff are something of a regular occurrence in Mumbai. "The public unrest and protest has really been physical at many instances in city and suburbs" (Municipal Corporation of Greater Mumbai 2009: 7). These outbursts, however, were not simply some sort of cathartic release, an overflow of always already simmering anger from marginalized and frustrated people who are starved of water, harassed by state officials, and criminalized by an excitable media. While people are indeed often marginalized, thirsty, and harassed, such incidents of violence (or, more often, threats of violence) are better understood as targeted responses to what are popularly conceived to be conscious and precise actions on the part of engineers and department staff to divert water either for political reasons or private gain (or both). For all the engineers' efforts to explain dry taps in either technological terms (e.g., airlock), as the result of natural disasters (absolute shortage due to scanty rains), or as the fault of criminal water theft (antinational terrorists and "mafias" in slums), the most commonly cited explanation for dry taps is simply "corruption."[4]

Violence and violent threats directed toward department staff are thus often described by their propagators in *disciplinary* terms: corrupt water department engineers and staff need to be threatened sometimes if they are to be kept in line. During one conversation with me, a neighborhood leader named Khan (who had recently turned down an offer to stand for the municipal corporation elections due to lack of resources with which to fund his campaign), reached behind his desk and grasped (without lifting) a two-inch-diameter *lathi* (a wooden club) as he spoke to me: "If I were the corporator, I would go down there to the water department and beat the engineers—I would beat the [hydraulic engineer] himself! I wouldn't kill them or anything, just hit them a little. Then they'd understand that they have to do their work properly. That's the only way they can be taught to listen; that's how things work here." Department engineers explain the challenges they face in pressurizing the distribution network in largely technical terms—caused by forces that are out of their hands—yet residents, politicians, and even some department staff express confidence that the water department retains tight control over the distribution network. In this context dry taps are explained as the result of either private profiteering by department engineers or politically motivated tampering. Both phenomena, of course, are variations on the more general explanation that water shortages are produced by "corruption."

In the context of regular experiences of infrastructural breakdown this corruption explanation plays a crucial role in mediating popular understandings of the water department as all-knowing and all-powerful. Popular discourse suggests a general belief that rational and complete knowledge of the water grid actually *exists* among department engineers and planners but that corrupt engineers and laborers simply do not act on their knowledge and power to produce water in certain neighborhoods. For their part department staff stick to the official narrative that they have complete command over the distribution system; breakdowns and shortages are the result not of fractured knowledge or powerlessness but rather "hydraulic complications" or technical difficulties. This explanation is often echoed by the media, among residents (irrespective of class or caste), and among political classes. The corruption discourse allows for a widespread belief in the coherence of the water department's knowledge and authority over the distribution network to coexist alongside everyday experiences of breakdown, shortage, and volatility. As the city's water distribution system grows increasingly volatile and unwieldy, notions about corruption have thus kept pace, with recurrent shortages and stoppages inspiring increasingly fantastic and paranoid ideas about mafias, terrorists, and larger-than-life conspiracies.

Hydro-Puppeteers

When I approached Korelekar to request permission to accompany the chaviwallas on their rounds he happily obliged. "I am also new to M-East," he told me. "I wish that I too had time to go on rounds with the chaviwallas." The chaviwallas open and close valves in three shifts: a morning shift, from 8 a.m. to 3 p.m.; an afternoon shift, from 3:30 to 11; and a night shift, from 11 p.m. to 7 a.m. I arranged to spend a week on each of the shifts. Perhaps inspired by my research interests, Korelekar instructed one of his subengineers to collaborate with one of the senior-most chaviwallas in drawing up a list of valve opening and closing timings, valve sizes, and number of turns. Maintaining a written record of valve manipulations is part of the job of the *mukadam* in charge of the chaviwallas; however, in the past decade or so the water distribution zones and timings have been tweaked and redrawn so often that recording practices have been abandoned. Knowledge of which valve is opened and closed at which time— as well as where these valves are located, to which main they are attached, and so on—is the exclusive province of the chaviwallas. Although there are a few engineers who have made an effort to acquire as much of this knowledge as possible, the specificities of the valves are such that there is much that can be learned and known only by those who actually turn the keys. For example, one chaviwalla explained to me that the threads on many of the older valves are worn in such a way that "the first few turns sometimes do not do anything."[5] So even engineers who know the number of turns it officially takes to open a valve may know nothing of the number of required unofficial turns or even the *direction* in which the key needs to be rotated in order to open or close a valve. The written list of valve openings and closings was for Korelekar's own edification, but when we met a few days later, he had made me a copy so that I could follow along with the chaviwalla's work as we circulated through the ward.

I arranged to go on rounds with the chaviwallas after having spent nearly a year researching in various sites across Mumbai's M-East Ward. I thus embarked on my valve adventure carrying with me the multiple and conflicting impressions and expectations born of many months hearing of chaviwalla exploits. The valve operators hold a special mystique in the water department, where engineers express both awe and envy at the depth and command of their knowledge. Indeed while making rounds with the valve operators was not originally on my methodological list of things to do, it quickly became apparent that these somewhat invisible operators play a crucial role in producing water flow and in the city's hydraulic imaginary. For instance, during the months I spent studying the comings and goings of municipal water tankers (which, as the object of much media attention and popular accusations of corruption, was something of a misguided fixation of mine during the early months of research), a sympathetic junior engineer supervising the tanker-dispatch procedure advised me in confidence that if I *really* wanted to understand the water department and the distribution system, I would have to find a way to access the knowledge of the chaviwallas. "Most decision-making power is in the hands of the chaviwallas," he asserted. "They can easily turn a little extra here or there, and they know how to even out the pressure by manipulating valves in other areas." Such sentiments and suppositions were expressed with such frequency that they came to inform my own attempts to make sense of the mysterious comings and goings of water. At one point during the run-up to the Legislative Assembly elections over the summer of 2009, I caught myself privately contemplating the somewhat paranoid possibility that valve manipulations might have orchestrated the water problems of one particular cluster of houses in Shivajinagar, home to a powerful opposition party worker. While my research with the chaviwallas eventually convinced me that such a level of precision is hydraulically impossible (since manipulating *any* of the area's valves would necessarily affect a much broader area), the realization of my own subconscious contemplation of such possibilities suggested something of the power and pervasiveness of the notion that the chaviwallas are veritable hydro-puppeteers. I thus began my chaviwalla escapades with both excitement and trepidation, anticipating confrontation, drama, and revelation, as well as the answers to many of my questions about where and how water is made to flow.

Once in the jeep, however, it quickly became clear that the work of the chaviwallas is exceedingly mundane and completely illegible. I followed along as best I could with Korelekar's handy list, while the chaviwallas did their best to be patient in answering my endless, often directionless questions:

> *Me:* Is this the valve described on the list as "shirt shop"?
> *Chaviwalla:* Yes.
> *Me:* Where's the shirt shop?
> *Chaviwalla:* I don't know.
> *Me:* When you open this valve, where does the water go?
> *Chaviwalla:* G Sector.
> *Me:* Where's G sector?
> *Chaviwalla:* Down the hill.
> *Me:* Oh.

So the days passed, and I did my best to make sense of their work and to take note of anything new, different, or out of the ordinary. Every once in a while someone would approach us on the street to report dry taps or short supply, but these interactions were by and large uneventful. On one occasion, while the 2009 monsoon played truant and an increasingly cranky city beseeched the skies to release their bounty,[6] a man approached the jeep and informed the chaviwalla that his tap had been drying up half an hour earlier than usual that week. The chaviwalla responded somewhat brusquely that if the fellow had read the newspapers, he would know that the department had instituted a citywide water cut until the rains came. Embarrassed, the man apologized, explaining that he had not read the papers as he does not know how to read, and quickly went on his way. It was thus with some surprise that I showed up at the water department in time for Shift 2 one July afternoon to hear that I had missed some excitement the previous day: "Yesterday we went to Trombay and a crowd of women had gathered, waiting for us. They yelled at us not to close the valve; they stood on top of it and prevented us from closing it." Since the chaviwallas had been unable to close the valve, some adjacent neighborhoods had gone without water. "One day is okay," the chaviwalla said, "but today we are going to have to deal with them." The evening proved a particularly generative research encounter, which I recorded in my field notes:

Sitting in the jeep before we leave to go on our rounds, one of the laborers—a young man named Pravin—explains to me that the women who had been standing on top of the valve the previous evening live in the neighborhood up the hill from the valve. They haven't been getting water for the past week or so, so they're angry and they stand on the valve to prevent it from being closed—they think that when the valve is closed then their water stops. But see, Pravin explains, "that just makes it worse because those areas up the hill won't get water until after we close that valve; the valve is open to supply the areas downhill, so once we close it, then the water will reach the uphill areas. But they don't understand that. We tried to tell them yesterday, but they don't believe us, so they wouldn't let us close it." Yesterday, Pravin tells me, the third shift closed it, once the water in the whole zone was already turned off and the women had gone home. I ask, But isn't that valve in front of the police station? Yes, Pravin says. So they didn't help? "Why would they help?" he says. "Our own boss doesn't help us, why should the police help?" Did you ask the police for help? No, he says. Unless it gets bad we wouldn't do that. And besides, "the women didn't do anything bad, they just stood there on the valve and told us not to close it. There's no need to involve the police."

Pravin tells me that Korelekar might be joining us today to try to calm down the people in Trombay—to explain to them that preventing that valve from being closed is actually making things worse for them. Savant (the driver) snorts, "Korelekar's not coming, he never comes to these areas. He only comes when there *isn't* a problem!"

Finally a junior engineer arrives—a new recruit named Tambe.[7] He stops by the jeep to tell us to wait for him, then he goes into the office. He leaves and the laborers groan, Why are they sending him?? He's a new man! He doesn't know anything! How is he going to calm the public?

Tambe comes back with the chaviwalla—a man in his late thirties named Patil—and off we go. We drive up to the reservoir to check that the outlet valve has been opened to the right degree. It's supposed to be at 30 degrees for an hour, then at 40 degrees after that—they've just changed it in conjunction with the water cuts. If it hasn't been done correctly, the chaviwalla explains, it could cause the shortage in Trombay. This is why Tambe is with us, I guess—to check on the valve and then go to Trombay with us to calm down the public.

At the reservoir, we climb down next to the outlet pipes and Patil and the engineer look at the dial—it says 30 degrees. They're speaking in Marathi so I don't understand what they're saying, but Tambe makes some phone calls, and people seem tense. There's an older man who is in charge of managing the reservoir outlet valves—probably in his fifties since he's not retired but looks much older. He's clearly not a senior person, and he seems to have made some sort of mistake, he looks terrified.

We get in back in the jeep. "We have time," says Savant (the driver), let's go get a snack. If we're going to get beaten up in Trombay, at least let's get beaten on a full stomach.

They laugh.

We go to the canteen and get a snack. While Tambe is waiting in line for his food I ask Patil and Pravin, What that was all about, up at the reservoir? Pravin explains, "The valve is supposed to be set at 30 degrees, but you can't see the dial clearly from up top." When we went down below we saw that it was actually set at 15; from up top it looked like 30, but when we went down we could see it was at 15. So we opened it to 30. "The man up there, he just made a mistake," Patil says, it wasn't on purpose but he's afraid of losing his job. Poor guy, he felt really bad, but it's a big mistake. You can't make mistakes like that! People don't get water when you make mistakes like that. . . .

We arrive in Trombay at 8 p.m., the jeep pulling up beside a crowd of mostly women. "They're here to welcome us," Patil says, cynically, tiredly. Tambe is visibly frightened.

Tambe: (anxiously) What can I say to them?!
Savant: Don't tell them about the reservoir mistake.
Tambe: No, no, of course not!

The possibility of real, honest error on the part of the BMC is not an acceptable narrative, it seems.

We get out of the jeep, all five of us: Patil, Tambe, Pravin, Savant, and I. The crowd surrounds us. There's a tall guy there with glasses. He greets us and sees me and says, "Come with me for a minute." I'm suspicious, but "Just come," he says. I come. Then, turning to the group of women, he announces, "This is a researcher! We've brought her tonight especially to understand your problems!" I'm shocked—the women aren't that naïve, are they? They're yelling and standing on the valve, a whole pack of them. To their credit, they don't seem much to believe Glasses's claim that he's responsible for my presence, but they engage me tentatively—whoever I am, maybe I can be useful; I arrived in the BMC jeep, after all.

They're from Sanjay Nagar, they tell me (the area up the hill). There's no water up there, not since three days. Hmm, I nod, unsure of how to respond since apparently we can't tell them that the reason their taps have been dry is that a worker in the reservoir made a mistake because the numbers were hard to see from the place where he usually stands. I say, "Well, the BMC has sent an engineer to try to figure out what the problem is—they heard your complaint and they're trying to fix it." A woman says to me, "They do this every month! They'll fix it but then they start their *natak* [games] again." I ask, How long have you had a water problem? "Two years!!" one woman yells. "This woman says three days," I say. "Well, three days no water at all, but since four months we are having extreme problems." They're yelling and yelling, trying to get my attention. Look! One old woman holds up her hands, which have short nubs where fingers might be—she has leprosy, another woman explains; Sanjay Nagar is a leprosy colony. "Everyone else gets water, but not us, we have to fill pots from hand pumps or else get water from a truck. How are these women supposed to pick up pots when they have no fingers?" she says. "How can they carry water when they can't hold pots?" For emphasis, another woman holds up her finger stumps, and her feet are all bandaged up. Pravin is behind me, but no one is talking to him; Patil and Tambe have gone back to the jeep. I go over to talk to them, and Patil explains that there's nothing they can do until the women get off the valve. "If we close it then the water will go to them, but they don't believe it. We tried to explain. They don't believe us." Patil sighs. "They told us that if you go with them to Sanjay Nagar to see their dry pipes then they'll let us close the valve. They want you to go up the hill and wait with them to see if the water comes." It strikes me as a bizarre kind of hostage proposal—like they want to keep me until their water demands are met.

Me: Okay, then I'll go.
Patil: (shaking his head) No madam, don't go!
Me: I'll be right back.
Patil: (without hesitation) Okay, but just go and come right back.

The women are happy. They let Patil close the valve, and I walk with them up the hill while the woman leading the pack—who seems to be a neighborhood leader of some sort—calls out for my benefit "See, no water!" as we pass various taps. She explains that she is the head of an area *mandal*—a self-help group that advocates for the community of women with leprosy. As head of the mandal, she has prohibited motors on the water pipes today, she tells me, because the people at the top of the hill haven't been getting any water.

We walk to the top of the neighborhood; there's no water in any tap. It's still early—it's been about twenty minutes since Patil closed the valve—but I'm starting to get nervous, wondering What if it doesn't come? I announce, confidently, "I think it's going to come." We walk to the top of the hill. There are a few hand pumps that produce sweet water. "People use those, it's groundwater," the woman says, "but we can't drink it." We walk back down a little ways and I see that—thank goodness—there's water! The water has come! I'm relieved. I was starting to doubt Patil's theory, but of course he knew, the chaviwallas always know. "The houses at the bottom are starting to get water," I say, "now it will come up higher too." "No no!" she insists, "there's no pressure!" I'm confused. "But look, it's coming!" I say. "Clearly it's coming! Just wait a few minutes."

Really, it does look like there's plenty of water coming, but she stops in every household and says aloud for whose benefit I'm not sure, "See, no water no water!" even though water is coming—maybe not at high pressure, I don't know, I can't really tell because I don't know what pressure is usually like here. Near the top of the hill we hear the buzz of a motor; the woman pokes her head in the doorway and tells a man who is filling his water barrel, "No motors today!" He says something dismissively (in Marathi) and we walk away while he is filling his barrel, his motor still buzzing.

She smiles at me and we walk back down the hill. Now she wants to take me all around the neighborhood, to keep showing me that there's no water (and thereby, it seems, showing her neighbors that she's managed to bring the attention of some foreign researcher to their neighborhood's water trouble). I repeat that it looks like the water is coming, maybe not to the houses all the way to the top of the hill, but clearly opening the valve has allowed water to flow in this direction.

The women on our parade through the neighborhood are not satisfied with this state of affairs; they seem to think that it's easy o give more pressure, that the chaviwalla could make the water reach the top of the hill if he wanted to but that their neighborhood is being denied water intentionally. I walk down with them. There's a crowd of women still there—it's gotten bigger. The women waiting at the bottom are asking the ones who came with me down from Sanjay Nagar, "Is there water? Is there water?" My tour guide says, "No no! No water!" I'm baffled—I say, "Yes, there is! It's coming! I saw it!"

We go back and forth like this for a moment—"No water!" "Yes water!"—and then I give up; it's absurd. I take my leave, telling the women that the chaviwallas are waiting for me: "We've got to open and close other valves." The woman who had taken me on the tour gives me a big, warm smile and thanks me and gives me her phone number— "Come back anytime!" Then she turns back to the crowd and shouts excitedly, "Let's go to the corporator!" The women cheer and they're off on a big march. This strikes me as funny since the water has just come.

I walk ahead, toward the police station, and Patil is there, coming to find me. He laughs, relieved to see me. "The engineer left because the crowd started to grow," Patil tells me. "He jumped in an auto and ran away." He smiles, having a laugh at the timid engineer's expense.

Back in the jeep, they ask what happened up the hill. I tell them: the water was coming—not all the way up the hill yet, but clearly it was coming. They didn't want to wait, though; they just went and stormed off to the councilor. Patil nods, unsurprised. "Yes, it's a lot of politics," he says. Then he adds, "Sanjay Nagar is a criminal area. All those connections are illegal—they don't pay bills; they don't even have meters. How can they expect that the BMC should give them water when they don't pay?" I'm stunned, confused. I ask him, "Wait, do you think it *was* on purpose that they didn't get water?" Patil shrugs. "Who knows? We opened the valve, but beyond that it's impossible to say."

Patil's final words are striking. While he in no way suspected the man at the reservoir of intentionally tampering with the valve, in suggesting that Sanjay Nagar cannot "expect" water pressure in their "illegal" connections he clearly did not dismiss the possibility that somehow, somewhere in the distribution system, the shortage was intentionally engineered. Moreover he did not seem concerned with reconciling these two contradictory positions; his final comment that "it's impossible to say" indicates that in spite of his own intimate knowledge of the valves, pipes, and flows, as well as his own extensive experience navigating the social and political forces directing flows of water, the distribution system exceeds any one person's ability to comprehend or command the network as a whole. Yet while Patil, Tambe, Pravin, and Savant seemed more or less convinced that the problem in Sanjay Nagar was the result of an honest mistake (Patil's final comments seem to reflect his broader perspective on the politics of the distribution system—as well as the pervasiveness of the legal-illegal binary—more than suspicion about this particular instance), this explanation was not one that could be used to appease Sanjay Nagar. When Tambe asked anxiously "What can I tell them?," Savant warned the green engineer not to mention the mistake at the reservoir.[8] Let them think the department is corrupt but not incompetent.

During the time I spent making rounds with the chaviwallas, I found myself increasingly preoccupied with a need to decipher the precise workings of the underground flows and to know whether, how, and why any particular water shortage or plenty may have been intentionally engineered. At one point I drew all the valves I knew of onto a map, overlaying each water supply zone with translucent paper onto which I traced meandering blue lines in an attempt to render visible—to actually see with my eyes—the spatial relationships between flows of water to different areas. These efforts were frustrated by the deeply fragmented nature not only of my own knowledge of the underground network but of the grid's very knowability. For instance, I was immediately confronted with the problem of reconciling conflicting accounts of the locations of pipes and flows. In an attempt to resolve this, I began to use different shades of blue to represent "rumored" flows and "official" supply. Yet this effort was complicated by the reality that even "official" knowledge of the grid is multiple, conflicting, infused with rumor, and in some sense based on speculation—either mine or someone else's. In retrospect it became clear that more important than finding out what really happened was the irresistible draw to speculate on what may or may not have happened. In the episode at Sanjay Nagar, for instance, my tour guide's insistence that the chaviwalla could make the water flow if only he could be made to *want* to can only in part be taken at face value; perhaps the woman believed that the chaviwallas could work such hydromiracles, but then again, perhaps she did not. Probably she was not sure; she likely did not give the question much thought. For practical purposes, what she and her followers believed or did not believe to be the ultimate cause of the shortage mattered little; the water shortage could have been caused by anything at all. Indeed scant attention was paid to the task of deciphering final causes, and the woman who led me on my tour of Sanjay Nagar— clearly a woman with some political ambition—seemed herself not entirely convinced of her own assertion that the chaviwallas could increase the pressure at will. Careful consideration of the incident reveals that the woman actually directed very little attention toward making any direct requests of the chaviwalla; on the contrary, she barely spoke to him at all. Instead, leveraging the notion that the department staff *might* be able to produce greater water pressure, she leveraged the possibility of departmental mischief in order to gather a crowd. Gathering the women on top of the valve and preventing the department laborers from doing their job allowed the woman to demonstrate and perform the extent of her authority.

Once the engineer explained to her that closing the valve would allow the water to flow, the event reached something of an impasse; the women's rally on the valve had gotten the attention of the department engineers, who were attempting to ameliorate the shortage. In this way my own appearance on the scene changed the stakes of the confrontation somewhat and presented a new possibility: first the man with the glasses and then my tour guide attempted to recast my presence in the neighborhood as evidence of each of their abilities to command the attention and resources of the state. After all, I arrived in the BMC jeep, suggesting I might have good connections and access to reliable information. Associating themselves with me, these neighborhood leaders suggested to the crowd of participant onlookers that they *themselves* might also command these resources. Up on the hill the woman was clearly less interested in the water's arrival than in making herself seen parading a foreign researcher through her neighborhood. Indeed the arrival of the water provided something of a comic foil to the whole affair, with her repeated announcements that there was no water punctuated by gestures to men and women who were filling their vessels from pressurized taps. By insisting that the chaviwallas could provide "full pressure" to make the water reach the top of the hill if they so desired, the woman simultaneously invoked the idea that the department exercises complete control over the distribution system, while suggesting—with her march to the corporator—that the department's unwillingness to increase the water pressure is evidence of the elected official's impotence in moving the corrupt state.

Corruption as Meaning Making

In a classic formulation Nye (1967: 416) defines *corruption* as "behavior that deviates from the formal duties of a public role (elective or appointive) because of private-regarding (personal, close family, private clique) wealth or status gains." In line with this definition, corruption has conventionally been theorized by social scientists and policymakers in terms of *boundary* transgression: corruption is the corruption of the imaginary divide separating public from private, lawful from unlawful, rationality from traditionalism. A conventional understanding of corruption as exceptional, deviant, indeed *corrupting* action presumes the existence of a unified and coherent state, one that is distinct from society and thereby amenable to subversion by private parties in violation of formal law. Scholarship has thus focused on the adverse effects of corrupt actions on social and economic outcomes (e.g., underdevelopment and inequality), on declining social and political trust and legitimacy, and on the subversion of the broader public good (e.g., public infrastructures) by the exigencies of particularism.[9] By the same token, others have pointed to ways corruption can facilitate economic and political *efficiency* by circumventing bureaucratic torpor or ineptitude.[10]

As a growing number of theorists (e.g., Anjaria 2011; Jauregui 2014; de Sardan 1999; Parry 2000) have noted, however, conventional understandings of corruption as exceptional, deviant, indeed *corrupting* behavior are insufficient for making sense of the *everyday* nature of so much of what is described as corrupt. One strand of scholarship has thus trained attention on the *discourse* of corruption, showing how the disdain with which the corruption epithet is hurled testifies to the internalization of a particular state idea: the notion that state employees ought to work not for their *own* good but for the good of a broader public (Parry 2000). Gupta (2005) points out that the corruption discourse testifies to a more basic belief in the existence of the state (corrupted or otherwise) in the first place. Another approach has turned an ethnographic eye to the everyday practices that people describe as corrupt. In his work on "ordinary corruption" among street hawkers and the police in Mumbai for example, Anjaria (2011: 64) shows how "power . . . works more through moments of contingency than through a systematic rationality of rule." Noting a disproportion between the scale of actually existing corruption and the larger-than-life discourse about it, Parry (2000: 37) notes that rumors that "nothing can be accomplished without it" work to plump the purses of those who can convince others of a capacity to mediate. Officials become corrupt, Parry suggests, "because everybody assumes that they are" (45).

The angry crowd from Kamla Raman Nagar that burst into Korelekar's office and the women who blocked the operators from closing the valve seemed to be acting on a conventional understanding of corruption as the use of public office for private gain. Disciplinary threats of violence are directed against those who would violate rules and norms designed to protect the public good. Yet at the same time, such moralizing characterizations of Mumbai's water department as corrupt are also puzzling: those who make such condemnatory accusations almost invariably *themselves* engage in activities and arrangements that can be described in these very terms. Khan, for example, the lathi-wielding social worker who would teach the department staff to "do their work properly," is the person through which all broker-mediated water connection-transfer payments in his neighborhood are routed (work for which, needless to say, he takes a small commission). The ethics of this kind of work are complex and situated: I once saw Khan forge Korelekar's name on a connection-transfer application, an act that he committed out of self-described "generosity" since cutting out the assistant engineer would reduce the cost—if increasing the risk—of the procedure, which was being carried out by a family of limited means.[11]

There thus appear to be two distinct uses of the word *corruption*: on the one hand, it is used to refer to morally reprehensible actions by public officials (engineers, laborers, police, politicians) who exploit their offices for private gain; on the other hand, people also describe as corrupt the myriad activities that involve the creative mobilization of resources (sociopolitical networks, financial means, knowledge and expertise) in *mitigating and managing* the ethical, financial, and hydraulic risks posed by the first kind of corruption (e.g., Khan's forging of Korelekar's name).[12] Given the moral and legal ambiguities that infuse the everyday work of getting water, allegations of corruption can be understood as a form of meaning making—a means by which people render intelligible the particular encounters and experiences that they then describe as corrupt. The corruption idea thus mediates the relationship between people's everyday encounters with illegible, unpredictable flows of water and various kinds of knowledge about the forces, actions, and activities that might be influencing those flows. Talking about corruption is the means by which people make sense of the city's erratic water flows, whereby the material, legal, and moral perils of getting water are rendered navigable. Like a roadmap, corruption narratives work as a knowledge resource that has important implications for what people then do to get water. Corruption narratives permeate the knowledge networks and symbolic systems that animate everyday infrastructural practice—the interplay, that is, between water knowledge and water-getting action—as people speculate, surmise, and pass judgment on the constantly reconfigured constellations that might be responsible for making water appear or disappear in this or that instance and then articulate these understandings in everyday talk about corruption. The facility with which one can read, interpret, and generate compelling explanatory narratives about the urban waterscape thus amounts to a kind of hydro-ethical literacy.

The knowledge that comprises this sort of literacy can be generated in any of three ways. First, people can have personal experiences of activities that they then describe as corrupt. Those offering accounts of their own corrupt acts include both state actors (water department staff and elected representative) and nonstate actors (residents, industry representatives, plumbers, political aspirants). While admitting complicity, those offering firsthand accounts of corruption overwhelmingly identify themselves as its *victims*. Second, if Mumbaikars are forthcoming in relating self-described corrupt actions, they are equally so in relaying secondhand accounts; in such instances people describe what they may have heard of the corruption-related experiences and actions of *others*.[13] Third, there are *rumors* of corruption in which corruption narratives are offered as a means of accounting for water's mysteries: pressure fluctuations, tanker sightings, connection cuttings. Such things are made sense of by weaving together snippets of information and hearsay. Rumors of corruption often take on exaggerated, mythic, even heroic proportions, with moral assessments either disgusted or enthralled—and often both simultaneously. Corrupt acts are sometimes characterized as ingenious and creative achievements yielding fantastic flows, and at other times (or even simultaneously) as depraved, immoral, or selfish, responsible for wreaking havoc on the water supply of others. Characterizations of corruption—by both residents and department staff and engineers themselves—tend to draw simultaneously on all three of these ways of knowing corruption as people make sense of their own personal experiences of water flow and stoppage using stories, rumors, and discursive categories that circulate more broadly.

Mafias of Mind

In the context of this widely held belief that dry taps are caused by corruption, as water supply in Mumbai becomes increasingly erratic (as Waikar fumed, "Even posh buildings in the suburbs are not getting water!"), ideas about corruption become equally so. For example, during the winter following the scant rains of 2009, the various ward offices of the water department implemented a citywide water cut that involved a mind-boggling series of calculations resulting in an elaborate choreography of shortened water supply timings and valve operations.[14] Since there is no one-to-one correspondence between a change in supply *duration* and a change in *volume* of water supplied,[15] the altered timings (which happened to coincide with both parliamentary and Legislative Assembly campaign seasons) became the subject of heated political debate, accusation, and suspicion. The water department responded with ongoing tweaking and retweaking, as well as renewed, high-profile actions against the so-called illegal water connections in places like Shivajinagar-Bainganwadi, and by responding to reports of shortage by increasing the number of water tankers available to each ward-level assistant engineer. Formally speaking, each ward-level assistant engineer has access to a single municipal tanker, each of which can fill and deliver around four 10,000-liter loads in a working day. The water cuts, however, saw some areas dry up dramatically, and demand for emergency supply by tanker led the department to contract a few private tanker companies in order to facilitate the delivery of emergency supplies. Meanwhile senior engineers in the head offices downtown were called for weekly press conferences, and fantastic reports about water "mafias" and the corruption-related causes of water shortages began to appear almost daily in the city's papers.

In reading these news stories and in conversations with research participants, I could not help but notice that accusations of corruption were frequently made in reference to activities that were by and large routine, standard, and in accordance with official procedure. One afternoon my neighbors Mr. and Mrs. Surve asked my opinion on a recent TV news exposé about the city's water tanker "mafia." In the newscast (which I too had seen) an investigative reporter presents an account of how municipal water is "stolen from the BMC's pipelines brazenly and in broad daylight": "[This is] why you might be going without water for several hours a day." Researching for the story, the journalist had gone undercover as a water tanker customer, claiming to need a 10,000-liter tanker of potable water for a family wedding function. In the first part of the clip, the undercover reporter is shown approaching the driver of a privately owned water tanker as he is filling his truck from a municipal filling station, described by the reporter as "stealing water" from the mains. In the second part of the clip, the reporter is shown at one of the city's ward offices, where he makes an official request for a municipally owned tanker to supply additional water to his family function by claiming that his own pipes have inadequate pressure. The ward office staff tell the reporter that there is no municipal tanker available to supply the water to his function but that he can contact one of the private tankers to deliver the supply. The reporter phones one of the tanker companies and is asked which "kind" of water he wants: ordinary water or BMC water? The third part of the clip focuses on the M-East Ward in particular, where the reporter visits one of the area's surface wells scattered across the formerly agricultural lands of Trombay, from which, he tells us, some private tankers fill their water. However, one particular well is not actually a well at all! The video shows us what *looks* like a well, while the reporter interviews a young girl filling a bucket; the reporter asks the girl whether the water is BMC water and she says yes. The reporter then tells us that the well is fed by a water main that—with the help of department engineers who turned a "blind eye"— had been opened to fill this fake "well" with municipal, piped water supply. We are told that water trucks fill their tanks from this well, stealing water from the municipal main and then selling it for a "fat fee."

Mr. and Mrs. Surve were inclined to believe the news story since the municipal authorities are "very corrupt"; they found the media story about the fake well and the tanker mafia at least plausible, if somewhat exaggerated. Aware that I had spent a number of months riding around the city in both municipal and private water tankers, they were curious to hear my opinion on the matter. By way of an answer, I related to them what I had learned of the process by which municipal water supply is distributed by tanker. A party desiring a water tanker goes to the ward office to present a letter to the assistant engineer, explaining that there is a shortage and requesting a municipal tanker of water. The assistant engineer is available to receive complaints from the public during a set window of time each morning. (In M-East this window is generally from 9 to 11.) Each of the city's wards has a single tanker available for use in that ward to meet the emergency needs of areas that are experiencing water shortages.[16] One tanker can make about four deliveries of 10,000 liters per day, so the assistant engineer allocates these four tankers based on an understanding of which areas of the ward are currently experiencing pressure problems—that is, areas that are experiencing shortage because of some trouble with the distribution system. These tankers are delivered at no cost to the receiving party. Given the quantity of water in the tankers, the assistant engineer has to send it to recipients that are prepared to receive and store it: community centers (e.g., mosques, temples, schools); residential areas and housing societies (those with shared tanks that can accommodate 10,000 liters); or low-income neighborhoods where some neighborhood leader requesting a tanker oversees the distribution of the water to residents' storage containers. Among these potential recipients, the tankers are, generally speaking, allocated on a first-come-first-served basis.

If the assistant engineer is not able to allocate one of his ward's municipal tankers to a particular party requesting a tanker, he can recommend that the party be permitted to *purchase* the 10,000 liters of water for Rs 118.[17] In this case the collection and transportation of the water become the party's own responsibility; he can move the water to his home by whatever means he chooses. With a letter from the assistant engineer to this effect, the party then visits the deputy hydraulic engineer of the zone (in another office in a different part of town), who is the official sanctioning authority. If the deputy hydraulic engineer approves, he signs the assistant engineer's letter. The party then takes this letter to the office of the assistant engineer (Maintenance) of the zone, who is in charge of the tanker-filling station (in a third, separate location). The party pays Rs 118 to the cashier in the office, and the assistant engineer (Maintenance) gives the party a *challan*—a receipt of sorts that acknowledges that the assistant engineer (Maintenance) has seen the permission and received the payment and authorizes the party to fill the designated amount from the filling station.

The party then takes the challan to the office of one of the private water tanker operators. (In the eastern suburbs these offices line the road outside the filling station.) He gives the challan to the tanker operator of his choice and then goes home to wait for the tanker. The tanker enters the gates of the filling station, where the driver shows the challan to the security guard. (The security guards tell me that they recognize the tanker drivers, so they do not actually check the challans; in any case they know that the challan will be checked by the junior engineer, who files them before issuing gate-exit passes.)[18] The driver parks the tanker under the filling-station pipe and enters the office, where he gives the challan to the junior engineer managing the filling station. The junior engineer files the challan and issues the driver a gate-exit pass. The driver climbs onto the tank and opens a hole in the top into which he inserts a plastic hose connected to the filling pipe. A water department staff person then opens the valve, and the tanker is filled with water. (Given the staffing shortage, the tanker drivers often perform this simple valve operation themselves.) The driver then leaves the filling station, showing his gate-exit pass to the security guard as he leaves.

As I then explained to Mr. and Mrs. Surve, in practice there are a few variations to this general procedure. Since the formal process involves travel among four different locations—which can be quite some distance apart—these variations primarily involve shortcuts. The groundskeeping secretary for a university in M-East, for instance, related a slightly different procedure for how the university arranged for its regular supply of municipal tankers:

> We had requested fifteen tankers per day, as per our requirements, but the [assistant engineer] only recommended ten. Then I took that letter to the deputy hydraulic engineer, but he only recommended five tankers. Then we brought our signed letter to the tanker company and gave them a copy. Then I went home. The tanker company pays the Rs 118 and then we repay them that, plus Rs 900 for a delivery fee. I have to go every week to the BMC. But this last time they gave us permission for tankers for the next fifteen days; this is the last time because we're getting a new connection.

Of the twenty or so customers who described to me the procedure by which they received a private tanker of municipal water, none paid the Rs 118 himself (which would be in accordance with the formal procedure described by various engineers); rather a copy of the signed letter is generally given to the tanker company, which pays the fee and collects a flat rate from the receiving party, as in the university secretary's description.

Additional shortcuts are also possible for certain customers. If the party needing water is a regular tanker recipient (some large industries have ongoing arrangements for tanker supply) or has personal or political connections, then much of the running around for permissions is obviated by communication over the telephone. The office calls the zonal deputy hydraulic engineer, who calls the assistant engineer (Maintenance) to authorize the tanker. Then the ward office calls the tanker company with the instructions to pay the Rs 118, fill the tanker, and take the water to a certain address, where the driver will collect the charges (the Rs 118 plus market-rate delivery charges).

Sometimes a customer goes to the ward office and the assistant engineer does not approve the request. As the owner of one private tanker company—a gruff, no-nonsense, extremely forthcoming (if not quite friendly) fellow named Thakkar—explained, "There's another possibility": "If they don't listen to you, then you can call us, the tanker company, and we go to the ward office and do the fighting. We convince the ward staff—they listen to us—then we pay the 118 and get a receipt, go to the yard, pick up the water, and bring it to you." As a fee for this service—the fighting and running around for approvals—Thakkar told me that he charges a "premium" of Rs 2,000.[19] He expressed disdain for water transport companies that charge more—as much as Rs 2,500—an excessive price, he insists, that gives all the transport operators a bad name. (Our interview took place shortly after the NDTV report inspired a slew of rumor-infused newspaper articles about the "tanker mafia.") The Rs 2,000 flat-rate charge, he tells me, is quite sufficient to cover his expenses—his employees, drivers, gas, truck maintenance, and so on—while earning a reasonable profit. (These charges probably also include any "speed money" that the tanker operator might have had to pay; although Thakkar does not explicitly mention this, his account of how he "convinces" the ward staff suggests that something a little more persuasive than Habermasian "communicative acts" may be exchanged during these hypothetical "fights.")[20]

While Thakkar describes these "premium" jobs as deliveries to those who have been turned away by the water department, my research discovered that many (if not all) such customers had never in fact attempted to gain the proper permissions; people who were willing to "run around" collecting permissions were generally able to get water at the standard rate, as in the case of the university secretary. The secretary explained that for almost two years the university had been paying Rs 2,800 per tanker to a transport company. Unaware of the "official" procedure, the groundskeeping staff had simply called a private transport company when the pressure in their pipes decreased, while attempting to secure approval for an additional connection from the water department. When a few hundred students fell ill with dysentery, the secretary tested the quality of the water supplied by tanker and discovered that the transport company had—intentionally or unintentionally—supplied the school with groundwater from a freshwater well. At that point the secretary decided to approach the water department to see how he could guarantee that his tanker water was supplied from the municipal filling point. Since then he has spent an entire day, once a week, running around to the various offices to secure the proper approvals and paying the official rate (plus transport charges), for a total of Rs 1,018. Similarly, in the housing society where I lived our society secretary called tanker companies directly, sparing himself the full day of running around to gather the various approvals by outsourcing the approval-getting process to the tanker company and paying the additional fee; our society paid Rs 2,500 for each tanker ordered during a period of low pressure—the highest unit cost of any residential water purchase of municipal water that I encountered in my research.

These deliveries to upscale housing societies, businesses, and industries (which fetch a premium of Rs 2,000 to 2,800) do not, however, constitute the majority of private tankers' work. Records from the tanker dispatch office (as well as conversations with tanker drivers, operators, and department laborers) reveal that such trips constitute only a small minority of tanker operators' business. Of the seventy to eighty tankers that depart from the filling station in the eastern suburban zone, twenty to thirty (on any given day) are municipal tankers, while fifty to sixty are private. Of these private tankers, the majority go to area industries (table 6.1).

In the eastern suburbs a large amount of municipal water is delivered every day by private tanker to an industrial soap manufacturer. As one of the zonal engineers explained, "Soap factories need lots of water. That factory requires 850,000 liters per day, but because of low pressure we have not been able to give them that much for the past year. There was a proposal a year back to put in a new main directly from the reservoir to feed that factory, but until we can arrange for that, we allow them twenty tankers per day." For each of these tankers the factory pays Rs 530; given that the industrial rate is Rs 38 for a thousand liters, this amounts to a 40 percent price increase. The company pays a flat rate

TABLE 6.1. Total Tankers Filled on an Ordinary Day from Eastern Suburbs Filling Station, 2008

Municipal tankers: 29	Private tankers: 42
7 to the dumping ground for firefighting	5 to private M-East University
1 to M-West Ward slum	3 to slum rehabilitation buildings
2 to S-Ward slum	20 to private industry
1 to T-Ward slum	14 to private housing societies
2 to government office	—
2 to L-Ward private housing society	—
1 to L-Ward maternity home	—
1 to high-elevation housing society in M-East	—
2 to high-elevation slum in M-East	—
2 to other slums in M-East	—
2 to high-elevation school in N-Ward	—
1 to slum in L-Ward	—
2 to masjids in M-East Ward	—
2 to slum rehabilitation buildings in M-East Ward	—

The information on which this table is based was provided by BMC staff responsible for verifying and recording this information.

of Rs 1,000 for each tanker, leaving the tanker company Rs 470 to cover all costs: employees' salaries, gas, truck maintenance and repair. Needless to say, this does not leave much room for profiteering on the part of either the tanker companies or the engineers. One tanker company director characterized deliveries to private housing societies (which comprise fewer than a third of all private tanker deliveries) as cross-subsidizing "premium" work that makes his business viable.

During the water cuts following the failed monsoon of 2009, for instance, tanker-supplied water was so much in demand that the eastern suburbs zonal office of the water department contracted a private water transport company to deliver municipal water. The company that was given the contract is the oldest in the city, continuously in operation since 1964, the owner tells me, when his grandfather began to provide water by tanker to a tire manufacturer in the newly annexed suburbs. The owner, a man named Shah, explained that the 2009 BMC contract paid him Rs 1,080 per tanker, allowing for very little profit. He accepted the contract anyway because "the BMC will actually pay." He tells me that the problem in his business, which deals in both BMC and groundwater, is that the majority of his customers are building contractors who use the water for construction purpose. "But these builders, sometimes they don't pay. They always need water, so my trucks don't sit idle, but it's not a secure source of income."[21] By accepting the BMC contract, he can maintain an operation of some scale—which gives his company credibility and name recognition—while diverting some of his trucks away from the high-risk business of supplying groundwater for construction purposes. The handful of daily "premium" jobs that he manages to do make up for the other, lower-profit (sometimes even loss-incurring) jobs.

In light of these observations about how municipal water supply is distributed by tanker, Mr. and Mrs. Surve's inclination to believe the water mafia news story takes on new meaning and significance. While the first part of the news exposé characterizes as "theft" the filling from the municipal main of a private tanker, this activity is in fact a completely aboveboard, standard practice. Similarly when the reporter is told that there is no tanker available but that he can hire one of the private tankers, this is also a variation on official procedure. The news report is unclear on whether the reporter presented an official letter of complaint to the assistant engineer for his signature of approval, but in any case, when the reporter phones the tanker operator he does not mention whether he had first sought the approval of the engineer but simply asks for a tanker. My research suggests that were the reporter to have done all of the proper "running around" on his own, he most probably would have been able to obtain 10,000 liters of municipal water for his private function for somewhere around Rs 1,000—which, given the limited number of tankers that can fill from the municipal filling stations in a given day, would be quite a bargain.

In any case, if an estimated eighty tankers can be filled daily at each of the city's twelve or so filling stations (for firefighting, emergency supplies, supplemental industrial use, etc.), this amounts to 9.6 million liters per day—merely a fifth of a percent of daily water supplied to the city of Mumbai. Moreover as the filling stations can fill only a fixed number of tankers per day, even if every drop of this water were to be filled without paying the Rs 118 per tanker (i.e., "stolen"), it would not have any effect on water pressure in the pipes elsewhere in the city, since—paid or not—approximately 9.6 million liters are filled from these points (which are located on the trunk mains *before* water hits the various service reservoirs) every day. As for the financial losses, were these 9.6 million liters to be filled without payment, it would amount to a loss of around Rs 112,000 per day, or Rs 40.4 million per year, a relatively insignificant 0.12 percent of the water department's 2010 budget of Rs 31,750 million (Ashar 2010)—which, in any case, the department never seems to get around to spending. All of which is to say that the accusations made in the TV exposé—that water tanker companies steal water from municipal filling stations while the BMC authorities "turn a blind eye" and that these thefts are somehow responsible for water shortages across the city—are not borne out by the evidence.

How, then, should the pervasive idea of the tanker mafia (and other corruption fantasies) be understood? The third part of the TV clip, which suggests that underground pipes have been diverted into storage spaces made to look like wells, suggests one possible interpretation. I asked the owner of a small water-transport company for his opinion on the report. The man, a weathered-looking fellow named Vipin, had been in the business for about fifteen years, keeping his small operation limited to six tanker trucks. Vipin does not deal in municipal water but in water drawn from surface wells and borewells located on tracts of high-elevation land that he holds on long-term lease. His groundwater delivery business slowed down after the failed monsoon of 2009; his wells are not producing as much water as they normally do. I asked him why, in that case, he had not diversified into municipal water since demand is so high. He replied that in recent months even the municipal water business is not very good; now that the demand for tanker supply has grown, the filling at the yard is generally done on a contract basis. "Before, you used to be able to pay 200 or 300 rupees to the ward office and they would write some nonsense and you could fill at [the filling station]. Then you could sell the tanker for 2,000 rupees to some housing society and make a profit." He was never interested in this work. "I fear God," he laughed. I asked him whether this institutionalized payment is what the media is referring to when they talk about the "tanker mafia," and he laughed again, shrugged, and nodded. Puzzled, I pointed out that idea of a mafia suggests a level of organization and orchestration on the part of the water department and tanker companies that seemed to me rather unlikely. "It's true," he agreed, "there's no organization. I don't know why they say 'mafia.'"

Since Vipin is intimately familiar with the locations and filling points of the other private tanker operators in M-East (he was able to pinpoint a remarkable number of filling points on a map, the accuracy of which I checked with a number of personal visits), I trusted that if a fake well like the one described by the NDTV exposé in fact existed, Vipin at least would have heard of it. I recounted to Vipin the NDTV account of the well and asked him if he had heard of such a thing. He shook his head no. "But do you think it is *possible*?" His eyes lit up and he flashed a bright smile: "Yes! Anything is possible." He then switched to English for emphasis: "India is great . . . and Bombay is highest great!" Switching back to Hindi, he explained, "Because people in Bombay come from all different states of India, they are creative—they think cleverly and they will do just about anything. Anything can happen here—they tell you some man is dead, and then suddenly he is alive again!"

Corruption as Transparency: Flows of Knowledge

Corruption narratives, while often inaccurate in a descriptive or representational sense, nonetheless have powerful material effects, inviting intense speculation and opening up hydro-political possibilities. Speaking privately outside the ward office, a junior engineer named Katekar recounted how he had recently taken (unofficial) leave from his job with the water department in order to work in the private sector. The water department job took up too much of his time, he explained. "I have my own business and I couldn't keep up with that work." Katekar had entered the public sector on his father's request: "My father pressured me; he said that it's good to have a government job. My father had a government job and so did my grandfather. There is respect in having a government job. But it's useless—showing up nine-to-five and having to run around. . . . I don't like this work, running around and collecting payments." By joining the water department he took a fourfold pay cut from his work in the private sector. In order to make ends meet, he told me, an engineer must be able to earn a little extra here and there in exchange for special attention, extra effort, and—particularly in the context of the staffing shortage—overtime work.[22] A recently retired senior engineer recalled that when he joined the department in the mid-1970s an engineering position in the municipal corporation was more than competitive with the private sector. Since the mid-1990s, however, private sector salaries (as well as the cost of living in Mumbai) have increased dramatically. "Younger engineers have left," he sighed; he does not blame them. On the eve of his retirement from the water department he was asked to stay on in an advisory capacity. "But the salary was too little. I was offered five times as much to go into the private sector."

In some departments of the Municipal Corporation, "unofficial incomes" are earned as a matter of course; in Building Approvals, for instance, engineers freely admit that fantastic salaries are earned without much "running around." "This is not corruption," one Building Approvals engineer insisted (unprompted); "it's speed money."[23] With Mumbai's real estate market booming, the engineer explained, there is just so much work to be done that a builder will happily pay a little (or even a lot) extra to have an engineer work overtime to process his file. In the water department, however, earning a salary comparable to that which one could earn in the private sector takes some running around, attending to the never-ending work of improvisationally managing the highly dynamic landscape of pressure and flow and the elaborately choreographed and politically charged game of hydraulic Kho Kho. Working in the water department is exhausting, senior engineers maintain, and for this reason it has become a de facto "punishment department" in the Municipal Corporation,[24] where engineers from other departments are transferred when they fall into disfavor in other departments.

In this context, for more senior engineers, retaining some semblance of control over the distribution system requires keeping a tight rein on what happens to the distribution system as well as what is *known* about it. Katekar explained:

> An assistant engineer never likes to have a junior who is too clever or independent, because the [assistant engineer] can never trust him. See, if a plumber approaches a junior engineer for some work, then the [assistant engineer] wants the [junior engineer] to run to him and tell him what the job is. But if the [junior engineer] is smart and has his own information, he will draft the case report on his own, and he could make a fake report: instead of reporting a new connection, he could report a transferred connection, which has lower brokerage fees. So an [assistant engineer] will always suspect that he is being lied to by a clever [junior engineer]—even if it *is* just a transfer.

For this reason, Katekar explains, access to information—for example, the private maps discussed in chapter 5—is tightly controlled, with department staff constantly working to increase their own informational resources while hiding this information from their colleagues. "The key to being effective in the water department," an engineer named Barve explained, "is to make yourself necessary—to keep an eye on things and learn about the distribution system so that you know how to get work done." Gupta philosophized, "Good doesn't mean you're honest, and honest doesn't mean you're good." To "manage well" in the department, he explained, an engineer needs to "solve problems and work hard." Engineers who wish to be able to "solve problems"—that is, who wish to be able to produce water where and when it is required—must find ways of keeping *flows of knowledge* about the distribution system directed through their own offices.

Keeping one's office "in the loop" requires that, as much as possible, even legally ambiguous work be directed through the department. For example, if a housing society's taps mysteriously dry up, or if a new development needs additional resources for the ubiquitous extra few floors that have already been sold but for which no occupation certificate exists, provisions for the additional water will generally be made by the department itself, even though official policy is somewhat hazy in such cases.[25] The society or builder will hire a plumber to arrange for the needed work. The plumber will present a proposal to an engineer either at the ward level or at the head office, depending on the size of the new connection involved. In exchange for facilitating the intervention, the engineer will receive a payment of some sort. One engineer insisted that since any monetary gifts are made only *after* the work is complete, they should not be considered payments for corrupt acts—"bribes"—but rather as "bonuses" or tips awarded to engineers who are "cooperative." Most engineers are very cooperative, one developer explained, because they know that if they do not approve a particular work, approval will be obtained by some other avenue. An uncooperative engineer would lose out on his bonus, but more important he would be left ignorant of crucial information about the distribution system that might make it difficult for him to do his job down the line.

Engineers have many ways of keeping themselves abreast of interventions into the distribution system. Katekar, for instance, mentioned that "There are a few valves that are not supposed to be operated, but I know they are operated sometimes." When I asked him to explain how he knows this, he replied simply, "It's my area—it's my job to know." Over the years he has learned, for instance, that when a certain valve is "adjusted," a cluster of homes in an adjacent area will not get much water. "So I go and ask the people on that road, 'Did your water come?' They will never say yes of course, but by the extent of their complaints I can interpret what has happened. If they say 'Just a little water came,' I know that plenty of water came and that valve has not been tampered with. But if they complain a lot about water shortage, then I know that the valve has been adjusted. I can read their expressions. So then I go out with the chaviwalla and he fixes the valves." Whether the valves are manipulated by the chaviwallas or by private parties who have figured out how to open and close them is anyone's guess; Katekar suspects that most operations are probably carried out by the chaviwallas themselves. While he has not personally witnessed any unofficial manipulation of the valves, he surmises that such procedures are likely managed the same way additional water connections or transfers are managed—in transactions with which he has plenty of direct personal experience. The party needing more water will approach a plumber or a broker of sorts who knows how to make the water flow, someone who knows where the water is, knows who in the department to talk to, knows the going rate for these transactions. Since it might be impractical, intimidating, and even risky to approach a chaviwalla directly, Katekar suspects that the arrangements are mediated by the plumbers. The plumbers would negotiate the arrangement with ward-level engineers who then simply instruct the chaviwallas to change this or that valve. In this sense it becomes very difficult to distinguish official from unofficial valve manipulations since any special adjustment could easily be carried out during routine valve operations. Katekar's readjustment practices might therefore be interpreted not as the undoing of corrupt work but as simply part of the adjusting and readjusting that comprises the everyday work of watering the city. Other people (area residents as well as department staff), however, suspect that unofficial valve manipulations are carried out by the chaviwallas themselves, without being directed by engineers. One of the many drivers who chauffeur the chaviwallas, a man named Navir, described how watchmen and security guards sometimes approach the valve operators while they are on duty. Navir allowed that such communications may very well be just casual interactions—complaints of short supply or information-passing efforts—although he readily admitted that he had no way of knowing. "You can't tell just by looking at it what they are doing with a valve."

Indeed you cannot. One morning out on rounds, one of the chaviwallas operated a valve that I had not previously seen any of them touch. Anticipating my curiosity the chaviwalla explained, "That valve is not numbered on your list. I just closed it a little. The valve is controlled," meaning that generally the valve is left partially open so that *some* water is allowed to pass, while pressure to some adjacent area is augmented. "We don't usually touch that valve, but today I closed it a little because there's some leakage." A few days later, in the jeep with a different chaviwalla, we passed the "controlled" valve that had been changed. The driver, a man named Sartaj who had also been with us on the earlier occasion, burst out laughing as we passed the valve and recounted—for the benefit of the chaviwalla present—how the first chaviwalla had changed the valve setting, telling me it was because of "leakage." The second chaviwalla, who was not amused but was keenly interested, asked, "Which valve?" Sartaj pointed it out. Confused, I asked, "Why would leakage lead him to close the valve?" Sartaj erupted again in laughter, and the chaviwalla shook his head. "Probably the corporator complained," he replied. "The people in Sanjay Nagar weren't getting enough water," he surmised, extrapolating from the incident the previous week, when the women from Sanjay Nagar stood atop the valve to prevent its being closed. The driver agreed, adding, "There's someone who lives around here—some politician or some kind of important person, connected to some higher-up in the water department. When they open that valve, more water goes down the hill to his area." This must have been the reason Sanjay Nagar was experiencing short supply, the driver concluded; now, after the corporator complained, the valves were being put back to normal. I asked Sartaj how he knows about the "important person" down the hill, and he told me that he has been sent there on numerous occasions to deliver water tankers to one particular house. (He added that he often returned to the filling station with a mostly full tank since the house's storage facilities can accommodate only a fraction of the tanker's 10,000 liters.)

The kinds of semiofficial, broker-mediated activities that constitute the everyday distributional activities of the water department staff render the tasks of maintaining adequate knowledge of the network exceedingly difficult. Gupta (the senior engineer who played a starring role in chapter 1) described how, a few years before his retirement, the deputy hydraulic engineer of the eastern suburbs had to take leave for a month. Unable to find a temporary replacement for this notoriously unwieldy suburb, one of Gupta's colleagues "challenged" him to assume responsibility for the six-week period. "You won't be able to handle it," the colleague had teased, citing the challenges of the unruly, rapidly changing M-East Ward. Another senior colleague warned against the move: "Are you trying to commit suicide?" Gupta explained, "Anyone who goes there ends up looking bad." There are so many conflicting demands made on the system, and they cannot all be met; the resulting political unrest can only reflect badly on whoever is in charge. He accepted the "challenge," he told me, since it was only for a short time; he managed to "stay alive" with what he described as "sweet talk": "I just said 'Yes, yes, no problem' to everything everyone asked."

While the short duration of Gupta's stint in the eastern suburbs allowed him to survive by acquiescing to what a longer time frame might have revealed as mutually irreconcilable demands, for those who spend longer stretches of time in a particular area, sweet talk would soon prove unsustainable. For those who spend the entirety of their careers in a single ward—department staff and laborers as well as private plumbers, neighborhood brokers, and residents— maintaining the integrity and coherence of the distribution system is of paramount importance. One local plumber, a man named Yussuf, expressed striking ambivalence at the extent to which private actors (himself included) are increasingly unrestrained in their access to the distribution system:

The real problem in M-East started about fifteen years ago, in the mid-1990s. Before that, the engineers kept the department together, they used teamwork.[26] In those days they kept control over the plumbers. For my business of course it was bad because they were very strict. But they made sure that whatever money they made from my work was divided equally in the department. That way the ward engineers could even manage the reservoir; by including [the reservoir engineers], they could arrange for a little more water here, a little more there. . . . They kept control on the whole system; everyone was working together to keep the pipes pressurized. The engineers let the plumbers make a living because they needed us, and also because they earned some too, but they didn't let us have free rein of the supply. . . . Recently it has just become a free-for-all. Now the engineers know so little about the distribution system, they have no idea how to manage the network; they have absolutely no idea. We make a proposal and they just say "Okay okay" and sign [the form]. In the old days the engineers took a bigger cut. We didn't make much in those day, but we did fine. Now that the department has lost control of the network, we earn more and the engineers don't earn as much. Sure, my business is great, but the situation is bad. For instance, I don't think that any of the earnings from our work goes to the reservoir anymore.[27] How can the reservoir people give more water when they don't know where it is needed? And anyway, why would they take the trouble when they are not getting anything? So there are so many [water] connections but no one makes sure there's water in the pipes! It's really bad—it makes [the plumbers] look bad, and then people don't trust our work. We have gotten a bad name. That's bad for business.

In this atmosphere, Yussuf sighs, even if the engineers wanted to do the work on their own, most of them would not be able to do much without the plumbers' knowledge. In this context even clearly perfectly routine works are regularly directed through the plumbers.

If someone is poor and they want to process their application on their own—do the running around after engineers and approvals themselves—these days sometimes the engineers won't even let them do it. They send them here and there until eventually they go through the plumber. For six months people are taken around like this! It used to be that if someone is really poor and persistent, then the department would do that person's work. There's a god, you know! But these days no one cares; there is so much corruption, everyone just wants to earn money.

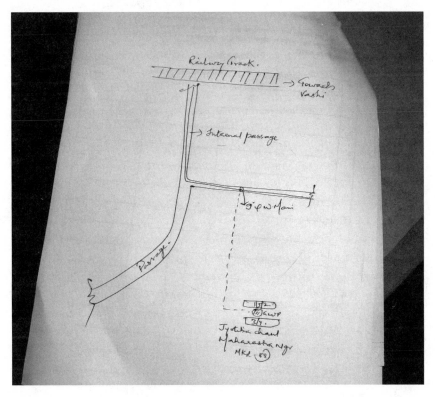

FIGURE 6.1. Plumber's drawing: application for new municipal water connection. Photo by author. Courtesy of Municipal Corporation of Greater Mumbai.

While plumbers thus blame the corrupt and self-serving department staff, engineers and laborers in turn hold the plumbers responsible for the situation. Katekar explained, "There are a few fellows—local informants—who go combing the neighborhoods looking for customers who want connections. Then they send these customers to the brokers.[28] The broker goes to the BMC with a bunch of documents, carrying with him a signed photocopy of some other plumber's license." Katekar clarified that according to official procedure, the junior engineer handling the case is supposed to go to the site and check all the documents and decide on a location for the connection, but in most cases the plumber comes with a hand-drawn map (figure 6.1); the plumbers are familiar with the distribution network, and most of the junior engineers are new to the ward, so there is indeed little trouble convincing them. And in any case, Katekar concluded, "Once the maintenance people go out to make the connection, the plumber anyway sometimes convinces them to put it in a different place." Whatever relations of power, knowledge, authority, and cash might underpin the arrangement, most decisions regarding the placement of new connections are handled by the plumbers. Sitting in the Maintenance Office one morning, I saw a man come in with a proposal for a new water connection. The staff person managing the office apologized to the man, instructing him to speak to one of the plumbers outside, calling out to one who happened to walk by the door. The man thanked the maintenance staff person and followed the plumber into the courtyard. "Why can't you manage his case directly?" I asked. "Because we only know the official charges," the staff person explained. "We don't know anything about the unofficial charges." I must have looked confused, because he added bluntly, "It's corruption; they all have to be managed by these plumbers."

Conversations with plumbers, residents, brokers, engineers, maintenance staff, and politicians offered remarkably consistent and somewhat standardized accounts of the corrupt procedures by which various hydraulic interventions (additional connections, connection transfers, valve operations, water tanker approvals, etc.) are accomplished. These accounts of corruption were readily offered, unprompted; they were often less apologetic or confessional than helpless, and sometimes were cathartically angry. Katekar expressed frustration that, unlike his father, he must dirty his hands "running around" in order to make a decent living in the public sector. Katekar chose instead to work in the private sector. (His shift to the private sector is somewhat ironic since the projects on which he works—designing hydraulic systems for high-end residential and industrial parks—will likely receive water connections through the very activities that he finds distasteful.) Plumbers meanwhile express dismay that they are made to look dishonest by an unpredictable distribution system that saps the water out of new connections as quickly as they are made. Senior engineers try to avoid postings to particularly troubling, fast-growing areas like M-East, where the breakneck speed of urban transformation has rendered the distribution system so unruly that, as Gupta puts it, "anyone who goes there ends up looking bad." Maintenance staff working long days under a punishing sun—repeatedly digging up the same buried pipes—feel justified in accepting tips from plumbers as compensation for the additional work.[29] In all these instances "corruption" cannot be reduced to a specific set of activities or behaviors—the exchange of favors, the awarding of bonuses, the minding of gaps. Rather each actor describes his or her own actions as being informed or shaped by the larger force of corruption that is beyond his or her control—that simply exists.

The common refrain that water flows are orchestrated by corruption thus works as a kind of explanation—an effort to link fragments of experience through a particular narrative logic. Both municipal employees and the general public are overwhelmingly skeptical of the water department's technological explanations for what are experienced as inexplicable water flows, shortages, and stoppages. Instead the activities involved in the everyday work of getting water and of mitigating the risks of infrastructural breakdown provide a practical and discursive lexicon that renders intelligible the mysterious volatilities of the pipes. People draw on their own personal experiences, secondhand accounts, and rumors to construct explanatory narratives: Sartaj recalls being sent on a particular water-delivery mission and concludes that the "controlling" of an area valve must have been manipulated in order to quench the thirst of a politically connected bigwig; Katekar extrapolates from his own experiential knowledge of cash-lubricated, broker-mediated transfers to surmise how valves may be changed through similar means; a Shivajinagar social worker accuses Balekar of ethnolinguistic preferential treatment toward Maharashtrians, drawing on decades of anti-Muslim (and anti–North Indian) vitriol and violence served up by the city's ruling Shiv Sena party to conclude that his area's dry taps must be the result of deliberate malfeasance by a Marathi-speaking valve operator;[30] municipal councilors representing the working-class suburbs create narrative order and political mileage out of hydraulic chaos following in the wake of the premonsoon (and preelection) water cuts in 2009 by accusing the water department of corruption in prioritizing the water needs of Island City elites over that of the slum-swollen suburbs. Indeed corruption might be described as an "empty signifier" (Laclau 1996: 44, following Saussure), its meaning specified by context: by who is using the word, by what its use seeks to explain, and to whom. This is not to discount the myriad ways in which personal or political connections, cash payments, ethnolinguistic chauvinism, and sociospatial elitism (among other things) are brought to bear on water and its infrastructures. But as we have seen, these categories in themselves are distinctly unreliable as predictors of water flow. World-class constructions might boast infrastructural connectivity, but these kinds of claims cannot be taken at face value; by the same token, while the new discourse of slum would characterize water supply to popular neighborhoods (particularly Muslim-dominated areas like Shivajinagar-Bainganwadi) as *by definition* legally circumspect and hydraulically tenuous, the slum narrative itself wreaks infrastructural havoc. Corruption narratives cannot be interpreted as descriptions of some independent reality. Rather they must be considered meaning-making practices that render the city's capricious hydrologies intelligible in ways that animate political, social, and infrastructural action.

SEVEN

"IF WATER COMES IT'S BECAUSE OF POLITICS"

Power, Authority, and Hydraulic Spectacle

Department at Work

In July 2009, during the run-up to the Maharashtra Legislative Assembly elections, cholera broke out in Rafique Nagar, a long-established slum neighborhood at the northwest corner of Shivajinagar-Bainganwadi sandwiched between a fetid creek and the Deonar Dumping Ground.[1] I entered the M-East Ward office one morning, having arranged to go along with the maintenance staff on one of their unauthorized connection–cutting actions, and found the water department office strangely empty. "They've all gone to Rafique Nagar," explained a junior engineer who had stayed behind to finish some paperwork. After the cholera deaths, he explained, the local corporator had called for a "joint action" by the ward engineers, so the health department, pest control, sewerage, and water had all gone to Rafique Nagar. I too headed there, hopping in a rickshaw and wandering into the tangle of lanes until I caught up with what looked like a parade. Picking my way through a stream of people, I came upon a team of hacksaw-toting water department laborers in their grayish-brown uniforms. The laborers trailed a short distance behind a gaggle of engineers following in silence, behind the duo at the head of the pack: Korelekar walked alongside a heavyset man in a bright, white, embroidered button-down, whose large dark sunglasses and gold rings made him look as though he had just stepped off the set of a Bollywood gangster film.

The man was Suresh [aka "Bullet"] Patil, the area's elected municipal councilor; I had seen his face once before, a few months earlier, smiling down from a large billboard along the road through Lotus Colony that connects Rafique Nagar with the highway. I had followed the path of a three-foot-deep trench at the edge of the road, inside which a twelve-inch-diameter water pipe looked to have been recently laid, a bright blue plastic tube announcing the promise of renewal for the neighborhood's dry taps. Just above the trench Bullet Patil's gaze floated above a block of Marathi-language text:

> As a result of a successful struggle, it pleases me to inform all the citizens of electoral district 129 that on the 5th Day of September, the Corporator, Suresh Patil, led an andolan [demonstration] on Ghatla Wall,[2] and for five hours prevented the water department engineers from closing the valve (which allowed the water to flow into Lotus Colony for these five hours). As a result of this successful andolan, the Additional Secretary has issued an order that Lotus Colony on Abdul Hamdid Marg have a new 12-inch pipeline laid. The Additional Secretary has assured that the work will be completed expeditiously and that the people of district 129 will have their water problems solved.

Curious, I had shown a photo of this remarkable billboard to Korelekar, inquiring about the events described therein. Korelekar had chuckled and said that while he did not remember the particular "andolan" to which the poster referred, preventing the chaviwallas from closing valves is indeed something that local politicians and social workers like to do on occasion.[3] As for the new twelve-inch pipeline for which Patil's billboard claimed credit, Korelekar (as well as planning department engineers) explained that the pipe was one of a number of similar mains that had recently been laid throughout Shivajinagar-Bainganwadi. Patil, however, was not alone in his effort to generate political mileage out of what may well have been (although no one is quite certain) routine water department work; a few weeks later I heard the district's incumbent Legislative Assembly candidate claim personal responsibility for the very same pipe.

In the wake of six cholera deaths our entourage snaked through the narrow lanes of Rafique Nagar, following a narrow sewerage trench of black, oily muck, along the inside edge of which—and dipping down into the blackness on occasion—ran clusters of one-inch-diameter black plastic water pipes. In a wider part of the lane, the ditch opened up to form a small lake of ooze, traversed by what looked like an elaborate macramé bridge of water pipes. A junior engineer explained that the plan was to cut all the plastic water connections; they crack easily and sewage seeps in, making people sick. We stood around in solemn silence, staring at the puddle. Korelekar's sunglasses fogged up as the slow stream of sweat escaping from the edges of his hennaed hairline responded to the mounting morning heat. Without breaking the silence, a young boy sprung gazelle-like to the far side of the sludge lake to get a better view, his footing sure as he landed on the sloped bank opposite. After some moments Korelekar and the other municipal staff murmured and nodded, and one of the hacksaw-wielding laborers stepped forward, kneeled at the edge of the lake, and began to slice through one of the plastic pipes. He had barely scratched the surface of the tube, however, when Korelekar (prompted by Patil) suddenly held up his hand, bringing the sawing to an abrupt halt as the crowd's attention turned to some commotion on the far side: a man had pushed his way forward through the crowd and was shouting his rage over the black expanse. "You're over here cutting our water connections," he fulminated, "but you're the one who arranged for all these plastic pipes in the first place!" Patil, visibly defensive and caught off-guard, responded in anger, "*You* all have put these illegal connections here and now you blame them on *me!*"[4] The altercation lasted a few minutes, ending in a protracted, angry soliloquy from Patil on the subject of his own magnanimity toward the neighborhood.[5]

The subject of cutting connections was finally dropped and the parade moved forward, away from the slimy puddle, turning up an adjacent lane. While Patil was engrossed in a conversation with some women from an area self-help organization, I approached Korelekar, who was standing a little way off: "Aren't you going to cut connections today?" Korelekar shook his head. "No. If we cut connections today it will hurt his image." Confused, I asked, "But didn't he invite you here in order to cut those plastic pipes laid inside the gutter because of the cholera outbreak?" "He invited us here because there is cholera. He wants to show the people that he is concerned, so he brought us all here, but he doesn't want to do anything unpopular. *We* want to cut the plastic pipes, but Patil doesn't want to actually *be* here when we cut the lines because some people might get angry." Patil was planning to stand for the Legislative Assembly seat in this district, Korelekar explained, and so he was particularly keen to demonstrate a swift response to the cholera outbreak, but he had to be careful not to do anything to upset anyone. I asked, "Do you think he invited you here knowing that he was going to stop you from actually doing anything? So that he could 'help' Rafique Nagar *twice*—first by bringing the engineers and then by saving the pipes from your actions?" Korelekar paused as he digested the question, then replied, "It's quite possible. But in any case," he added, his usually jovial tone suddenly betraying a hint of fatigue and cynicism, "there's nothing we can do. We're helpless. We have to stay here until he's finished." Another hour passed, leaving at least fifteen of the ward engineers and staff standing idle on the side of the road, waiting for Patil to finish his tour around the neighborhood. To pass the time I pulled out my camera and snapped a few photos of the crew. A subengineer laughed wryly and asked, "What will you title that one, 'Department at Work'?"

Politicians like Patil face a dilemma. On the one hand, whatever flows or does not flow out of his area's pipes will be interpreted as a sign of power—either his own or someone else's. Yet given the intractability of the distribution system, as well as the politically volatile discourses of legality that permeate water supply to slums, it is exceedingly complicated for Patil to facilitate a sufficient and lasting water supply to the residents of Rafique Nagar, at least in the immediate term. In this incident, in which a lethal water-borne disease had already claimed the lives of a handful of residents, Patil thus sought to demonstrate his ability to mobilize the BMC engineers while simultaneously distancing himself from any specific remedial action. Many Rafique Nagar residents expressed sympathy with the engineers' contention that the plastic pipes had facilitated the spread of disease and with the effort to cut plastic pipes, not least because a reduction in the number of pipes promised to increase pressure to those who remained. However, the protest at the edge of the sewage lake demonstrated that the action would not be without damage to Patil's reputation—political costs that, in the rumor-infused environment, were well understood to exceed Patil's own capacity to define, contain, or otherwise control.

In this context Patil's parade was an end in itself. The demonstration of his ability to rally such an extraordinary showing of ward engineers functioned as a performance of his authority, a testimony to the strength of his networks and thus of his potential capacity to leverage the resources of the state bureaucracy for any particular end. The unpredictability of the water distribution system coupled with the ambiguous legalities of infrastructural configurations produce volatile and risk-laden hydrologies that are characterized by protracted bouts of water shortage punctuated with surges of abundance. As chapter 6 demonstrated, everyday experiences of the erratic distribution system are thus rendered comprehensible largely through an ever more fantastic discourse of corruption. Despite official explanations of water trouble as the result of technical difficulties (such as airlock), natural disasters (such as insufficient rains), or absolute shortages (caused by increasing demand from population growth), dry taps (which are closely associated with water-borne illness during the rainy season, when the drainage ditches through which many water pipes are laid run high) are overwhelmingly described—in private conversations, in popular discourse, and in media narratives—as the result of an all-knowing, all-powerful water bureaucracy that is riddled with corruption. Performances like Patil's parade, in other words, functioned as a sign (and perhaps a warning) to area residents that it was in their interest to throw their political support behind the man who was able to demonstrate such a decisive ability to set the apparatus of the state in motion.

Hydraulic Spectacle

During the months leading up to the Assembly election in October 2009, Patil's water spectacles increased in both frequency and drama. In the predawn hours of a July morning in 2009, at the tail end of the valve operators' night shift, our lonely jeep full of snoozing chaviwallas (waiting for 6 a.m., when it was time to open the shift's final valve) was awakened by the roar of a shimmering white sport utility vehicle, the faces of those inside obscured by darkened windows. A rear door soon opened and out stepped Korelekar, who approached the jeep, spoke a few words (in Marathi) to Khade (the chaviwalla), and then returned to the suv, which promptly sped off. A few minutes later, after Khade had opened the 6 a.m. valve, we climbed back in the jeep, but instead of turning back toward the ward office, we continued north toward Shivajinagar.

> *Me:* Where are we going?
> *Khade:* To look at some valve.
> *Me:* Why?
> *Khade:* (shrugs).
> *Me:* Because of Patil?
> *Khade:* (nods, smiling)

We stopped in Shivajinagar, pulling up behind the parked suv at the intersection of BPD Marg and Road 2. The street was dark—it would be at least another half hour before sunrise—the quiet stillness showing little sign of wakeful activity in the neighborhood. The suv door swung open, and Patil slid out from behind the darkened glass, flanked by Korelekar. Khade selected one of the heavy metal valve keys from the back of our jeep, and walking over to the shoulder of the road edge of the road, he pointed to what looked like a crack in the dirt surface of the road. Kneeling down, he brushed the dirt off the top of the rectangular outline of a valve chamber—a steel trapdoor a few feet long by a few feet wide. Khade explained that the residents of this road had complained to Patil about water shortage. The valve connecting the road's nine-inch pipe to the distribution main along BPD Marg had not been operated in decades. Khade believed the valve was closed. The pipe was fed by a different feeder main, with water flowing in from the west; Patil, however, wanted the department staff to open the valve so that water could be supplied to Road 2 not only from the west but also from the east, through the line attached to the new pumping station.

Khade and his team of laborers squatted down on their haunches and began scraping away with their hands at the dirt and grime caked over the edges of the valve door. A subengineer made himself comfortable, leaning against the jeep. Korelekar stood nearby, looking somewhat disinterested. The driver fell asleep. All the while the laborers scraped and scraped, sometimes with their heels, sometimes using their bare hands to claw at the dirt. Khade banged the heavy metal valve key down on top of the door to try to loosen it. The action produced a loud clanging sound, and soon a stream of people began to emerge from the area houses to watch. "Our water is dirty," one woman yelled, seeing Korelekar. "It's black!!" "We have no water," added another, "no water at all for over a week." A third interjected, "Our water comes so slowly, just a few buckets and it smells like the gutter." I followed this third man back to his home to see what was coming out of his tap. Bending my face down toward a bucket, I see water that looked clear enough, but the man was right, it smelled like the gutter.

After a half hour of banging on the lid of the valve, a crowd of more than fifty people had gathered, some carrying tools: a pickaxe, a mattock, a crowbar, a long pole. At one point a resident himself took a turn, taking the pickaxe from the hands of the sleep-deprived chaviwalla to carve at the edges of the long-neglected steel square. The crowd was huddled in a horseshoe around the valve; the circle was completed by the hood of the SUV, in front of which, at the head of the valve, stood Patil, satisfied, watching the scene in a silent vigil that he broke only occasionally to issue digging advice to Khade. Finally, after an hour of prying and digging and clanging, they managed to wedge one of the edges of the thick steel door upward and out of the ground, quickly sliding a few small rocks underneath to keep the colossus from dropping back down and taking with it one of the laborers' fingers. They worked their way around the massive door, pressing back against the interloping crowd. On the count of three, five men lifted the huge steel lid, the space inside releasing a foul stench. The undeterred crowd loomed in, peering into the hole. Inside was indeed a valve, but not an operable one. "Its closed, locked," announced Korelekar, unsurprised. "We can't open it. We'll have to replace the valve." Patil nodded, satisfied, and climbed back into his suv while the laborers slid the huge steel lid back into place. Korelekar quickly took leave of Patil, squeezing in next to me in the back seat of the jeep as he directed the driver to drop him off at his next appointment: he was due at 8:00 at the office of the adjacent electoral district's (opposition party) corporator.

Patil's hydraulic spectacles seem at first blush to recall what political theorists call *clientelism*, described in one classic formulation as the "exchanges of favors for votes" (Rose-Ackerman 1999: 138). Yet closer consideration reveals that water-related activity departs from this characterization in a crucial way, insofar as nothing is actually *exchanged*. Indeed while Patil's actions are narratively framed (Goffman 1974) as an effort to improve the water supply to his area, neither of the incidents had any direct hydraulic implications whatsoever: neither was the valve on Road 2 replaced, nor did the M-East water department staff ever get around to cutting connections in Rafique Nagar.[6] While Patil's actions *look* like clientelism, in other words, the absence of any concrete (or rather, aqueous) action calls this reading into question. How, then, should Patil's actions be interpreted? What meanings are ascribed to these sorts of activities, and by whom?

Patil's hydraulic actions work not as clientelistic favors or exchanges but rather as spectacular performances of his ability to mobilize the resources of the water department. Given the opacities of the distribution system, the politically divisive issue of the cutoff date (Patil's district spans both older and newer areas, his electorate comprising both well-documented and less-well-documented residents), and the very real hydrological challenges of actually convincing the pipes to produce water, it is unclear what might even constitute a hydraulic favor. This is evidenced in the standoff in Rafique Nagar, in which Patil may have been planning (although this is unclear) to perform his ability to marshal official resources by cutting the disease-causing (if not necessarily unauthorized) connections but stopped himself from doing anything at all once the young man voiced his dissent by accusing the department staff—and Patil himself—of corruption (for allegedly having provided the connections and then for cutting them). In this context simply appearing in public with the department engineers must be understood as a performance of Patil's power, actualized in his ability (and thus presumably future potential) to move the water bureaucracy for ends that are left open to speculation and interpretation.

The corruption discourse holds that the network's volatile flows result from intentional action on the part of an all-knowing water bureaucracy. Since it is exceedingly difficult to deliver on hydraulic promises or favors in any comprehensive way—and thus politically risky to make large-scale promises at all—

efforts to garner popular support often involve efforts to take credit (often after the fact, as in Patil's billboard, claiming responsibility for what may well have been routine department work) for hydraulic outcomes, whether they be positive, negative, or both.[7] By parading the engineers through various neighborhoods, Patil produced a hydraulic spectacle: he leveraged the resources of the state (in this case, the engineers themselves) not in order to perform clientelistic favors but as a performance of his own authority.

While these hydraulic spectacles may have had little direct implication for water supply, some performances use water *itself* to produce such spectacle. For example, a few years earlier, during the run-up to the 2007 election, another of M-East's corporators had managed to arrange for an additional, much larger pipeline to be laid through one of his neighborhoods where water pressures were particularly low. While the opening of the ground and the laying of the pipe, as one ward-level engineer recalled, was done with much fanfare— earning the corporator much credibility as an effective wielder of authority— the pipe itself, once commissioned, actually resulted in a *decrease* in area water pressures. With pressure in the feeder main insufficient for even the old, six-inch main, the laying of an additional, nine-inch main had simply lowered pressures even further. The original plan had been to remove the original six-inch main, but some area residents who were fortunate enough to have decent pressures in their taps and were thus were understandably reluctant to let the engineers tamper with their hydraulic fates opposed the transfer of their connections to the new nine-inch main. Faced with this opposition, the corporator had stayed the department's hand from transferring all of existing connections and from decommissioning the six-inch main. One afternoon I witnessed Korelekar authorize the transfer of one housing society's connection *back* from the new nine-inch main to the original six-inch main, from which he had transferred the connection a few years earlier. The society secretary voiced his frustration: "Can't you just put all the water into either one main or the other?" Korelekar responded in stride, "I'll tell you what: you convince all the societies along the road to choose either one or the other main; then we can decommission one."

Hydraulic Performance and Its Audience

During the run-up to the Maharashtra Legislative Assembly elections in 2009, two major political parties organized tit-for-tat *rasta-rokos* (roadblocks). In each instance crowds from Shivajinagar-Bainganwadi stopped traffic, vowing not to move until water department engineers promised to solve the neighborhood's water problems. The two mass demonstrations came in the wake of a citywide water cut, an effort by the Mumbai water department to conserve resources in upstate water reservoirs following two consecutive failed monsoons. The water cuts involved a mind-boggling series of calculations and an elaborate choreography of shortened water supply timings and valve operations (since, as engineers explained, there is no one-to-one correspondence between a change in supply *duration* and a change in *volume* of water supplied), which resulted in certain areas of the city experiencing severely reduced water pressures and timings, with some taps drying up altogether. The water cuts, which happened to coincide with parliamentary and Legislative Assembly election seasons, quickly became the subject of heated political debate, and water engineers found themselves targeted by media-empowered politicians hurling accusations of corruption and partisanship. The water department responded to angry cries for explanation from one or another corner of the city by tweaking and retweaking the valves and by unleashing a series of raids on the so-called water mafia, confiscating pressure-enhancing suction pumps and sawing through the water connections of area water vendors' retail businesses. It was in the wake of the raids in Shivajinagar-Bainganwadi that area residents filled the streets, banging empty pots and demanding water.

Before the assembled crowd headed out on a march to the traffic intersection on the nearby highway, I spoke with a local leader from the Samajwadi Party, the political party organizing the protest, in its Shivajinagar-Bainganwadi office, asking him to explain the goals of the impending roadblock: What particular demands were they making?

> *Me:* You mentioned that this rasta roko was inspired by the water department's raids of last week—the confiscation of individual suction pumps on water taps and the cutting of illegal connections. The water department says that by cutting illegal connections and taking motors, they are trying to improve water pressures in the neighborhood. Is your party asking the water department to keep on cutting the connections and confiscating motors in order to improve water pressures? Or are you just asking the department to leave the neighborhood alone?
>
> *Party Leader:* We want water, that's all!

I rephrased the question, probing for what kind of remedial action (hydraulic or otherwise) might satisfy the party leadership, but again encountered only vague but emphatic resolve: the crowd would block the highway intersection until their demands were met! Given the intractability of the water distribu-

FIGURE 7.1. Samajwadi Party roadblock meets police in riot gear. Photo by author.

tion system and the politically volatile discourses of illegality that permeate water supply to Mumbai's popular neighborhoods and slums, the party leadership studiously dodged any articulation of a coherent water-related demand. I posed the question to the district chief of the Samajwadi Party and to his secretary, neither of whom was able to articulate a coherent position. The party leadership, in other words, sought to hold highway traffic hostage to their water demands while simultaneously distancing themselves from any specific corrective action to actually address the neighborhood's water problems. At the same time, while the rasta roko itself was organized completely devoid of practical hydraulic demands, the event nonetheless had a clearly desired trajectory, albeit one that, as the following account demonstrates, did not go quite as hoped.

A few hundred residents—mostly women, toting empty water pots for emphasis—showed up for the march, which proceeded eastward on the main road along the southern end of Shivajinagar-Bainganwadi toward the intersection with the highway near the taxi stand, where we were greeted by a hundred or so police officers in riot gear (figure 7.1). The Samajwadi Party leaders directed the crowd of women into the middle of the highway, stopping traffic and seating the women in a tight cluster in the middle of the intersection, where they continued to bang on their empty pots and yell "Pani do! Pani do!" (Give us water! Give us water!) The wall of police soon advanced toward the seated women, and after some minor scuffling, the Samajwadi Party district chief, perhaps realizing that the police intended to cut short their show, cried out over the megaphone, "Let's go to the pumping station!"—a request that might be loosely interpreted as "Let's get out of the road so that at least we can make some noise before we get arrested."

The women, however, remained seated; ten minutes or so passed until the party leaders were able to corral the women to the side of the road, near the gate of the pumping station, where they stood in a tight cluster on the shoulder of the highway while party leaders and local elected representatives took turns with the megaphone:

> District Chief: We don't want violence, but if the police don't cooperate then we are not responsible for any violence that results. Instead of interfering with our peaceful protest, why don't you [police] call the [municipal corporation's water] engineers?

One woman turned to another standing beside her and spoke over the rumble of the now freely flowing traffic and the din of the megaphone, "Instead of standing here on the side of the road yelling, they should lead us over to the [municipal corporation] ward office! We women were told to come here to sit in the road![8] But then when we sat down they told us to move!" The second woman sighed and nodded her agreement with her friend's annoyance: "We're wasting our time here." The first woman concluded, "I have to go home and cook lunch." "You go," her friend replied. "Later I'll tell you what happened."

> Councilor: We are not going to leave until we get promises of water! We are going to stay here until our demands are met! We won't leave until you call the BMC! I'm not moving!

It was later explained to me that the intentional use of women to block the traffic was intended to stave off a forceful response from the police.[9] However, seeing that the police were intent on preventing the roadblock, the party leadership had changed course, directing the women to the side of the road so that they would not be violating any traffic laws.

The event was clearly choreographed to produce a desired outcome: the police would request an appearance by the municipal water engineers, or at least a verbal promise or two over the phone, which the police would then communicate to the crowd so it would disperse. This was the trajectory of what area residents had described as a "successful" roadblock in a nearby neighborhood a few months earlier. The woman's comment "We're wasting our time. I have to go home and cook lunch" indicates that the participants themselves had a particular narrative in mind—a sense of what kind of action might produce an expected outcome (the appearance of an engineer). By the same token, her friend's response—"You go. I'll tell you what happens"—gestures toward the character of the event as a performance, as something that is *watched*, something that has a particular and anticipated narrative structure but whose final outcome is not yet certain. The crowd blocking the road was thus not only the *medium* of this mass political performance but also its *audience*.

The theatrical and performative dimensions of social and political life have long attracted the attention of social scientists, with classic works emphasizing the symbolic and representational dimensions of political spectacle (e.g., Geertz 1980) as well as the regime-legitimizing and (re)integrative work of ritual and performance, what Turner (1980) theorized as "social drama." More recent scholarship building on the insights and interventions of poststructuralism has attended to the *performative* and *citational* (Derrida 1977) dimensions of political life. The theater theorist Richard Schechner (1985), for instance, draws on a Derridean notion of citationality in his discussion of how meaning-laden "strips of behavior" are building blocks of performance. "Performance," Schechner writes, "means: never for the first time. It means: for the second to the nth time. Performance is 'twice-behaved behavior'" (36).

In line with this characterization of performance as "twice-behaved behavior," Hansen's (2004: 25) ethnography of political spectacle in Mumbai describes "public rituals" (protests, rallies, roadblocks) as "citational practices, drawing on a vast reservoir of popularized national history and religious myths and imagery." Public performance, Hansen suggests, is the semiotic grammar through which political authority in Mumbai is articulated: "To be someone, to enjoy respect and authority is not a given fact, but needs to be reproduced through reiterative performances of various kinds" (22).[10] Yet accounting for the citational syntax and performative character of political spectacle does not explain how symbolic displays are *received* or the extent to which any performance succeeds in actuating the authority it sets out to produce. Performativity, in other words—understood in Butler's (1993: 2) terms as the "reiterative and citational practice by which discourse produces the effects that it names"—is not the same thing as *performance*, which, as Goffman (1974) pointed out long ago, must also consider the question of audience.

Back in Mumbai the Samajwadi Party's public performance unfolded in ways that clearly departed from the narrative frame that the event's organizers, as well as its participant-audience, seem to have had in mind. For twenty minutes or so elected councilors and party leaders took turns on the megaphone, alternately challenging the police to arrest them and beseeching the police to phone the water department. Then suddenly, without any apparent provocation or change in circumstances, the police charged the crowd, striking out with wooden clubs (*lathis*) as they seized politicians and protestors, herding them into police vans while the rest of the crowd vanished. In the commotion someone hurled a rock through the windshield of a public bus. A few days after the incident I spoke to one of the elected councilors, a man named Naviq, who had been arrested and held for two days before his family managed to secure his release after posting a large bail payment.[11] "It was awful," Naviq told me. "They booked us under so many offenses—destroying public property because of the bus, then everything from rioting, to inciting violence, unlawful assembly . . . everything." While the possibility (and perhaps intention) of getting arrested is implicit in an act of mass civil disobedience, Naviq's account suggests that the event's organizers had hoped that their drama would be matched by an equally theatrical police response and prompt release from custody.

Perhaps the police action was a little too real for comfort, yet Naviq's explanation for why the event went awry suggests that the incident yielded a somewhat different interpretation of the relationship between the theatrical and the real: "It was because of our MLA (state-level Legislative Assembly representative)[12]—he represents the same people I do, but he doesn't want to work together; he wanted to sabotage our protest. He's very powerful, and he's getting ready for elections. . . . He has known the [zonal] assistant commissioner of police for a long time [because he] was a councilor for five terms; he knows everyone. . . . So he had directed the police to arrest us and book us under everything—to make us look bad, to make us look ineffective."

On Naviq's reading, the failure of the roadblock was not adjudicated by real (as opposed to theatrical) law enforcement but rather by the question of *who* was ultimately able to enlist the city's law enforcement apparatus in this bit of political theater. The notion that the police crackdown was an intentional act of "sabotage" by the opposition party MLA is clearly one possible—and widespread—interpretation of the day's events. Moreover the analysis is not that far-fetched; a few weeks later, when asked why his department had not responded to the protest by making an appearance so that the crowd would disperse,[13] a ward-level water engineer explained that the assistant municipal commissioner had phoned him on the morning of the protest, summoning him to the head office for a meeting that had been called by the area MLA on the issue of water shortage in the ward. "The MLA demanded increased inflow into the [local] reservoir," Korelekar told me. "But really, the MLA called us away because he knew that this Samajwadi Party was having a roadblock and he wanted to sabotage it." He smiled helplessly. "What can I do?"

The Samajwadi Party's rasta roko, with its citational narrative structure and its dramaturgical form, in some way conforms to Hansen's (2004) account of political spectacle as performance, along the lines of Schechner's (1985) "twice-behaved behavior." Yet the deviation from the script anticipated by members of the crowd ("They should lead us over to the ward office!"; "When we sat down they told us to move!")—who were scuttled out of the intersection, confronted with police aggression, and disappointed by the nonappearance of any engineer—invites further analysis. The arrests and the nonappearance of the engineer were interpreted not only as "sabotage" of the Samajwadi Party's show but as an effective *hijacking*; conversations with participant-observers in the aftermath of the event reveals the Samajwadi Party's humiliation was overwhelmingly attributed to the Congress Party's Legislative Assembly incumbent, whose own authority was thus bolstered.

Apparently to hammer home this point—to leave little doubt as to who was responsible for the Samajwadi Party event's failure—the Congress Party staged their own rasta roko a few weeks later, cordoning off the entire block in front of the Municipal Corporation's ward-level office, where they assembled at least a thousand people (mostly women) to chant slogans and hold signs. The event was carefully choreographed, following a seamless script that was pulled off largely without a hitch: high-quality, professionally printed signs displayed slogans such as "Shame on the BMC!"; "If the Municipal Commissioner won't give water then he should vacate his seat!"; and "One two one two throw out the chief engineer!"[14]—slogans that accused the Municipal Corporation of intentionally withholding water from the people of Shivajinagar-Bainganwadi. A scattering of police constables, notably without their riot gear, stood by calmly while Congress Party leaders circulated through the sea of signs, passing out quarter-liter containers of water to the throngs of seated women (figure 7.2).

After Congress Party workers handed out the water, a truck pulled up producing a few hundred lunchboxes that were passed through the crowds. Shortly after lunch not simply the ward-level engineers but a deputy hydraulic engineer himself made an appearance, stepping up onto a podium, which, having until that point remained unused, seems to have been prearranged for this purpose. The MLA projected his voice over the crowd, proclaiming that the present allocation for the local reservoir should be increased from 107 million liters per day to 135. The deputy hydraulic engineer responded (somewhat flatly) that the department would give 115. The MLA shouted, "This is

FIGURE 7.2. The Congress Party's spectacular roadblock. Photo by author.

not enough!" and raised his fist in punctuation, while elected councilors and party workers rallied around him. After a moment the police (who until then had been standing by calmly) stepped forward to nudge the politicians into the waiting police vans. The MLA again shook his fist (or was he waving?) out of the rear end of the police van. A brass band played exit music as the vans drove off. As a whole the event seemed to have gone without a hitch. The only apparent divergence from the script was the appearance of an ill-fated donkey, which Congress Party escorts had tried to direct onto the scene. The police (who later explained that the donkey's appearance was simply going too far in disrespecting the Municipal Corporation) ushered the confused animal into a police van and sped him off. While the donkey's fate in police custody remained unclear, the politicians fared well enough; when I asked one councilor a few days later how long they had been kept at the station, he responded with a laugh, "Two hours."

Two similar acts of mass civil disobedience thus met with dramatically different responses; indeed some of the same individual participants may well have been present in each of the two crowds, which drew their constituents from the same neighborhood of Shivajinagar-Bainganwadi. How can we account for the divergent trajectories of these two events that seem so similar? In the first case, the narrative structure of the event was subverted by the action of the police, who met the protestors prepared for confrontation (as indicated by the riot gear), treated political leaders harshly in custody, loaded them with criminal charges (many of which were still pending as of 2013), and released them only after they made substantial bail payments. The event, we can safely conclude, did not go quite as hoped. In the second incident, the law-violating roadblock was presided over by a relatively small and docile police force—this despite the fact that the Congress Party's rasta roko was significantly better attended as well as more egregious in its violation of traffic laws. (Recall that the Samajwadi Party's event was violently broken up while the crowd was gathered on the highway shoulder.) By contrast, at the climax of the Congress Party's rasta roko, the Congress MLA managed to produce for the audience a senior water engineer. This deputy engineer's office is an hour's commute from the site of the roadblock, indicating that the engineer had made prior arrangements to attend the staged event at a preset time: just after lunch. The engineer made a token hydraulic concession, agreeing to increase the water allocation to the local reservoir to 115 mld. Yet significantly, as I would later learn, an increased water allocation to the level of 115 mld had *already* been implemented by water supply planners a few months earlier, when additional supplies had finally become available from a source-augmentation and network-extension project that had been many years in the making. That the engineer would credit this routine supply increase post hoc to the MLA's roadblock suggests his willing (if not necessarily heartfelt) participation in the performance.

Since we can safely presume that the MLA (if not the audience) already knew about the 115 mld water allocation to the local reservoir, why did he not simply make that number the target of his request? Asking for 115 mld would have allowed him to simultaneously make a successful demand of the water department and, presumably, avoid arrest altogether. The MLA's patently untenable 135 mld demand suggests a two-part explanation. First, the volatility and opacity of the city's water distribution system renders it exceedingly difficult for engineers themselves to convince the pipes to produce water in places and at pressures that they might wish. If the MLA had made a demand to which the engineer could actually have agreed, then the MLA would implicitly also be accepting responsibility for any continued low pressures in area taps. Thus by asking for 135 mld knowing he would receive a "promise" of 115 mld, the MLA performed his ability to mobilize the apparatus of the state (by making the engineer appear in the first place, and then having the engineer agree to an incremental increase of 8 mld, additional water that could actually be proven, should anyone care to check), while simultaneously distancing himself from continued water stress in the neighborhood. Second, by making an unreasonable request, the MLA was able to "reject" the engineer's offer and thereby court arrest. That the MLA's arrest was preplanned is attested to by the triumphal band that serenaded his police-escorted exit with lively, almost circus-like music. Thus while the MLA made the apparatus of the state dance to his tune for a time, the finale of the drama restored narrative order by "enforcing the law."

This discussion of roadblocks as political spectacle and performance suggests that the intended audience for these roadblocks was not only (or even primarily) government officials but rather the crowd itself.[15] Notably neither roadblock was particularly well covered by the news media, an absence that might be accounted for with a two-part explanation. First, print media in Mumbai is responsive (at least in part) to the dictates of the consumer market; it is likely that these roadblocks in an out-of-the-way suburb were simply not interesting enough to warrant serious attention. Second, since it would not have been terribly difficult to arrange for coverage had it been so desired by the organizers, the dearth of media coverage thus suggests that the targeted audience was largely the one present: the Shivajinagar-Bainganwadi crowd itself. While the narrative logic (the script) of these events might on the surface point to the municipal authorities as the primary target ("We won't leave until you call the BMC!"), the clearly prearranged arrival on the scene of the engineer (in the case of the Congress event) as well as the reality that the stated demands of both events were, in the end, not *really* demands, suggests that water was less a goal of the event than a pretext of performance.

Yet if the crowds gathered not to press water demands on the authorities but rather as an audience for their own spectacle, then what impelled them to turn up at all? What was it that people turned up to watch? Participants may have been attracted by material incentive: they were fed lunch (in the case of the Congress event), and according to area social workers, many of the participants in both events were paid in cash to come. Indeed in contemporary Mumbai crowds are generally paid—with food, cash, or both—to amass.[16] One social worker offered the following account of how cash distributions work: The party leadership distributes money to area party workers and prominent local residents for rallies and protests. "On each block there will be one or two important people [*har galli me ek-do main hai*]. The party gives the money to those people, and then it's up to the *main* to figure out how to get the public." While some residents might ask for (or be offered) money in exchange for participation, he explained, others might simply come at the invitation of a trusted neighborhood leader or out of curiosity to see "what happens." I asked a longtime political party worker named Rakesh, "If everyone here knows that everyone else is paid, what's the purpose of the crowd? Everyone knows it's all just a lot of acting!" Rakesh explained, "People need to see a crowd; they need to see how much public you have."[17] I pressed, "But everyone knows you're *paying* the public!" Rakesh replied, "People don't mind that the crowd is paid. The public will come for money also. There's no shame in this. Anyway, why will the public come if you aren't going to pay them? You look powerful if you can manage such a huge public! You show you're wealthy and strong by showing you can get the public."

In the theater of contemporary Mumbai's political life, this account suggests that "getting the public" is an end in itself. "What shows sells," a party worker named Ramu put it. "You have to show that you're winning. Money can help you win, so showing money means that you're strong, that you're winning."[18]

If the hordes are hired, then is the size of a crowd simply a proxy for the wealth of its organizers? Rakesh demurred, "Money alone cannot produce a crowd." Rather "to get the public, people have to believe that you can get work done." And indeed it seems people joined the rasta rokos largely out of curiosity, out of a desire to see "what happens." That is, while the only *direct* accomplishment of the MLA's roadblock was the performance itself, the significance of the spectacle must be understood in relation to the MLA's demonstrated capacity to "get work done"—an accomplishment that speaks to broader hydropolitical landscapes in which neighborhood residents access water on an everyday basis.

While the divergent outcomes of the two roadblocks seem at first blush like a relatively straightforward case of party favoritism,[19] further consideration reveals more subtle dynamics at play. As the Samajwadi Party corporator explained, the police crackdown on the rasta roko was not predetermined by the shared political affiliation of the area MLA and the home minister. (Were it so simple the party leadership would not have attempted the roadblock at all.) According to this corporator's understanding, this kind of police-mediated sabotage of their spectacle would not go "as far up" as the home minister, who presumably has enough to do at the state level without concerning himself with a roadblock on an out-of-the-way street in a far-flung corner of Mumbai. Rather the MLA "has known the [zonal] assistant commissioner of police for a long time [because he] was a corporator for five terms." By this assessment it was the MLA's personal networks of contacts—"He knows *everyone*," as the councilor put is—forged over more than two decades in public office that facilitated the hijacking. Yet at the same time, the MLA's ability to orchestrate the cooperation of the local police had limits, as the donkey drama suggests; the police and the engineers seem to have gone along with the performance only insofar as aligning with the Congress Party MLA shored up (or at least did not compromise) their own authority. Congress Party workers' efforts to shame the Municipal Corporation with the donkey was effectively overruled by the police, demonstrating that even this largely scripted performance was—like everyday life itself—infused by moments of contingency and decision. Indeed my account has suggested that it is largely in order to watch how these contingencies play out that the crowd-audience turned up: in order to watch how the drama would unfold and to see "what happens" when some political actor seeks to perform (and thereby actualize) his material authority over the roads, pipes, and police.

Hydraulic Mediations

Successful hydraulic performance is thus underpinned by effective networks of knowledge. But what does it mean to "know" people? Who or what, precisely, must be known—and how is this knowledge produced? Patil himself began his political career drawing on the social and political networks forged during his many years as a police constable. Recalling the 2007 Municipal Corporation election, one neighborhood leader explained that Patil had run a "good campaign" as social worker. "He helped out neighborhood kids who got in trouble with the police," one resident recalled, "and convinced the police to return confiscated motors [water pumps]." If comprehensive hydraulic promises are hard to fulfill, knowledge-brokering hydraulic mediations are a particularly effective way for political aspirants to evidence and perform their authority.

Given the illegibility of the water grid and the ambiguities of legality, one common way for a political aspirant to articulate authority is by complaining about the so-called corrupt or illegal activities of political competitors or other kinds of local power brokers. One afternoon, for example, as I was leaving Korelekar's office, I ran into Rakesh, the social worker from the Mankhurd neighborhood of Maharashtra Nagar. Rakesh is not affiliated with any particular party ("I work for my stomach," he insisted) but was in this instance standing alongside three towering, gym-chiseled young men in blinding white shirts that I recognized as social workers affiliated with the Maharashtra Navnirman Sena (MNS) party. A few weeks later, speaking with Rakesh in Maharashtra Nagar, I asked what he had been doing at Korelekar's office. He explained that the MNS boys "were complaining about some illegal water connections in their area—connections from which local people were selling water."

Me: But why were they complaining?

Rakesh: Because selling water is illegal!

Me: Why do they care? Everyone sells water. What do they want?

Rakesh: They wanted the BMC to come and cut the connections.

Me: Did the BMC come?

Rakesh: (nodding, then laughing) See, they make the complaint so the BMC has to come and cut the connections.[20] That way the MNS boys show how strong and influential they are. Then the water sellers will come to [the MNS boys] to have the taps reconnected, and they'll pay money to the MNS for protection.

Me: So have they been reconnected?

Rakesh: (nods yes).

I asked Rakesh what he himself had been doing at the BMC since, after all, he is not affiliated with the MNS. "I was complaining about a sewerage thing. Some Congress people were building stairs over a sewerage line. It's illegal." He shook his head and laughed. "It's just politics."

Significantly a complaint about some irregularity does not necessarily result in the consolidation of the complainer's authority. Rather the outcome is contingent largely on the creativity with which each actor is able to leverage his or her own networks of knowledge—of things as well as people—against the opacities of the city. For example, a young man named Rashid who owned a number of the water connections in the (declared) slum neighborhood of Ganeshwadi described the relationship between knowledge and complaint in relation to water. When the six-inch-diameter distribution main feeding Ganeshwadi's handful of metered water connections dried up a decade earlier, the neighborhood was left entirely dependent on by-the-can purchases from the nearby neighborhood of Sundarwadi, where Rashid and his brothers then lived. At that time Rashid was employed by a local water vendor (someone who had managed to arrange for a handful of connections to the nearby distribution main) to oversee sales to the bike-and-can crowd and to distribute water to members. When Ganeshwadi's connections dried up, Rashid and some friends decided to go into business for themselves, arranging through a local plumber for pipes to be laid from a more distant water main and for the requisite *hafta* payments to the police and the water department staff.[21] Over the following years, as the neighborhood's population grew and demand from the bike-and-can customers increased (many customers coming from Shivajinagar-Bainganwadi), he arranged for more of these kinds of unmetered connections in Ganeshwadi, which, due to its relative proximity to a number of large distribution mains in different supply timing zones, became one of the most consistent and reliable water markets in the area.

I asked Rashid whether the police and the water department staff have a general sense of how many water connections actually exist in Ganeshwadi. "Do you pay hafta for each of your pipes?" I asked, "or do you pay per *business*— as a vendor—regardless of how many pipes you have?" The water engineers really have no way of knowing how many connections exist in Ganeshwadi, he told me, because "each vendor pays a flat rate." I ask, "So say, for example, you have five pipes and your neighbor has only two. Would you still pay the same rate?" He explained:

> Here's what would happen. The guy with fewer taps might go to the police and complain. He will say, "I'm not paying as much as that other fellow since he's got twice as many taps as I do." So then the police will come to me to demand more money, but instead I'll make them an offer: if they can convince the guy with the two taps to give his taps over to me, then *I'll* give the police the hafta that they want for the business on those two pipes. So then the police are on my side. They threaten my enemy, scare him a little—they say they're going to arrest him or something. Then I go to him and tell him that I'll do him a favor. I say, "Look, I'll take over your taps for you and give you 5,000 per month to manage each of them." He says okay; he even thanks me! And the police are happy too because I pay them what they wanted. Then, after a few weeks, I close down those two pipes. When the police ask what happened, I tell them the water dried up. Taps dry up all the time, the police know that—they live in Bombay too. Maybe they won't believe me, though, so they might keep an eye on the two pipes for a while, but then after a month or two, I open them again. So now I'm just paying for one business but I've gained two pipes! And the other guy? He's become my worker; my enemy now works for me! I keep paying him 5,000 per month, but now he works for me.

According to Rashid's account, the hafta payments themselves are negotiated in a cat-and-mouse game fueled by the illegibility of the distribution system. While police informants keep officers abreast of who the vendors are[22]—and even how many pipes various vendors have—the illegibility of the pipes means that knowing how many connections anyone has (as well as whether or not a pipe produces any water) is simply not possible, particularly if an officer wishes to preserve and protect his own hafta-mediated flows of information.

And besides, Rashid said, most of the water vendors *are* the police informants; Rashid himself has worked for the police since he was ten years old.

Rashid's account was echoed by a number of neighborhood-level power brokers of various sorts. A businessman from a neighboring ward who was affiliated with the Shiv Sena, a man named Vidhu who worked not in water but in the transportation business—explained that municipal elections are generally won by whoever has the most people on the ground "keeping an eye on things." As if to emphasize this point, during this particular meeting Vidhu and I were approached by a man on a motorbike who Vidhu later explained had been "operating" trucks in "his area," a piece of information that Vidhu had acquired from one of his own men. The operator informed Vidhu of his business in the area and arranged to meet later to work out the details. After he left, Vidhu said that the fellow probably knew he had been complained about, so he sought to work out an arrangement directly, before Vidhu (or the corporator in whose area he works) complained to the police. Vidhu explained that, whatever party people may be affiliated with, all the work goes through the corporator: "People all work together in this city. This separate party thing is just for competing for the posts." In his area Shiv Sena has the best network of men "keeping an eye on things." While Vidhu has been affiliated with Shiv Sena since the early 1990s, he confessed that he personally does not actually vote in Mumbai but rather in his home district in rural Rajasthan. When I asked him which party he votes for he held up the palm of his hand and flashed a bright, cheeky grin: "Congress!"[23]

"Competing for the posts" involves demonstrating effective knowledge of and command over what goes on in a particular area, and then using this knowledge to direct business "through" one's own office. For their part, municipal engineers respond to complaints for the reasons that Vidhu described: once an engineer is informed about some ostensibly illegal activity, failure to act on the complaint renders the engineer himself complicit in the illegality and thus vulnerable to complaints of corruption. One subengineer, a man named Yadav, recalled how his own lack of "cooperativeness" a decade earlier had gotten him transferred to another posting.[24] Upon learning from his network of informants of the large-scale water-selling activities of an area vendor, Yadav confronted the seller, who in this case also happened to be the area's elected municipal councilor: "She used to get multiple connections made and then sell them to people. When I refused to let her have her multiple connections she threatened to have me transferred. I said to her, 'Don't think that you can overpower me—I'm also from this area and I have my own network of contacts.' I told her, 'If you have me transferred, I'll trace each one of your connections and have them cut.'" After this standoff, he had some of her connections cut. In retaliation the vendor-councilor filed a complaint at the police station, accusing Yadav of trying to extort money from her, that he had cut her water connections because she refused to pay a bribe. Yadav recalled, "I said to the police, 'By accusing me of extorting money she admits those connections are unauthorized, but can you prove that I extorted money from her?'" On this reasoning the police dropped the charge. Soon, though, she complained to other area corporators, alleging that Yadav had "insulted her as a woman." Yadav's well-respected reputation inside the water department inspired the senior-level engineers to ignore these complaints for some months. Eventually, however, "the department and the [Indian Administrative Service] officers just got tired of the complaining, so they had me transferred. The higher-ups, they weren't as invested in me, so after the complaints went to the municipal commissioner, he just had me transferred. The [senior engineers] tried to keep me, but in the end they all just didn't want to bother anymore." These kinds of complaints function much in the same way as the spectacular hydraulic performances discussed earlier: the outcome of a complaint is not known at the outset; instead creative assemblages of information about the goings-on in a particular area are leveraged in a competition to perform authority. Significantly the success of performances actualized through the mechanism of complaining about corrupt activities of this or that engineer hinges on the vagueness and illegibility of the hydraulic network, as well as its legal contradictions and ambiguities.

Spectacular hydraulic performances, these accounts suggest, articulate and perform actionable authority. On the one hand, as in the standoff between Yadav and the corporator, the ambiguous nature of the water connections' legal status (judging from Yadav's account, the connections may very well have been *authorized*—if perhaps in someone else's name) were fought out over whose network of personal contacts was stronger: Yadav did not claim to be able to prove that the woman's taps were illegal but instead threatened that his knowledge of the area exceeded hers; he could "trace each of her connections and have them cut" irrespective of any relation to law. Conversely, the corporator alleged that Yadav had acted illegally and then made good on her threat to have him transferred by leveraging her own network of contacts. The result was decided not by any relation to who may or may not have done what—or the relation of such actions to law—but by whose networks of knowledge and authority were more *effective* in moving the state apparatus to support his or her position.

In this way, allegations of corruption are not references to particular, legally exceptional *actions* but rather, perhaps, articulations of a different relation between action and law—or legality—than that envisioned by a liberal-democratic, bourgeois political imaginary. Liberal formulations theorize law normatively, as an ongoing process of consensus formation on the substantive content of a legal and administrative system—a system whose specific purpose is to secure the rights of individuals to participate in reasoned debate on the moral rightness of that system. The articulation of what is legal is thus understood as the institutionalized will of a (sovereign) people, with the enforcement of the law simply a procedural matter. This understanding of what is legal or illegal, however, bears little resemblance to the sociomaterial lives of these concepts in Mumbai—evidenced, for instance, in Yadav's interaction with the corporator. In Mumbai everyday performances of hydropolitical authority interact with myriad official and unofficial activities that actually make water flow through the city, thereby producing a materially opaque and legally wooly distribution system fraught with legal, political, and hydraulic contradictions. In this context any particular hydraulic action simply cannot guarantee water in any particular time and place for very long before flows are redirected. Thus, to shore up their reputations political aspirants must engage in *continuous* hydraulic performances and must also find a way to demonstrate that some hydraulic event signifies their authority rather than another's. It is not uncommon, in other words, for some would-be water wielder to effectively act on water, only to have the spectacle of that act hijacked by someone else entirely.

Reading Water: Signs of Whose Authority?

I was standing near the municipal water tanker as it refilled the empty tank of a Kamla Raman Nagar masjid one morning in April 2009 when a young man approached me to offer his take on the morning's events. A Samajwadi Party social worker had arranged for the tanker, he told me, shaking his head dismissively, "but the sp is useless; maybe they can get us a tanker sometimes, but they can't get water to come into our *pipes*." I asked the young man, who gave his name as Kalim, to explain why the water had dried up in Kamla Raman Nagar's pipes. He paused, then said, "I think there's some problem with the pipe . . . but there's also a problem with the party." The Shiv Sena controls the bmc, "so unless we have a Shiv Sena corporator nothing will happen." But if the Sena is in control of the water, wouldn't they make *lots* of water flow to your area, then take credit for it in order to show you how strong they are—to win your votes? He shook his head. "If they gave us water the Congress and sp would take credit for it. So they withhold water in order to make Congress and SP look weak." Just as the concrete outcomes of hydraulic spectacles are not predetermined, interpretations of spectacle are equally up for grabs.

In the weeks following the tit-for-tat Samajwadi Party and Congress road-blocks, rumors flew as people tried to make sense of the relationship between these hydraulic theatrics and the ongoing volatility in their taps. Speaking with a senior inspector of one of the local police stations, I asked him his opinion of why the pipes had been drying up all over Shivajinagar-Bainganwadi. "It's because they're not turning on the pumping station all the way," he answered matter-of-factly. Why not? "See, it's all politics. The elections are coming." I asked him to explain. "Well, we have one party in power here in the city—which controls the BMC [Shiv Sena] and another at the state level [Congress]. The Congress criticized the BMC in their *morcha* [mass protest], so the BMC is trying to make Congress look bad—this is a Muslim area, a Congress area. So the Sena government is cutting the water. That's what I think." A neighbor-hood water vendor had a quite different theory: "The problems started with the change in supply timings. It's all the fault of the SP and their morcha—the supply timings change happened after the morcha. They must have demanded it." A third, particularly insightful account came from a resident of the chawl in Shivajinagar-Bainganwadi described in chapter 5, where water supply, after some initial volatility after the supply-timing change, had actually *increased* through the spring of 2009: "Elections are coming, so the SP had a morcha. After that less water came. There was a lot of *mach mach* [arguing] between the parties, and then the SP paid off the BMC to give more water. That's what everyone is saying. Also, the boss changed,[25] and that's why we get more water now. He was very corrupt. He used to give our water to other places."[26] So which party made the water come? "No one knows. Because of the elections all parties say 'It's because of us,' but no one really knows." A woman standing nearby, overhearing her words, summed up: "See, if water comes, it's because of politics, and if water doesn't come, it's because of politics."

Given that "no one really knows" which party makes the water come but everyone knows that it comes "because of politics," much effort was made by local-level social workers (who all suddenly became party workers at election time) in the run-up to the 2009 elections to provide concrete (or rather, aque-ous) evidence of this or that party's material authority over the pipes. One way claims were evidenced was through the provision of municipal water tank-ers. The provision of water by tanker—because it travels above ground—is a particularly compelling way for a party worker to ensure that his party's (and his own) name is attached to the water that his actions produce. Thus in the

FIGURE 7.3. Arrival of a tanker. Photo by author.

months before the election the tanker dispatch office was overrun with social workers who, having waited diligently and patiently in the ward office for all the proper letters and authorizations, sought to ensure that their tanker be dispatched promptly. Once the gate pass was signed and the tanker left the filling station, the social worker, who generally arrived on a motorbike, would race back to the neighborhood on behalf of which he had requested the tanker, preparing the informational ground for the aqueous arrival to come. As the tanker neared its destination, the tanker driver would call the social worker on his mobile phone, requesting the social worker to come out onto the main road and direct the truck to its destination. This guiding work served two functions: first, because addresses can be somewhat imprecise, tanker drivers wanted there to be no dispute as to which party was authorized to receive the tanker; second, the social worker would generally make a big production of the tanker's arrival, clearing the narrow roads of pedestrians, shooing away children who sought to open the valve and fill a pot or two while the truck inched along a road, and generally making it unequivocally known precisely who deserved credit for the tanker's arrival (figure 7.3).

Even with these safeguards, however, delivery did not always go as planned. In April 2009 a Congress Party worker named Malik, who had been regularly arranging by phone for tankers to Kamla Raman Nagar, called the dispatch office to ask about the estimated time of arrival of his tanker, which had been authorized to one of the area's numerous masjids. Shortly after the call, a young man arrived; giving his name as Karim, he told the dispatch staff that he had come on behalf of Malik, to be sure the tanker arrived at the right masjid. The young man hopped in the tanker, rode with the driver to Kamla Raman Nagar, and directed him to the masjid. An hour or so after the load had been delivered, Malik called the dispatch office again, inquiring about the whereabouts of his masjid's tanker. The dispatch staff said that it had been sent with a man claiming to be his social worker. Needless to say, Karim, who was not yet affiliated with a political party, became something of a neighborhood hero; he soon became a regular at the dispatch office, delivering tankers to masjids all over Kamla Raman Nagar, eventually in the name of the Samajwadi Party.

In the high-stakes context of the upcoming election, social workers went to creative and even audacious lengths to attach their names to water. One young social worker named Abdul took to riding not only in tankers whose permissions he had arranged but in *any* tanker bound for Shivajinagar-Bainganwadi. Abdul seemed to have worked out an arrangement with a couple of the drivers (one in particular). On a few occasions, as the tanker neared the intersection a few hundred meters outside Shivajinagar-Bainganwadi, the driver would phone Abdul, who would be waiting at the stoplight. He would hop into the passenger seat for a ride through the neighborhood. As the truck snaked through the narrow lanes, Abdul would yell out the window, "Tanker coming through! Move to the side!," all the while his arm waving out the window, occasionally banging his hand on the outside of the door to make a loud bang, drawing the attention of passersby. If the tanker was to be claimed by another social worker, Abdul would jump out a block or two before the arranged rendezvous point. It was thus not always necessary to actually *deliver* water but simply to be seen as associated with its delivery. During the run-up to the 2009 Legislative Assembly elections, Abdul was in high demand, with party campaigns competing for his services, offering significant fees in exchange for tankers delivered to various party workers to be distributed in water-scarce neighborhoods—evidence of this or that social worker's hydraulic authority.[27]

Everyone's a Social Worker

The number of young men and women self-identifying as social workers has dramatically expanded in recent years; as one young man put it, "These days, *everyone's* a social worker!" Social work, described earlier as "knowledge brokering," is a way for an enterprising person to generate employment while opening up his or her own future business or even political prospects. Abdul, for instance, the child of an indisputably poor North Indian Muslim family, began his own social work career at the age of eleven or twelve, when he volunteered as a neighborhood police informant. Spending afternoons loitering around the police station—bringing tea, running errands, delivering messages—Abdul soon found a way to make himself useful to a broader audience when the Shivajinagar police station's water connection went dry. With a letter from an inspector, Abdul took to spending long hours in the local water department office, securing approvals for station-bound water tankers. Since the police station could use only a fraction of the 10,000 liters in the tanker, Abdul took it upon himself (with the blessing of his contacts at the police station) to distribute the remaining water up and down the adjacent lanes to homes, schools, and masjids. Soon community leaders and masjid directors were seeking out his services, which Abdul performed happily, accepting *chai-pani* tips but not charging any fees.[28] He soon became a regular around the water department, where he would perform favors, fact-gathering missions, and informant services for the municipal engineers. He became well-enough acquainted with the ward staff that his wait times decreased; by the time I met Abdul he needed only to phone the subengineer in charge of tanker approvals to have his application approval called over to the dispatch office. As Abdul's trajectory indicates, establishing oneself as a social worker begins with acts of generosity: running errands for the police and water department earned him the privilege of distributing water around the neighborhood. Distributing water earned him the trust of community leaders, who began to compensate him for his services. His reputation as a reliable supplier of water made him an indispensable asset at election time, as parties competed to attach their name to his reputation, thereby winning the votes of the families who had come to trust in his abilities as social worker. My research revealed that social workers' histories tended to follow a similar pattern, with the bestowing of small favors and gifts eventually shoring up strong networks of local knowledge and authority that were increasingly compensated with tips or fees.

The reach and effectiveness of social workers' networks can thus often exceed that of any particular elected corporator. As political parties select their candidates from the ranks of area social workers, the authority of this or that politician is not an *effect* of the office that he or she occupies but rather *precedes* (and is in part constituted by) election itself.[29] A powerful social worker, in other words has little need for a corporator's office or signature to get work done, while conversely, an unknown corporator can accomplish very little without a network of social workers. The electoral successes and political fortunes of a candidate thus hinge upon his or her relations with area social workers, while social workers' own work is then facilitated by the corporator. As Vidhu, the social worker who works in transport, explained, he works independently, even spending from his own pocket to help area residents with school admissions, hospital bills, police trouble, and more. "But it's an investment that I get back because when [the local corporator] is reelected, then my work gets done." Aware that Vidhu's strength as a social worker is a result of his translocal knowledge as well as his network of political and administrative contacts, at election time residents who have come to rely on him will generally support whichever candidate he tells them is "ours."

While some social workers maintain close relations with particular parties—indeed many begin their career as party affiliates—others are often somewhat ecumenical in their partisanship, working with whichever party happens to be in office. A social worker named Khan had actively campaigned for the Samajwadi Party candidate during the 2009 parliamentary election but was standing firmly alongside the incumbent Congress Party candidate, Mr. Kamble, during the 2012 corporation campaign. He responded firmly when I asked about his party affiliation.

> *Khan:* I work for myself and for my people here. Kamble supports us.
> *Me:* But how do you convince people to vote for him?
> *Khan:* I just tell them how to vote and they do.
> *Me:* Why don't they just nod and then vote for who they want?
> *Khan:* They don't know who they want, so they ask me. They trust me
>   to tell them who will protect us—who will do their work.

In contemporary Mumbai elections are won or lost largely on the strength of these elaborate and intricate knowledge networks. Performances of authority allow these mediators to insert themselves into the decision-making apparatus of the state itself.

CONCLUSION

Pipe Politics

In February 2007 voters in the low-income, municipal housing colony of Nehru Nagar in Mumbai's eastern suburbs elected Sable, their local water department valve operator and neighborhood social worker, to represent them in the Municipal Corporation, throwing out the incumbent councilor who had been in the seat for twenty-two years and who was an established National Congress Party leader.[1] Sable won with a comfortable margin, campaigning on a promise to bring public resources to bear on the neighborhood's deeply deficient infrastructures. He told the reporters who flooded his one-room home that while resigning from his secure (if low-paid) public-sector job had been a difficult and risky decision, he was ready for a career change; in any case senior engineers in the M-East water department were growing impatient with his increasingly frequent leaves of absence for social work activities (Udwala 2009). The chaviwalla's tenure as municipal councilor would witness dramatic changes in Nehru Nagar: the inauguration of a new health dispensary (part of an effort to turn the tide on the neighborhood's long-standing battle with tuberculosis), the dredging of the neighborhood's gutters, the laying of a new below-ground water pipe, and the approval of a slew of new metered water connections, made possible by the new distribution main. In 2012, when Sable's electoral district was reserved for women, area residents happily voted into office his wife, Vandana.

The chaviwalla's story, in which authority based on intimate infrastructural knowledge wins elections and can then facilitate public investment, is not unique. At the time of research the political careers of nearly half of M-East Ward's thirteen elected councilors were connected directly to water. One corporator is said to have been elected because her husband was the neighborhood's premier water vendor; he consistently produced large quantities of water, convincing area residents of his credibility and involvement in networks of authority. Another is best known for arranging water-connection transfers; a third got his start as a neighborhood plumber; a fourth, the driver of a senior politician's nephew, is widely (if vaguely) said to have earned his own reputation "through water." Plumbers, vendors, brokers, and department laborers—as one resident of Shivajinagar-Bainganwadi put it, "Politics here is only about water."[2]

The extraordinary political salience of water in M-East stems largely from the way Mumbai's "slum and building industry" plays out in this part of the city. M-East's peripheral and somewhat unpalatable proximity to the garbage dump, the slaughterhouse, and numerous polluting industries has resulted in a dense concentration of low-income residential settlements. In the reconfigured policy context of recent decades such neighborhoods tend to be treated for policy purposes as slums, irrespective of the legal standing or planning history of the city's highly differentiated working-class housing stock. At the same time, the ward's vast tracts of formerly industrial land are situated at the southernmost edge of the inner suburbs, and they attract property developers for whom slum redevelopment housing is an extremely profitable way of generating flexible development rights, which can then be used in the city's higher-value areas. The marketization of development rights in M-East has unmoored geographies and planning regimes governing pipes from those of human settlement in a particularly dramatic way.

Here, as everywhere else humans live, people must—and do—get water. There are myriad ways in which water infrastructures are configured and reconfigured by everyday activities and infrastructural interventions that make water flow (or not flow) through the pipes. While attempts to transform Mumbai into a "world-class city" have resulted in what municipal engineers describe as hydraulic chaos, the opacity and volatility of the pipes is also bound up with the rescaling and reconfiguration of infrastructural expertise and the ways that the multiple forms and registers of knowledge animate competitions over election to public office. Just as actual control over the flow of water has been rescaled—increasingly mediated by neighborhood-level social workers, plumbers, and brokers of all kinds—the city's ever more volatile hydrologies have given water and its infrastructures increasing political salience. Those who wield infrastructural authority and can command water convincingly and reliably—by making water appear as well as through hydraulic spectacles—have become increasingly powerful political actors in Mumbai. And the material goals—legal, financial, infrastructural—toward which highly dynamic and contested "pipe political" actions are directed can diverge drastically from world-class urban fantasies.

Imran's masjid and madrassa at the edge of Bainganwadi gesture toward one sort of alternative developmental visioning. Yet the rescaling of authority over Mumbai's built spaces and infrastructures has implications that are much more profound. "We want to *develop* our area," explained an M-East municipal councilor named Fareed.[3] As councilor, Fareed has presided over the replacement and upgrading of the entire network of water mains in his district, a small-scale industrial neighborhood called Janata Colony, which is home to 300,000 people and thousands of manufacturing units. Small-scale businesses and industries—embroidery, garment finishing and piece work, and bag assembly—thrive in Janata Colony, and a great many of its upper floors are industrial spaces where migrants work, eat, and sleep. Yet the risks of urban upgrading amid world-class city making have thwarted investment in the neighborhood, threatening to drive out small-scale business and manufacturing on which Janata Colony's economy rests. At his election in 2007 Fareed announced that he would "allow" vertical development in the neighborhood, up to "ground-plus-two" stories. His self-styled "policy" was backed by his deep and broad networks of contacts with the Mumbai police, the Municipal Corporation, and the city's business communities (he remains staunchly unaligned with any political party) to keep at bay any politically motivated complaints that might threaten Janata Colony's legally ambiguous vertical growth. Fareed explained that his remarkable ground-plus-two policy was inspired by the regulatory framework enabling world-class redevelopment elsewhere in the city: a set of rules designed to facilitate a massive slum redevelopment project in the industrial neighborhood of Dharavi in central Mumbai.[4] To win the consent of owners of the many thousands of small-scale industries in Dharavi, the rules had been tweaked to allow for resettlement areas upward of 400 square feet per family. (At the time, the official SRA resettlement area hovered around 265 square feet, although it keeps changing.) "Janata Colony is not a slum; it is an industrial neighborhood like Dharavi," Fareed explained, laying out his calculations. The Colony has floors measuring ten-by-fifteen feet, and a ground-plus-two-story structure approximates the space permitted by the policy framework governing the state-backed Dharavi Redevelopment Project— but without handing over half of the land to an outside developer.

During his tenure in office, private investment in the Janata Colony's built spaces—homes, shops, factories—boomed and local business flourished. Not only did Fareed's tenure create an environment deemed safe for such investment, but the councilor also used the leverage of his public office to bring municipal resources to support the neighborhood's infrastructural growth. Working closely with social workers and plumbers, Fareed put forward a proposal to the M-East water department, which promptly incorporated it into the Municipal Corporation's budget in 2008. The engineer in the water department (our friend Sheth) who worked with Fareed and his plumbers on the proposal explained that there was nothing "irregular" about this process; while final proposals for budget plans are written by water department engineers, "every plan needs someone to initiate it." As Fareed put it, "We want to develop Janata Colony . . . but not by handing it over to some builder who will take half our land and call it 'development.'"

While chapter 7 demonstrated how hydropolitical spectacles, from roadblocks to new water mains, can have material effects that are related only tangentially (if at all) to an action's stated goals, Fareed's and Sable's stories demonstrate quite different ways in which webs of materially embodied knowledge, power, and political authority are being deployed in the contemporary city. Such dynamics have two sets of broad empirical and analytical implications. First, these kinds of pipe political processes call into question conventional categories through which infrastructural connectivity and urban resource distribution have often been theorized: as legally enforceable claims, as institutionalized rights, and as the very meaning and substance of democratic citizenship. (Thus we saw how the water department's efforts to increase private-sector involvement in things like valve operations and billing ultimately became mired in heated ideological debates among international water rights activists over the right to water as a common-pool resource rather than a market good.) Popular and academic accounts of infrastructure and access in cities of the Global South tend to take categories like law and right, formality and informality as points of analytical departure. People are said to obtain resources like water by claiming rights either through procedural channels or through informal processes—acts of theft, corruption, or political negotiation—that violate law. We are told that while rights-bearing citizens access infrastructures *formally*, as a simple procedural matter, the rightless resort to *informal* means. Informal infrastructural configurations are in turn either condemned as corruptions of rational-bureaucratic order or celebrated as subversions or supplements to the exclusionary capitalist, bourgeois processes of urbanization.[5]

What I show to be highly contingent *effects* of politics both critics and champions of infrastructural informality treat as empirically given starting points, thereby leaving a host of more fundamental questions unasked: Through what political, sociocultural, and materially embedded processes and practices are claims to legitimate access (whether rights-based or otherwise) articulated in the first place? What sort of access to what sorts of urban resources (land, water, housing) is being claimed? When, by whom, by what means, and to what effect? The framing of something as a right in the first place involves feats of theoretical gymnastics—the conceptual disentanglement of things from their actual sociomaterial contexts. The creation of Mumbai's market in urban development rights involved, first, the theoretical abstraction of buildable space from urban land and land-based infrastructures and, second, the highly contentious negotiations over the rules and calculations according to which these rights could be measured, valued, traded, and used to make claims to urban space. We saw how a particular (and quite peculiar) set of ideas was imposed as a legally enforceable regulatory regime governing a market in development rights, and how the implications of these tenuous framings and codings can be seen and understood only in their materially embodied contexts. The highly contingent and contested political idea that imagines itself as an inevitable unfolding of a universalizing principle—the world-class "development" that one engineer insists "you can't stop"—is shown to be a highly artificial creation.

Deep and sustained attention to the myriad ways water is made to flow through Mumbai reveals how people actually constitute themselves as citizens, consumers, or claims makers with different sorts of identities through everyday water practice. Effective claims to water, in other words, cannot be predicted or accounted for by prior categories of identity: class, community, rights, or rules. Instead these categories themselves are contingent, discursive *effects* of infrastructural practice. The categories of world-class and slum, for instance, do not represent distinct spatial infrastructure or sociolegal configurations (with the former legal, formal, and networked and the latter illegal, informal, and fragmented) but operate instead as globally empowered discourses with material-infrastructural and legal-institutional implications: we saw how the discourse of slum wreaked havoc on Shivajinagar-Bainganwadi's infrastructures and how the idea of world-class development was deployed to legitimate speculative constructions on highly euphemistic "humanitarian grounds." In this environment both the criminalization of slum infrastructures and the legal-institutional legitimation of world-class pipes are themselves highly precarious, even illusory processes. We saw how the criminalization of slum infrastructures mediated by cutoff dates obviates existing policy frameworks through which infrastructural investment and upgrading in nonelite neighborhoods can (and do) take place. The material practices through which world-class infrastructure is to be achieved are not only hydrologically unreliable; they frequently remain beyond the city's legal-institutional frameworks of water supply.[6] Taken-for-granted categories like legal and illegal, formal and informal, world-class and slum, in other words, do not *describe* but *produce* their objects.

While these categories are products of human imagination, they are not *unreal*; on the contrary, the institutionalization of certain claims (and the deinstitutionalization of others) has had profound implications. Indeed while these categories construct the phenomena they purport to represent, the irreducible materiality of infrastructures—and urbanism more broadly—means that the legal-political and material effects of the political-discursive practices necessarily exceed the performative capabilities of utterances. We saw that notwithstanding a real estate developer's boast that his luxury developments would get water "because this is a developed city," the world-class aesthetics of construction are not tantamount to uninterrupted infrastructural connectivity. The gulf between aboveground appearances and belowground realities have fueled fantastic conspiracy theories about the substance and scale of "corruption." The materially embedded nature of infrastructures means that even cash-infused efforts to make water flow are highly contingent on local networks of power, knowledge, and material authority. These networks have valorized (politically and economically) the intimate, embodied infrastructural knowledge that actually makes water flow, fueling a veritable explosion of infrastructural activity: bustling secondary markets, informational brokerage, and political theatrics. The multiple and dispersed forms of authority and expertise that are so crucial in mitigating the everyday risks of infrastructural breakdown have simultaneously shored up notions about official knowledge and state capacity. A global political discourse sees neighborhoods like Shivajinagar-Bainganwadi, Janata Colony, Kamla Raman Nagar, and Nehru Nagar as informal, illegal, and irreparably obsolete spaces ripe for redevelopment. Yet against Mumbai's pipe political materialities and contested urban imaginaries, the fantasy of transforming Mumbai into Singapore or Shanghai appears ever more illusory.

The new network of water mains and the profusion of metered water connections in Sable's neighborhood are not the result of patronage-based exceptions and subversions of formal, official processes and rights-based politics. Fareed's vision of development for Janata Nagar is not the corruption of a fantastical broader public good. Instead the intricate webs of knowledge, trust, and authority that shape informal political interventions can be (and increasingly are) articulated precisely through the formal institutions of electoral democracy, official procedures of municipal governance, and sometimes even policy frameworks that they challenge and reconfigure.

This is not a politics of concession, corruption, or clientelism, nor is it a politics of subaltern resistance or revolution. This is representative politics in full swing, whereby claims to urban land and resources are fought out on the battleground of electoral democracy. The result is not necessarily a prettier, more just or equitable city but rather one whose future is hotly contested. With effective knowledge and expertise being rescaled by the complex and dynamic sociomaterial reconfigurations of recent years, control over water in Mumbai is not in the hands of international experts and consultant surveyors touting political neutrality, transparency of knowledge, and high-tech gadgets. The bureaucratic and technocratic rationalities that are often theorized as the hallmark of modernity seem increasingly like media-fueled hydraulic fantasies. Meanwhile the socionatural processes and politics of urbanization and contestation through which the actually existing city *is* being made are animating and empowering new configurations and scales of sociomaterial and practical expertise. In Mumbai it is these new constellations of knowledge-empowered political actors for whom knowledge is power—or rather water.

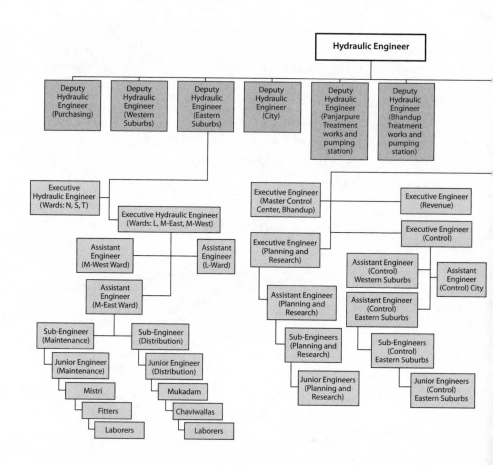

Department of Hydraulic Engineering

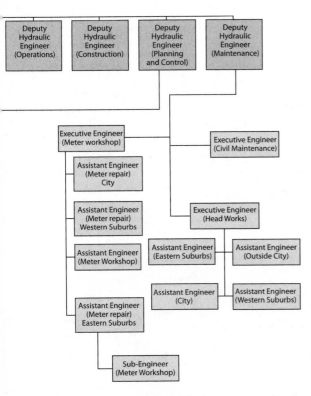

Organizational structure of the Department of Hydraulic Engineering.

Source: Department of Hydraulic Engineering, Municipal Corporation of Greater Mumbai.

NOTES

INTRODUCTION: *Embedded Infrastructures*

1   While Mumbai has a long and lively history of water-related contention stretch-
    ing back to the nineteenth century (see Dossal 1988, 1997; Kidambi 2007; Klein
    1986), this book shows how market reforms have introduced a very different set
    of challenges.
2   The 2011 census reported that 62 percent of Mumbai's population live in slums.
3   For a broad overview of Mumbai's economy, see Chapter 2.2 "Economic Profile"
    in the Municipal Corporation of Greater Mumbai's *Greater Mumbai City Develop-
    ment Plan (2005 to 2025)*.
4   In 2007 "The Mayor's State of Environment Report for London" reported the city's
    per capita consumption (an estimate that was likely provided by Thames Water
    itself rather than by some independent evaluator) at 156 liters per day. The Mum-
    bai Municipal Corporation (also not an independent source) estimates Mumbai's
    daily per capita water availability at around 160 liters (Greater London Authority,
    2007).
5   The term *world-class city*, which has become common parlance for Mumbai's
    urban transformation project, was popularized by a 2003 report by the global
    consultancy McKinsey and Company titled *Vision Mumbai: Transforming Mumbai
    into a World-Class City*. The report was privately commissioned by the policy
    advocacy group Bombay First, which was formed in 1992 (on the heels of India's

liberalizing reforms) by business elites at the Bombay Chamber of Commerce. Troubled by the mismatch between the city's perceived potential for investment and the infrastructure to attract and accommodate it, Bombay First contracted McKinsey and Company to produce a strategic plan for the city's transformation. The government of Maharashtra promptly approved the *Vision Mumbai* report, which soon became the roadmap for a $60 billion project dubbed Mumbai Makeover. The *Vision Mumbai* report enters our story in chapter 3.

6   For instance, Castells 1977[1972].

7   Lefebvre's formulations presented a fundamental challenge not only to Marxist ideas about the industrial city but also to Chicago School urban sociology. While sociologists took as a point of analytical departure the existence of the city—naturalizing cities as already existing social worlds operating according to ecologically analogous laws of development and change—Lefebvre's formulation called attention to urbanization itself as a process and to cities as particular and contingent manifestations of broader "urban society" (Lefebvre 2003; see discussion in Keil 2002). Understanding urbanization in Lefebvre's terms means that research attention must not be limited to the phenomenon of the city itself but must include the "socionatural" (Swyngedouw 1996) production of "heterogeneous spatiotemporal forms" (Harvey 1996: 52). Urban geographers and political ecologists have thus debated the appropriate scale of research and analysis for studying urban society and the dynamics of planetary urbanization (cf. Angelo and Wachsmuth 2014; Brenner 2013). While this book looks at infrastructures *within* a single city, the research design was inspired by neo-Lefebvrian formulations in employing *processual* analyses of urbanization and socionatural transformation; see the discussion later in this introduction.

8   For an important, critical review of the "world cities" and "global cities" literatures, see Robinson (2002).

9   See Harvey (1989) for a discussion of the idea of the "entrepreneurial" city. Robinson (2002) has pointed to the role that urban sociologists and geographers have had in furthering this policy agenda. The urban sociologist Saskia Sassen, who popularized the term *global city* with her book by that title in 1991, has become one of the most sought-after urban policy consultants in the world (Robinson 2002). Yet, as Robinson points out, while much work has been done on the particular parts of cities identified as "global," we know much less about *why* some cities attract these firms and others do not; scholars have thus resoundingly critiqued "the empirical basis for claims that 'global cities' are significantly different from other centers" (535).

10 The "global cities" idea and project have been critiqued from a variety of overlapping and divergent perspectives: political ecologists, for instance, have emphasized the unsustainable environmental contradictions of global urbanization (e.g., Heynen et al. 2006; Keil 1995; Swyngedouw 2004; Swyngedouw and Kaika 2008; Swyngedouw et al. 2002); urban political economists have called attention to inequitable distributional and spatial implications (e.g., Brenner 1998; Brenner and Theodore 2002; Harvey 2001; Peck and Tickell 2002; Sassen 1991); urban

theorists (e.g., Harris 2012; Robinson 2002) have emphasized how overemphasis on the global as an analytical device is not only empirically questionable but can inadvertently shore up elite-led world-class urban restructuring political initiatives themselves.

11 Along similar lines Smith (2002:443) describes how real estate has become the "centerpiece of the city's productive economy." See also Brenner's (2013) neo-Lefebvrian discussion of "planetary urbanization."

12 The term *creative destruction* originates with Joseph Schumpeter (1942), who drew on Marx's work while opposing political Marxism. David Harvey (2001) has popularized use of the term in an urban context.

13 Sassen's account follows that of Keith Hart, who in 1971 first coined the term *informal economy* to refer to hidden, unregulated dimensions of national economies escaping economic analysts. Hart (2010:377) notes that, "in the name of the free market, deregulation of national capitalism led to the radical informalization of world economy."

14 This line of argumentation is suggested, for instance, by the work of Chibber (2013).

15 "Under the current neo-liberal hegemony," Swyngedouw (2009:58) writes, "water rights are increasingly articulated via dynamics of commodification of water, private appropriation of water resources, dispossession tactics and the like."

16 This approach shares analytical terrain with Rademacher and Sivaramakrishnan (2013:1), who use an "urban ecologies analytic" to analyze the "dense networks of livelihoods and intimate connection that make urban life possible."

17 Smith's theory of self-regulating markets applied only to *commodity* markets; neoclassical economics has tended to cite him somewhat inaccurately.

18 The neoliberal ideology of "spontaneous market order" has thus been characterized as a "strong discourse" rather than something that reflects the realities of "neoliberal statecraft." Political economy formulations have therefore described neoliberalism as a form of "contentious politics" that aims to reorganize the global economy to serve economic interests of capitalist elites (Peck, Theodore, and Brenner 2009:52).

19 This understanding borrows from Foucault's call to study neoliberalism "not as ideologies, hegemonic projects, or governmental rationalities but as forms of 'critical reflection on governmental practice' " carried out by historically situated "thinkers" (Collier 2011:18).

20 Inspired by the success of Mumbai's example, some small towns in Maharashtra have begun experimenting with these tools.

21 This comment was made during an interview in 2010.

22 Commodities, following Thomas (2009:39), are here understood simply as "objects, persons, or elements of persons which are placed in a context in which they have exchange value and can be alienated."

23 See discussions in Appadurai 1988; Callon 1998; Thomas 2009.

24 The infamous complexity of real estate regulations in cities worldwide testifies to the pervasiveness and widespread awareness of the social and political challenges posed by urban infrastructural externality.

25 My approach shares methodological and analytical terrain with some neo-Deleuzian "assemblage"-type formulations (e.g., Deleuze and Guattari 2004; Farías and Bender 2010; Ingold 2000) as well as with some varieties of Latourian "actor-network theory" (e.g., Callon and Latour 1981; Latour 2005).

26 This discussion of infrastructure's various registers recalls the analytical distinction drawn by Lefebvre (1991:42) between *representations of space* (things like maps and models that serve as conceptual tools of instrumental rationality) and *representational spaces* (which are "directly lived" and thereby saturated with meaning); see Kanna (2011) for an illuminating use of these concepts in the context of Dubai. These infrastructural registers also parallel Orlove and Caton's (2010) discussion of watersheds, water regimes, and waterscapes as three sites to which an anthropology of water might attend.

27 My approach to materiality is inspired by the work of urban political ecologists (e.g., Bakker 2010; Gandy 1997; Heynen et al. 2006; Kaika 2005; Swyngedouw et al. 2002) who have called attention to the "inseparability of the social and the physical in the production of particular hydrosocial configurations" (Swynge-douw 2009:56); by neo-Heideggerian attention to the "vitality" of matter (Bennett 2009; Deleuze and Guattari 2004; Ingold 2000; Latour 2005); and by Peircian insights into the "irreducible" materiality (Keane 1997:12) of signs.

28 Thus Deleuze and Guattari (2004:454) enjoin us to "follow the matter-flow."

29 The M-East administrative ward comprises thirteen electoral districts at the municipal level and two at the state level, whose boundaries map onto those of M-East.

30 My account of unmapping Mumbai's water infrastructures shares analytical terrain with Roy's (2003:139) discussion of "unmapping" land in Calcutta.

31 Although I have changed the names of most persons and places throughout the book, I have used Shivajinagar-Bainganwadi's real name because of the distinctiveness and recognizability of the neighborhood.

32 With a few noted exceptions, names of places and persons have been changed.

CHAPTER 1: *"We Got Stuck in Between"*

1 My initial theory that the original occupants of the largely Muslim neighborhood located on this site must be descendants of migrants from the Palestinian city of Nazareth was soon belied when I saw another map that labeled the neighborhood "Hazara Godown," inspiring a new theory that the neighborhood must have been settled by Afghani migrants. The mystery was finally solved when I put the question to Mr. Khan, a local scrap dealer, who explained that the Hazara Godown is a warehouse for toxic chemical substances: hazardous *godown* (warehouse).

2 *Merriam-Webster's 11th Collegiate Dictionary*, for example, defines *map* as "a representation usually on a flat surface of the whole or a part of an area."

3 "Managing water as an economic good is an important way of achieving efficient and equitable use, and of encouraging conservation and protection of water resources" (cited in Budds and McGranahan 2003:91).

4 See discussion in Goldman 2007.

5   Bakker (2005, 2010) distinguishes further between *commoditization* and *com-mercialization*: the latter describes changes in "management practices" in line with market principles like "efficiency" and "profit maximization" (2005:544). Following Callon (1998), I use *marketization* to describe the material, ideological, and practical processes of framing a good as a commodity, which are inextricably intertwined with rationalities and principles underpinning management, pricing, and delivery of that good.

6   Under a concessional contract the private operator takes responsibility not only for daily operations (as under a management contract) but also for future plan-ning and investment financing. According to one study, the urban poor were presented with water bills demanding up to a quarter of their income (Schultz 2000).

7   The violence and drama of the Bolivian episode, in which impoverished city-dwellers were pitted against rapacious multinationals in a globally mass-mediated spectacle, contributed to a popular conflation of dynamics of marketization with the term *privatization*. Thus when water shortages and escalating prices led to a cholera outbreak in South Africa in late 2000, popular antiprivatization protests led to the cancellation of concession contracts, which were largely blamed for the shortages even though the disruptions and price hikes occurred in regions ser-viced by both public as well as private providers.

8   Engineers' accounts of the impetus behind the hiring freeze vary. While two senior engineers cited Delhi as the origin, others pointed out that, officially speak-ing, central government officials have no authority over the human resources offices of the Municipal Corporation; the hiring freeze, they maintained, was pushed by Indian Administrative Service officers (i.e., additional municipal com-missioners) at the state government level. These disagreements in the accounts of the hiring freeze are notable insofar as they gesture toward the somewhat spectral, highly intangible, and dispersed quality of the de-staffing impetus.

9   Indeed conversations with senior engineers reveal no aversion to accepting World Bank loans for the carrying out of this particular study, which—for reasons that will become clear in the following pages—was seen as much needed. While the antiprivatization literature tends to depict recipient governments either as victims who have been bullied into accepting loans or as complicit capitalists shamelessly profiteering from the sale of public assets, the recollections of Mumbai's depart-ment engineers reveal a more subtle set of power relations and exchanges.

10 The housing society where I lived during my tenure in Mumbai counted forty-eight buildings, many subdivided into multiple apartments (I occupied one of three apartments in my house), meaning there were likely to be at least 50 to 150 individual residences in our society that depended on our "one" municipal connection.

11 See appendix.

12 Department laborers and junior engineers were demanding increased Diwali bonuses in order to supplement salaries that increasingly failed to keep pace with the ballooning costs of living in the city. In addition, one senior engineer recalled,

junior engineering staff struck in a solidaristic response to a perceived injustice committed by the municipal commissioner against one of their peers. The number *eight hundred* is the one generally given in reference to the number of daily operated valves in the city, but as discussed in the following chapters, the operation of valves—by whom and in what way—is a constantly renegotiated process.

13 The political geographies of this hydraulic choreography are addressed in later chapters.

14 The matter of whose official responsibility it is to coordinate these operations is a matter of some dispute. While some senior engineers maintain that formal responsibility falls to the deputy hydraulic engineer (Planning and Control), others say it falls to the zonal deputies. As one engineer put it, "It is humanly impossible to track operations [of eight hundred valves] spread over twenty-four wards on a single day."

15 Another engineer explained that because the threads on the valves become worn over time, only the chaviwallas know how many turns are useful: "So maybe the first few turns are totally useless, but even the engineers don't know which valves have what kind of threading missing or worn."

16 Ductile iron is a combination of steel and cast iron.

17 The city's public bus provider was established in the 1870s under something like a build-operate-transfer contract between the (private) Bombay Tramway Company and the colonial government in Bombay.

18 The idea was to bring in an operator who would manage the tertiary distribution system, involving all aspects of distribution between the local service reservoir and the end consumers.

19 Kulkarni recalled that it was during one of these seminars that the World Bank's senior sanitary engineer from Delhi forged a close friendship with one of Mumbai's additional municipal commissioners, a man named Srivastava who eventually played a pivotal role in Mumbai's tryst with privatization. Kulkarni's comments echo Goldman's (2005) account of the global transmission of water policy frameworks.

20 In 2002 a fiery new chief hydraulic engineer demanded that meter readers provide details about meters listed as nonfunctioning, thereby compelling overworked meter readers to visit each and every nonfunctioning meter. "Suddenly," the now-retired engineer recalled, "the number of working meters in the city increased from 20 percent to 56 percent, so our revenues increased."

21 The Public-Private Infrastructure Advisory Facility is a "multi-donor trust fund" that is part of World Bank Group. PPIAF's stated aim is to provide "technical assistance to governments in developing countries in support of the enabling environment conducive to private investment, including the necessary policies, laws, regulations, institutions, and government capacity. It also supports governments to develop specific infrastructure projects with private sector participation" (PPIAF 2015).

22 A result of understaffing as well as rapid and dramatic transformation of the built landscape of the city, a dynamic that is explored in subsequent chapters.

23 The decades following the liberalizing reforms of 1991 had the unintentional effect of rendering BMC salaries increasingly less competitive with salaries in the private sector; many engineers abandoned the once prestigious government jobs in the BMC for more lucrative employment elsewhere.

24 While "unaccounted-for water" is not the same as leakage, the terms are frequently used interchangeably; see the discussion in the next section.

25 The "official" number of liters changes regularly, engineers maintained, because the *actual* volume of water provided varies; a certain volume must be maintained in the reservoirs in order to ensure water pressure in the mains conveying water all the way to south Mumbai. A letter from the water department to the municipal commissioner, No. HE 3761 MC, dated November 17, 2007, puts the number at 3,350 mld. Since 1999 this information has been collected and maintained using supervisory control and data acquisition technology.

26 Department engineers carefully maintain information about flows into and levels of service reservoirs—data that are recorded on an hourly basis by the executive engineer (Control) and his three assistant engineers (Control) for the city, eastern suburbs, and western suburbs. But since each reservoir does not constitute a hydrologically isolated *water zone*, reservoir-wise audits cannot be conducted.

27 In 1950, when Bombay City was merged with Bombay Suburban District, the area for which the Municipal administration was responsible more than doubled, from around 67 km^2 to 235.1 km^2. This area was again expanded in 1957 to incorporate another 194.25 km^2, for a total of 437.7 km^2. The Department of Hydraulic Engineering was thus—in a decade—rendered responsible for water provision to an area over six times larger (Mumbai Suburban District 2015).

28 Departmental accounts of the total number of connections vary on whether the total figure is meant to include the unmetered connections.

29 The water department maintains that 60 percent of the city's documented connections are "slum connections," which are billed at a subsidized rate. See chapter 4 for a discussion of the discursive politics and hydraulic implications of the category "slum."

30 Steel piping is much more expensive, particularly for connections that have to travel hundreds of meters to reach a pressurized water main; see the discussion in chapter 4.

31 Humanitarian Grounds connections are discussed in chapter 2.

32 Tankers' inclusion in NRW calculations is particularly complicated since many tankers are in fact revenue providing.

33 One of the four senior engineers who provided feedback on an earlier version of this chapter insisted that the reporting of leakage estimates to Delhi is not a standard practice; the report that I mention in this case was a condition for assistance received under a particular and time-bound central government scheme. The exchange is revealing of the ways these estimates are regarded among those who know the system most intimately.

34 This is a nonstandard but common practice since the challenges of receiving road-breaking permission often precludes the proper placement of consumer connections.

35 On July 26, 2005, Mumbai received 994 mm (39.1 inches) of rainfall in a twenty-four-hour period. This is the eighth-highest level of rainfall ever recorded on earth and nearly doubled Bombay's previous rainfall record from 1974, when 22.6 inches were recorded. The unprecedented destruction and loss of life from monsoon-related flooding in the city nearly prompted the municipal commissioner to resign. His reputation was rescued when Hurricane Katrina wreaked destruction on New Orleans and that city's flood-management debacles made the BMC's flood-management efforts look impressive by comparison.

36 See appendix.

37 Alok then explained that of these four hundred, "20 percent of the meters were stolen." Stolen? I asked for clarification: Do you mean that you installed four hundred meters, but when you went to read them 20 percent were missing? Or that they were stolen from the meter workshop before they were installed? "I don't know," Alok said helplessly, "I wasn't here. But the subcontractor said they were stolen."

38 Alok's account echoes Sharma's, who in explaining his growing skepticism regarding the auditing project cited these very technical complications: "We talked to the meter makers, and we said, 'Look, Mumbai gets flooded three to four times per year. Will your meter still work?' They all said, 'No, they won't work.' Not a single manufacturer told us they could make it work. So internally we realized the futility of the audit idea."

39 The senior engineers who had conceived of the pilot project maintained that it was they themselves who had selected K-East and that they had done so for two reasons: first, because it is "a good ward; it has all the problems: hills and slums and industries and bulk consumers"; second, for the eminently practical reason that one of the project leaders at that time was the acting assistant engineer of the K-East Ward.

40 Invited to the stakeholders meeting were representatives from the BMC's labor union, civil society organizations, municipal councilors, World Bank and PPIAF representatives, and members of the Castalia team.

41 *Sujal* translates roughly as "good water."

42 Under this proposal rates per unit of water would increase if consumption exceeded certain amounts.

43 Sujal Mumbai also involved some less controversial projects around supply augmentation and customer service improvement.

44 The characterization of the prepaid metering technology as a tool of neoliberal or neocolonial appropriation and exploitation seems to have been born largely from the case of Soweto, where a prepaid metering initiative had devastating implications for vast numbers of working-class residents.

45 Here it is unclear if Suraj was referring to a lack of connections to vernacular presses (Marathi, Urdu, Hindi, Tamil) or connections to community groups and neighborhoods. Subsequent conversations led me to conclude that his assessment referred to both of these.

46 The Shiv Sena and the Indian National Congress are the two largest and most influential political parties in Mumbai.

47　Proof of residence before the cutoff date renders a family eligible for rehabilitation in the event the neighborhood is declared to be a slum and demolished.

48　"Now, Sena Opposes Pre-paid Water Meters," *Indian Express*, December 18, 2007.

49　Meaning people without pre-1995 residence proof.

50　Senior engineers vehemently opposed the prepaid water meter initiative on much more practical grounds: since Mumbai's water distribution network runs on an intermittent system, it would be exceedingly difficult to guarantee that water that had been prepaid would reach those seeking to access it, potentially opening the door to a host of difficult-to-manage complaints.

51　A former World Bank official with considerable experience in India offered the following set of possible explanations for the rumor: "This sort of practice has gone on for years. I don't know whether it was specifically done with water engineers, but I know quite a few IAS officers who came to the Bank. [The IAS] have pretty liberal policies on giving leave to their officers. It is unlikely that the practice had anything to do with loan conditionalities. . . . For the most part, this process is a bit like admission to a selective school in the [United] States: if they are IAS you know they are very bright. But they can use their shine and/or connections to move to an international version of what they do at home. Not a bad step in a career."

52　I interviewed the former additional municipal commissioner twice and followed up with a few e-mail correspondences.

53　A year after the Standing Committee rejected the proposal in 2008, the department did float such a tender, which was written internally by members of the department. The project bore the (somewhat unwieldy) title "Study of Mumbai's Water Supply System, Water Audit, Computation of Unaccounted for Water, and Leak Detection." But as Gupta explained, "We asked for too much." Indeed the tender generated only one response, and that too was half-hearted. "The contractor kept on changing the bid," Gupta said, and the project never even made it to the Standing Committee for deliberation.

54　This account echoes Bakker's (2003) characterization of water as an "uncooperative commodity."

55　The Bank representative from Delhi, a little flustered, offered, "Slum upgrading has a lot of dimensions." Indeed it does; this highly contentious political terrain is taken up in the following chapters.

56　The implementation of India's New Pension Scheme on May 1, 2009, finally ended the hiring freeze, and in spring 2010 the chief hydraulic engineer called for the hiring of two thousand laborers and eight hundred engineers. However, as Gupta explained, "no one is bothered; everyone is too busy now to deal with recruitment, so they just pass the file from one desk to another."

CHAPTER 2: *The Slum and Building Industry*

1　Floor space index (FSI) is a ratio of buildable space to the size of a plot of land, essentially guiding the allowable height of a building. For instance, an FSI of 1 would allow a plot of land of 100m² to accommodate a building with 100m² of square footage; an FSI of 2 would allow that same plot to accommodate a building of 200m².

2 While accounts of the origins or normative implications of the Indian state's failure to make development-facilitating investments in infrastructure might differ dramatically, the empirical accuracy of the description has gone largely unchallenged.

3 Bombay's burgeoning suburban population exploded almost overnight when the British signed the Indian Independence Act in August 1947, simultaneously ending colonial rule on the subcontinent while partitioning Hindustan into India and Pakistan. The weeks following Partition would see a migration of unprecedented magnitude, as 12.5 million people fled across the newly created border, fleeing a storm of communal violence that raged on both sides. Bombay received an estimated 100,000 refugees from present-day Pakistan, most of these families settling in "camps" on the outskirts of the city. M-East Ward received a large number of these Sindhi families, who were given housing in an area that would come to be (and is still) known as Sindhi Camp.

4 The report is undated, but historians (e.g., Shaw 1999) maintain that it was released sometime in 1947, the year of independence.

5 The act was amended from the colonial Town Planning Act of 1915. The 1954 Town Planning Act required the Municipal Corporation to draw up a land-use plan for the city; it was applicable only to lands under municipal jurisdiction, leaving the rapidly urbanizing peripheral areas unregulated. To remedy this situation, in 1966 the newly formed Maharashtra state government passed the Maharashtra Regional and Town Planning Act, which provided for "the establishment of regions and constitution of Regional Planning Boards, for the preparation of regional plans, designation of sites for new towns, establishment of development authorities to create new towns, preparation of development plans for the municipal areas, and town planning schemes for execution of the sanctioned development plans."

6 According to the 1966 Maharashtra Regional and Town Planning Act, which replaced the Bombay Regional and Town Planning Act of 1955 after the state of Maharashtra was formed, acquisition of private land for development planning purposes must proceed in the way specified by the LAA. Under the LAA market value determines the rate at which private land can be acquired for public purposes.

7 The challenges that the water department faced parallel those encountered by the Municipal Corporation in implementing the 1967 development plan, discussed below.

8 Engineers describe modeling of the distribution system as an "iterative process" whereby calculations are repeated with varying input data in order to achieve the desired result (i.e., pressures and volumes at the ends of pipes). The factors influencing the distribution are so complex that there is much debate on the relative merits of modeling versus trial-and-error hydrological interventions.

9 While the historical accuracy of this account can of course not be verified, it serves to illustrate the kinds of debates over the relative merits of practical and theoretical knowledge that continue to occupy department engineers.

10   In the interim years, however, the politics of master planning had changed some-
     what. While the 1964 development plan was drawn up by the Municipal Corpora-
     tion itself, with the creation in 1975 of the state-level Bombay Metropolitan and
     Regional Development Authority, the task of preparing regional development
     plans to guide future growth (population and economic) through zoning and
     infrastructural development was removed to the state level. Thus the 1984 master
     plan drawn up by the BMC's Development Planning Department (the plan was
     prepared in 1984 but was not approved until 1991) did not deal with zoning deci-
     sions but with detailing land use at the level of already zoned plots. For example,
     in a zone that the MMRDA regional development plan declared as "residential," it
     fell to the BMC to decide which plots should be reserved for schools, playgrounds,
     hospitals, and so on, as well as to actually *acquire* the plots—through the provi-
     sions of the central government's Land Acquisition Act of 1898 (in which land can
     be acquired using the powers of eminent domain, with landholders compensated
     monetarily). Much of the MMRDA's work involves infrastructure: trains, roads,
     and monorails. Since infrastructure work invariably requires the displacement
     of slum neighborhoods on public land, the MMRDA was granted powers in 2003
     as the Slum Rehabilitation Authority for neighborhoods affected by its proj-
     ects. Until 2003 rehabilitation of slum dwellers affected by MMRDA projects was
     handled by the state-level body Maharashtra Housing and Area Development
     Authority.

11   The large-scale, unplanned population transfer and land-use zoning violation
     committed by the emergency-empowered state itself in the case of Shivajinagar-
     Bainganwadi (discussed in chapter 4) is described by engineers as an *exception*
     during these years; in the 1970s, it seems, what Chatterjee (1997) describes as the
     imperatives of democratic legitimation gave rise to ongoing negotiation over issues
     of urban land use and other entitlements, generally precluding such large-scale
     dispossessions and dislocations and the lasting hydraulic challenges they present.

12   While the Town Planning Act specifies that land acquired under LAA is to be *used*
     by the local body—the Municipal Corporation—the power to actually *acquire*
     private land under LAA belongs to the special land acquisition officer in the state
     government's Office of the Additional Collector. Land acquisition and use for
     purposes of the development plan therefore required coordination between these
     various levels of government. The rates were set at the time that plot reservations
     were declared in 1967, with a fixed 12 percent annual increase—a rate that lagged
     behind actual rates of inflation (Nainan 2012:66). Forcible acquisition of lands,
     scholars have noted, was politically impracticable (see Benjamin 2007, 2008;
     Nainan 2012).

13   The act, passed in 1976 during a hiatus from constitutional democracy known as
     the Emergency, restricted landholdings to 500m^2; holdings exceeding that amount
     were to be handed over to the state authorities.

14   See ULCRA, Section 19.

15   By the time ULCRA was repealed in 2007, however, only 15 percent of land identi-
     fied as "surplus" had actually been acquired by the state, the vast majority of

landholdings having been granted exemptions or with acquisition proceedings stalled in court.

16 See Nainan (2012) for a wonderfully detailed account, which is based on oral histories.

17 Notably M-East Ward's FSI was limited to 0.75 due to the concentration of highly toxic industries in the area.

18 The version of liberalization that the 1991 development control rules instantiated cannot be reduced to the sudden unleashing of market forces; rather the *idea* of global capitalism was put to work in Bombay by a precarious and shifting coalition of actors—charismatic individuals, political parties, landowners, builders, voters—under the charismatic leadership of Sharad Pawar, a Congress dissident known as the "Maratha strongman." Building on long-time alliances with the media and powerful political and economic networks (that famously included Shiv Sena's chief Bal Thackeray), Pawar presided over the instantiation as official policy of this very particular set of policy tools, which was implemented in the name of leveraging the resources of the private sector to ostensibly populist ends.

19 For other explanations for the project's failure, see Singh and Das (1995:2477–81).

20 The politics of Shiv Sena's Slum Rehabilitation Scheme and its hydraulic implications are taken up in chapter 4.

21 There are still more ways of generating additional FSI, such as the redevelopment of "heritage" buildings; see Phatak 2007.

22 Any development larger than 20,000m^2 is required to undergo environmental assessment. This is approximately five acres, about a quarter the size of Vashi Nakka compound, discussed below.

23 Neighborhoods on low-value land meanwhile, despite their efforts, cannot seem to attract builder interest. See Anand and Rademacher (2011) for a discussion of the aspirational dimensions of slum rehabilitation in Mumbai.

24 Particularly the Mumbai Urban Infrastructure Project and Mumbai Urban Transportation Project, ongoing World Bank–funded projects approved in 2002 that are being carried out by Indian partners (MMRDA and various nongovernmental organizations).

25 "They have a choice about their displacement," a representative of one NGO somewhat cynically explained. "They can go to [the resettlement colonies of] Lallubhai, Vashi Nakka, Gautham Nagar, or Indian Oil."

26 If the originating location of the TDR is in the Island City, then it can be used either in that ward or in the suburbs to the north; if the originating location of the TDR is in the suburbs, then it can be used at any location to the north of the originating site.

27 Between 2000 and 2010 the ward saw the construction of more than 100,000 tenement rooms for up to half a million project-affected people; many of these rooms have never been filled and are likely to crumble in obsolescence rather than ever be used to house people. The empty buildings haunting M-East already show significant signs of wear; they have been vandalized (with even light fixtures removed), and the concrete structures are themselves cracking—a result,

one contractor privately admitted, of the poor-quality materials routinely used in these speedily assembled constructions: substandard cement-sand ratios, for example, the use of brackish water, and in one case even the use of prefabricated concrete blocks rather than reinforced concrete in critical areas of construction such as rooftop water tanks. While the SRA officer Shinde proposed that projects continue to be approved in the name of "future need," whether or not these buildings will survive into any hypothetical future is certainly debatable.

CHAPTER 3: *"You Can't Stop Development"*

1   In the wake of the government of Maharashtra's approval of McKinsey and Company's 2003 *Vision Mumbai* report, a partnership was formed among the government, the World Bank, USAID, and the development NGO Cities Alliance, with the goal of facilitating Mumbai's "transformation into a world class city" (Mumbai Transformation Support Unit 2011). Calling itself Mumbai Transformation Support Unit, the initiative turned the *Vision Mumbai* report into a road map for urban transformation, placing particular emphasis on massive investments in infrastructure (especially transportation infrastructure—railway, harbor link, airports) to facilitate the growth of "high-end services" (IT, media, entertainment, and telecommunications), to attract investment (particularly in real estate), and to create "hygienic and aesthetic surroundings" that will increase land values.

2   Both the Maroshi–Vakola–Ruparel water supply tunnel and the Middle Vaitarna Dam project will need to be completed, the department asserts, before water supply can be granted. While the projects were originally to be completed by December 2011, delays pushed back time lines.

3   See, for example, "Mumbai Demanded Water" 2009; Tatke 2010. Congress Party leader Rahul Gandhi had visited the neighborhood of eighty thousand to mend political fences over a police shooting incident in 1997, but residents were reportedly more concerned to share with Gandhi their complaints about lack of water supply and sewerage.

4   Bhide (2013) reports that over 70 percent of slum resettlement housing generated by the two largest projects, the Mumbai Urban Transport Project and the Mumbai Urban Infrastructure Project, are located in M-Ward.

5   One builder-affiliate explained that because the slaughterhouse is thought to be ritually polluting, wealthier, higher-caste Hindus will not live in its proximity. There is thus much speculation among builders on the removal of the municipal slaughterhouse outside the city, which—in conjunction with the much discussed closing of the Deonar Dump—is expected to produce exponential rises in real estate values.

6   Shivajinagar-Bainganwadi's hydraulic misfortunes are outlined in chapter 4.

7   Development plan roads are designated on the 1984 development plan but are not yet built.

8   That is, 20 liters per person per day. The World Health Organization calculates the bare minimum daily "basic water requirement for human needs"—including drinking, sanitation, cooking, and bathing—at 50 liters per person per day.

9   This history is contested within the department; ward-level engineers maintain
     that the Trombay High-Level Reservoir received no additional supply to help
     them accommodate the project-affected people, while some (though not all)
     supply planners insist that there was in fact augmented supply. In order to clear
     up this mystery, I examined records of daily inflows to the Trombay High-Level
     Reservoir from each year from 1997 until 2009, taking random samples from
     the same month of each year (October 1997, October 1998, etc.). The data are
     as follows: 1997: 95 mld; 1998: 115 mld; 1999: 116 mld; 2000: 110 mld; 2001: 110
     mld; 2003: 106 mld; 2004: 101 mld; 2005: 106 mld; 2006: 102 mld; 2007: 111 mld;
     2008: 116 mld; 2009: 109 mld. The numbers are revealing and explain some of the
     disagreement among engineers about the numbers. Ward-level staff who worked
     in M-East in the late 1990s recall abundant water during those years because
     in 1997 the supply-augmentation scheme Mumbai-3A was completed before all
     of the distribution infrastructure was in place. Excess water thus flowed to the
     Trombay High-Level Reservoir not intentionally but because higher levels in
     the master balancing reservoir meant higher water pressures in the intake pipe
     feeding the Trombay High-Level Reservoir. By the early 2000s, however, the
     distribution network had been extended to accommodate the additional supplies,
     and the Trombay High-Level Reservoir's intake fell again, somewhat. As the data
     make clear, the water department—as promised in the correspondence with the
     Municipal Commissioner's Office—was able to provide additional water only in
     2007. The period during which Lallubhai was allotted, 2004–6, corresponded with
     the decade's *lowest* reservoir levels.

10   This practice is an on-again-off-again phenomenon, as the valves of the empty
     buildings are not supposed to be open. With the establishing of the Deonar Police
     Station in one of Lallubhai's empty buildings in 2009, resident complaints have
     led to the shutting down of this business.

11   See Anand and Rademacher (2011) for a discussion of aspirations of (quite literal)
     upward mobility infusing slum redevelopment.

12   A good number of allotment recipients seem to have rented out their flats right
     away in order to move back to neighborhoods where they have jobs. It is thus
     necessary to make a distinction between people who never moved into their flat
     to begin with and those who moved later on because of water stress.

13   A posh area in Island City.

14   While the White Paper (Municipal Corporation of Greater Mumbai 2009) itself
     does not calculate the daily per capita supply estimates—I have generated these
     numbers myself using population and zone-wise supply estimates given in the
     White Paper—the astonishing equality of per capita provisioning for the eastern
     and western suburbs demands attention. Following the failed monsoon of 2009,
     zone-wise estimates became a rallying cry for suburban councilors, who pointed
     to imbalances between city and suburban per capita supply as evidence of "cor-
     ruption" and preferential attention paid to the hydraulic needs of the Island City
     over that of the suburbs. (See the discussion in chapter 6 of corruption narratives
     as meaning-making practice.) In February 2010 the water department announced

a citywide 15 percent water supply cut; after a particularly disappointing monsoon of 2009 failed to raise water levels in upstate reservoirs to desired levels, water supply planners sought to use existing supplies sparingly in order to prevent water stress during the hotter months ahead. Yet the cuts sparked heated responses (described by engineers as "shouting") by municipal councilors, particularly those from the western suburbs, who complained that their districts were already suffering inequitably low supplies. The department accounts for the disproportionate amount of water supplied to the Island City as a function of water pipes laid long ago, particularly those feeding older industries, and bulk users. This attempt to depoliticize the issue with a technocratic explanation was unconvincing to councilors in the western suburbs, who demanded instead that a zone-wise water audit be conducted. While a "scope of work" plan was written up for such an audit, the issue was apparently resolved (and the "shouting" councilors appeased) before the survey was carried out. The sensitivity of the issue, however, is clearly reflected in the startling equivalence of the per capita supply estimates to the eastern and western suburbs suggested in the 2009 White Paper (Municipal Corporation of Greater Mumbai 2009), which was written at the height of the political feuding over the 15 percent water cut. The number 212 can be arrived at in a variety of ways. For instance, while the White Paper reports per capita supply in the western suburbs as 1,318 mld, senior engineers from the Planning and Control Department consistently gave me a lower number: 1,250 mld. The question of accuracy (in the sense of correspondence with reality) is beside the point; as discussed in chapter 1, there is general agreement—among engineers, the politicians, and the media—that numbers (both water and population estimates) are wildly inaccurate. The point, rather, is that numbers nonetheless are rhetorically powerful and thus politically useful. (See the discussion in chapter 7 of the performative and theatrical dimensions of hydraulic numerology.)

15 Constructed in 1984 in conjunction with the commissioning of the Trombay High-Level Reservoir that feeds the area of Gowandi containing Shivajinagar-Bainganwadi.

16 This is a reference to the material of the main, which is glass-reinforced plastic (GRP); most of the city's large outlets, by contrast, are made of iron. GRP pipes are available in unconventional sizes, such as 800 mm, the diameter of this particular main. Until 2005 or so the water department used primarily cast iron pipes, the joints between which are secured with lead. In recent years the department has switched to the almost exclusive use of ductile iron, which is significantly more expensive but is preferable since it can be joined with a different—and noncarcinogenic—material. The department experimented with GRP, which is hydraulically comparable to ductile iron and much more economical, but found that this lightweight, somewhat fragile material tended to rupture under the heavy traffic and general conditions of Mumbai. It is likely a result of both the lower cost as well as ease of use of lightweight GRP that the MMRDA constructed this particular main out of this less durable, cheaper material. While the mains do not yet show any aboveground sign of cracking (not that aboveground

signs are very telling), the area north of the railway tracks is a largely industrial zone, with the Ghatkopar-Mankhurd Link Road the site of heavy-vehicle traffic. The use of GRP piping in such an area is thus particularly shortsighted—which is of course not at all out of character with the world-class modality of planning that I have been describing.

17 The area is marked on the development plan as a "general industrial zone."

18 Bathtubs and Jacuzzis are allowed at luxury hotels since they are billed for water at a higher unit rate.

19 "We only use natural resources," the contractor somewhat perplexingly offered. This discourse of sustainability is echoed in the discussion of rainwater harvesting below.

20 The wells have not been covered up, however, but left open for use in case of emergency.

21 As per the 2002 General Rule, a builder cannot be granted an occupation certificate by the Buildings Approvals Department of the BMC unless the water department has indicated that the builder has met this condition.

22 A representative of another of the city's largest builders confirmed that this is standard practice. A senior geologist with the geological survey of India named Gooptu, who was on deputation to Mumbai, explained that the law really does not make much sense in Mumbai, where the groundwater is so high already; the notion of "recharging" groundwater with rainwater harvesting makes no sense in a city where groundwater is replenished a third of the way through the monsoon. In any case, he added, the idea of using rainwater for gardening purposes is absurd since gardens do not need to be watered during the rainy season. Gooptu dismissed the BMC's rainwater-harvesting initiative as fueled largely by political theatrics and expressed frustration that his own time and expertise were being thus wasted.

23 This number, notably, is the official per capita supply norm for nonslum residential areas. So while such generous supply might be unfair, it cannot be described as irregular or illegal.

24 Indian Oil is a bit farther, but still less than two kilometers.

25 Nestor's taps are pressurized by the sump-and-pump system; their connections to the distribution system are pressurized only intermittently.

26 This recalls Coronil's (1997) discussion of the "magical state."

CHAPTER 4: *"It Was Like That from the Beginning"*

1 The 2011 census measured Mumbai City's population at almost 12 million, and that of Mumbai Urban Agglomeration at more than 20 million.

2 The word *slum* has an inglorious past; its millennium-era revival by the development industry—a trend perhaps most prominently evidenced in the United Nations' 1999 Cities without Slums campaign—has thus been hotly debated. For discussion, see Arabindoo 2011.

3 This report is perhaps best known among social scientists for the lengthy treatment it receives in Davis 2007.

4 According to Section 51 of the Maharashtra Land Revenue Code, "If the person making the encroachment so desires, [the collector may] charge the said person a sum not exceeding five times the value of the land so encroached upon and to fix an assessment not exceeding five times the ordinary annual land revenue thereon and to grant the land to the encroacher on such terms and conditions as the collector may impose subject to rules made in this behalf, and then to cause the said land to be entered in land records in the name of the said person." Regularization seems not to have caught on with anything like the zeal that slum declaration would see. This was probably due to the financial layouts involved in regularization as well as the fact that regularization was lesser known, buried as it is in Land Revenue Code. During my research I encountered widespread misunderstanding among city officials and city residents about the meanings of these two legal terms as well as the differences between them.

5 This section is based on oral histories given by current residents.

6 Zari is a kind of embroidery that is common in Muslim women's clothing in Mumbai. Mumbai's zari industry exports heavily to Arab states in the Gulf.

7 A great many of these long-established working-class neighborhoods predate the 1967 plan and its zoning and development control rules. In 1976 the government of Maharashtra created the Maharashtra Housing and Area Development Authority to oversee and coordinate the work of the various statutory bodies responsible for housing issues in the city.

8 Similarly elusive are any written accounts of how and why this particular location was selected for the new colony. The discussion in chapter 2 of the political and financial obstacles to land acquisition for public purpose suggests that perhaps the undecided status of the reclamation site rendered it an expedient and practical choice.

9 I had already spent nearly six months trying to track down the original plans from the water department, to no avail.

10 I am fairly confident that the absence of any original plan for Shivajinagar-Bainganwadi—if indeed one ever existed—was not manufactured for my benefit. On reflection, the best explanation I can offer is that Shivajinagar-Bainganwadi was built during the Emergency; any plan for the resettlement colony would thus not have needed approval by the Municipal Corporation's Standing Committee of elected councilors, which may explain why it has escaped the otherwise meticulous filing systems of the Corporation's record keepers.

11 The Hindi word *pucca* translates as "cooked"; *katcha* translates as "raw."

12 BEST stands for Bombay Electric Supply and Transport Company, which is a public undertaking of the Municipal Corporation.

13 *Jhopadpatti* is a commonly used word that might be literally translated as "hut-ment." In Mumbai (as elsewhere in India) there are many different words used to refer to areas now increasingly called slums. In Mumbai *slum* and *jhopadpatti* are used interchangeably also with the word *bustee*, which translates roughly as "settlement." While it is tempting to treat *slum* as a foreign word with a clearly negative valance and to celebrate others like *bustee* and *jhopadpatti* as value-neutral native

categories, neither is it the case that native categories are value neutral (*jhopadpatti* is sometimes used by residents of wealthier parts of Shivajinagar as an epithet cast at poorer areas like Saibabanagar), nor does *slum* carry an unequivocally negative connotation. When I was searching for an affordable apartment to rent in 2011, for instance, one broker cheerfully queried, "In building or in slum?"

14 This discussion recalls Benjamin's (2008) concept of "occupancy urbanism."

15 Mumbai was not unique in this respect; Benjamin (2007:550) lists fifteen separate ways that land has been claimed in Bangalore.

16 While neighborhood leaders insist that Kamla Raman Nagar was officially declared a slum in the early 1980s, municipal and state-level officials were not able to provide me with records of officially declared slums. Officials from the Office of the District Collector expressed doubt that Kamla Raman Nagar was ever officially declared a slum; since it is located on government land (given on long-term lease to the Municipal Corporation), one official reasoned, there was simply "no objection" to infrastructure provisioning in the area. Slum "declaration," he explained, has been used as a policy tool primarily for facilitating government intervention into infrastructurally deprived neighborhoods on *private* lands, where landowners might have objected; it was simply not necessary to use the policy tool of declaration to move the municipal authorities to make infrastructural investments. Whether or not Kamla Raman Nagar was formally declared a slum, any absence of formal declaration clearly did not hinder it from becoming a recipient of slum-upgrading initiatives, evidencing the improvement-oriented conception of slum that prevailed in the preliberalization years.

17 Authority to declare slums remained with the district collector until the early 1990s, when the government of Maharashtra passed a general rule reassigning this responsibility to the state government's Department of Urban Development. Accusing the Collector's Office of indulging vested interests, the government of Maharashtra centralized slum declaration powers. The (perhaps unintended) consequence of this centralization move, however, was that every slum in Bombay had to be registered by a single, already overburdened office. Needless to say, slum declaration, while still a legally practicable policy, is largely a thing of the past.

18 The circular states, "Precaution will be taken that hereafter water supply to the illegal constructions shall not be approved" (Government of Maharashtra 1996).

19 For discussions of the rise of caste, class, and regional politics in India, see Jafrelot 2000.

20 Corbridge and Harriss (2000) describe liberalization-era Hindu nationalism as an "elite revolt" against the rising political and economic power of regional caste-based parties.

21 See Hansen 1999:5.

22 Maharashtra chief minister Prithviraj Chavan, who has made a point of refusing to meet with real estate developers, has been sharply criticized by politicians as "naïve and impractical." One exasperated Congress Party MP was overheard by a reporter from an English-language weekly complaining to his colleagues, "Which builder will give you money during elections if his work is not done?" (Khetan 2011).

23 Identification either formally through declaration or operationally through the activities of the Slum Improvement Board.

24 The Slum Act refers not to individual slum residences but to "slum areas." I am grateful to Simpreet Singh for this observation.

25 In an effort to clarify the eligibility requirements of the Slum Act, in 2002 the government of Maharashtra passed an amendment stating that in order to be eligible for compensation in the event of demolition, households have to prove that they have been in "undisturbed occupation" of a slum house since before the cutoff date; households who engaged in any form of transfer were thus rendered ineligible for rehabilitation (Bhide 2002). More recently a January 2012 government resolution sought to legalize transfers, allowing that more recently arrived owners of pre-1995 structures might become eligible for redevelopment schemes by paying a "transfer fee" and then providing two kinds of proof. First, the owner must prove that the *structure* has been in existence since before January 1, 1995. This proof could take the form, for example, of a property sale agreement shored up by a court affidavit, accompanied by the pre-1995 residency proofs of the former owners. Second, the new owner would need to provide proof that he has been the resident of the structure for at least one year. However, until the development control rules Section 33.10 (governing "eligibility for redevelopment schemes") is amended, the 2012 government resolution states that "any transfer will be considered 'conditionally eligible.'" At the time of writing, it is unclear when or whether the development control rules will be amended to allow for transfers.

26 In those days, I am told, people desiring billed water connections could generally secure them without too much hassle; the real struggle was convincing the taps to produce water.

27 Appendix E is present from the first version of the Water Charges Rules that came into effect in April 1981. While the earlier versions of Appendix E do have a stipulation requiring that "unauthorized structures" must be shown to have existed prior to 1974 to be provided water, this did not prevent the water department from regularly providing water to newer areas—as in the case of Kamla Raman Nagar—under the provisions of the Slum Act. Indeed the Slum Act provision for "improvement works" such as the laying of water mains and provision of taps in underserved areas (i.e., slums) is not governed by any cutoff date.

28 That Shivajinagar-Bainganwadi's homes are infrequently registered in the names of the occupants can be accounted for by the difficulty in procuring identity documents and the ambiguity in the cutoff date. Both of these challenges can be overcome, I was told, via broker-mediated and cash-lubricated (or "paper-weighted") negotiations with the Municipal Corporation bureaucracy.

29 The Municipal Corporation's ward-level colony officer keeps such a record of householders residing in municipal housing colonies.

30 As discussed in note 25, the legal status of transfers may soon change, pending amendment to the development control rules (section 33.10). However, as the 1996 circular prohibiting water supply to "unauthorized structures" does not concern itself with the legal status of *residents* but rather with that of *structures*,

what change the new transfer rule might effect regarding the implementation of the 1996 cutoff-date rule remains to be seen.

31 That is, documented transfers that are followed up with regular bills.

32 A housing activist who filed under the Right to Information Act for official estimates of the number of Bangladeshi refugees in the city was told that there are 626 Bangladeshis in all of Mumbai (National Alliance of People's Movements 2005).

33 The notion would be almost humorous (if disturbing) in its absurdity, reducible perhaps to the quirkiness and theatrical tendencies of the city's political life, but for its discursive similarity to popular debates in international policy circles. For example, the United Nations 2006–2007 report *State of the World's Cities* warns that "Poverty, underdevelopment and politically induced fragile or anarchic states have created fertile conditions for new and old threats to our daily security. The world's cities—and the people who live in them—have become lightning rods for international terrorism, transnational crime and increasingly violent lawlessness" (United Nations 2006–7:22).

This sentiment was echoed during the UN's 2006 World Urban Forum by the president of Britain's Town and Planning Institute, who cautioned that "cities not only suffer the effects of terrorism, but if their unplanned growth leads to marginalized people, that can lead to terrorism itself."

34 Monthly rental rates in Shivajinagar-Bainganwadi ranged from Rs 500 to Rs 3,000 in 2010.

35 This is a rumor that water department engineers unintentionally help to spread by responding to middle-class complaints of low pressure by ramping up raids on the "water mafia" and the cutting of illegal connections in neighborhoods like Shivajinagar-Bainganwadi. This was apparent during the winter of 2010, when a failed monsoon impelled the water department to cut supply hours to some middle-class neighborhoods. In response to angry cries for an explanation, the department scaled up their antimafia actions in M-East. This was admittedly a "cosmetic action," I was told, but it pleased the middle classes.

36 My discussion here builds on the posthumanist critiques of representationalism coming from the field of science and technology studies, which has questioned the existence of a mind-independent world of objects with essential characteristics, demonstrating instead that the world is made (or "becomes") through actions that are simultaneously material and discursive (see Barad 2003).

37 Ghertner (2011:280, 285) has described a similar dynamic in Delhi as an "aesthetic mode of governing," wherein the appearance of "planned-ness" becomes "an attribute of urban space key to determination of legality" that enables government intervention into "otherwise ungovernable terrain."

38 Cities Alliance, one of the UN's nongovernmental partners that has been involved with Mumbai's makeover project, admits to identifying slums simply by looking for highly subjective "miserable living conditions" (United Nations 2003:10).

39 These indicators define the "minimum criteria" for being counted as a slum for UN Habitat's measurement and cross-country comparative purposes.

40 The performative enactment of Shivajinagar-Bainganwadi as an illegal slum by means of a shift in the political technologies animated by the slum label recalls Deleuze and Guattari's (1984:9) notion of "incorporeal transformation."

41 The Collector's Office has carried out similar censuses in 1976, 1980, and 1985. The senior official to whom I spoke did not know whether Shivajinagar-Bainganwadi was included in those earlier censuses nor what the criteria for inclusion were.

42 Catching himself, the officer elaborated that of course they surveyed only illegal *single-story* structures, not illegal *buildings*. While many buildings are constructed without proper authorizations, he explained, illegal buildings cannot be counted as slums because you cannot bring a building under slum redevelopment.

43 The fuzziness of the slum concept in Mumbai has given rise to political and legal battles between builders and residents: while the increased FSI allowed by the 1991 amendments to the development control rules allows for the redevelopment of both slum and nonslum structures, developers have a strong interest in rebuilding any particular neighborhood *as a slum* since slum redevelopment generates highly profitable additional development rights. Journalists thus report on incidents in which older housing societies going in for redevelopment (to take advantage of higher FSIS allowed by the development control rules) have been handed notices by the Slum Rehabilitation Authority that, unbeknownst to them, their homes are slums. Angry residents, needless to say, are challenging such declarations in the courts, since redevelopment of their buildings as slums would dramatically reduce both the value and the square footage of their new homes (e.g., Bharucha 2009; Masurkar 2009).

44 "There is no power relation," Foucault (1977:26) writes in an oft-cited passage from *Discipline and Punish*, "without the correlative constitution of a field of knowledge, nor any knowledge that does not presuppose and constitute at the same time power relations."

45 This discussion of how Mumbai neighborhoods become slums through the techniques of survey recalls Mitchell's (2002) discussion of how the political technologies of cartography in colonial Egypt enabled territorial governance and rule. Mitchell's analysis shows how power operates both at the level of discourse— shaping the concepts, norms, and evaluative frameworks through which reality is represented in maps—and through the procedures, forms of expertise, and techniques of measurement, computation, and representation by means of which knowledge of the world that a map professes to represent is itself produced in the first place.

46 The masjid is a collaborative effort among a Mumbai-based religious trust, a transnational team of Italian architects, and an assortment of local contractors and civil engineers for which Imran's Bainganwadi office is the local coordinating center (see Wagle 2012).

CHAPTER 5: *"No Hydraulics Are Possible"*

1 See appendix.

2 Road widening and repaving are part of the government of Maharashtra's Mumbai makeover plan.

3 The road was constructed sometime in 2007. The colony provides housing to a scattering of current municipal employees, including municipal slaughterhouse workers, firefighters, and public school teachers.

4 The cupped end of the sounding rod is placed on the ground near where the leak has been reported; the skinny end is placed beside the sounding man's ear.

5 Later an engineer explained that leaks from water pipes are more audible than leaks from sewage pipes because the contents of water pipes are under higher pressure.

6 Deonar Municipal Colony has its own small storage and pumping station, which is supplied by the Trombay High-Level Reservoir by at least three feeder mains at least three separate times each day.

7 The road-breaking crew insisted that their work was complete and there was no reason for them to wait around with the M-East laboring crew for the assistant engineer.

8 I suspect that many more such maps are in circulation both in M-East and other wards across the city.

9 I thanked him but declined his offer.

10 The role that social workers and brokers play in facilitating access to state institutions and resources is the subject of much anthropological interest in India, where the ubiquity of this sort of mediation is said to reveal the "blurred boundaries" (Gupta 1995) between state and society.

11 *Bhai* is the Hindi/Urdu word for "older brother"; see the discussion in Hansen (2005:189).

12 There are actually nineteen homes on the chawl, but I include some homes on the adjacent lane that have long shared in the chawl's water arrangements. Of these thirty-one homes, three are second-floor additions that are rented out on a month-to-month basis; two are home to varying numbers of migrant *zari* workers, who use the open, loftlike space both for sleeping and for piecework.

13 While jerry cans generally have a standard forty-liter capacity, sizes were not standardized and some were notably much smaller than others.

14 Despite the financial incentive to do so, only a small fraction of connection owners make the high-risk-high-return decision to sell water to the bike-and-can crowds, since the higher returns on by-the-can sales are offset by risk-related costs such that, in the long run, there is little discrepancy in water-related incomes earned by each. It is thus necessary to consider the *noneconomic* motives that vendors might have for making this entrepreneurial choice—motives that have more to do with the relationship between hydraulic spectacle and political authority that I explore in chapter 7.

15 And perhaps, she added contemplatively, if she turns off her motor after she and her upstairs tenants have filled their barrels, this might allow more water to reach the dry taps connected farther downstream on the distribution main.

16 This explanation glosses over the crucial point that the integrity of pressures in Island City taps is herein prioritized over pressures in Shivajinagar-Bainganwadi. When I raised this point, engineers responded by insisting that the problem of

water supply in the suburbs needs to be addressed "systematically" rather than with an intervention that would disrupt the entire hydrology of the Island City.

17　Supply planning engineers in the head office expressed exasperation that ward-level staff were leaving open Valve B; the whole purpose of the pumping was, after all, to preserve the levels in the reservoir by *not* supplying water between 6 and 8 a.m.

18　This can happen especially if there is a "hump" or a higher spot along a main, so at such places air valves are generally installed.

19　These charges are technically paid in order to be released on bail. However, since charges rarely result in actual criminal prosecution, they simply function as fines, which is how they are described by residents.

20　Notwithstanding this fellow's reputation as a crass real estate wheeler-dealer, his water meter reported his house's water consumption as perfectly average.

21　The leak on the highway persisted for another month or so. When I mentioned the leak in an offhand way during a meeting with a senior engineer, he grew visibly embarrassed and immediately made a phone call to inquire about the status of the repair. He learned that the job had been held up because the department had not yet been granted road-breaking permission from the maintenance department. Another phone call was made, and permission was granted. He explained to me, almost apologetically, that the ward-level staff was very busy; echoing the society secretary, he said that unless someone sees a complaint through to completion, it will not be prioritized. On my way home from the meeting that afternoon, a road-breaking crew had already fenced off a section in the center of the highway and was busy jackhammering. By the following day the daily floods had stopped.

22　The society also has a freshwater surface well, whose waters can be used for gardening. The well has a pump and distribution network of pipes that supplies a small amount of water to each house. The secretary was looking into possibilities for filtering the well water to make it potable.

23　Additional lines were granted not only to this one building but to all three of the buildings rehousing Shenoy's former countrymen—families that are still on the voting list in the now demolished neighborhood. This kind of collaborative log-rolling among corporators of different parties on the same ward committee is quite common. In this particular case, Shenoy explained, the local corporator hoped to impress the Lallubhai residents with his effectiveness in the hopes of directing future work through his own offices.

24　An employee for one of Mumbai's most ubiquitous builders told me, "Our company has in-house employees for service approvals right from the beginning. Those companies that do not have in-house service approval departments, they outsource the approvals [acquisition process] by paying fees to architects or licensed plumbers."

CHAPTER 6: *"Good Doesn't Mean You're Honest"*

1　The reports of the day's events are conflicting: one staff member who witnessed the event said that a mob "broke in and beat Korelekar"; Korelekar himself denies there was any violence but reported that a crowd of angry people burst into his office.

2 Other chaviwallas, a number of whom have served the department longer than Balekar (who is relatively junior), expressed frustration and resentment at the extent to which their own expertise is overlooked, their own skills unseen. A senior chaviwalla named Naviq explained that while he might not be as vocal or assertive as Balekar, his understanding is deeper and his commitment and loyalty to maintaining the integrity of the distribution system stronger.

3 Responding to the allegations that he had manipulated the valves without authorization, Balekar explained that for emergency purposes he keeps a valve key at home; sometimes his boss calls him during off-duty hours with emergency valve-related instructions, so having a key at home allows him do this work without having to travel all the way to and from the ward office to fetch the key. If people see him doing these manipulations outside of the regular hours of valve operations they assume that he is up to no good. Notably no one to whom I spoke reported either having seen the chaviwalla manipulating any of the valves in question or of knowing anyone who had witnessed any such activity.

4 The English word *corruption* is the most common word used by Hindi and Marathi speakers in this context.

5 The chaviwallas are unable to explain precisely how they know this information, offering simply that they "just know." Their knowledge amounts to what Polanyi (2009:18) describes as "tacit" ways of knowing: "It is not by looking at things, but by dwelling in them, that we understand their joint meaning."

6 The media reported feverishly on Israeli "cloud-seeding" technology during these months.

7 Tambe, incidentally, was the junior engineer who, after seeing my copy of Kamat's map, proposed to meet outside the office to "help each other."

8 Here it is important to distinguish a narrative of technological and hydro-logical challenges (such as long distances from reservoirs or airlock— hydrological dynamics that are discursively naturalized as properties inhering in the pipes themselves) from *human* error. The first is acceptable; the second is not.

9. See Evans 1989; Nye 1967; Rose-Ackerman 1999; Wade 1985; see also discussion in Gupta 2005.

10. This kind of account suggests an economistic reasoning that "private vice does indeed result in public benefit" (Parry 2000:28); see discussion in Bardhan 1997; Huntington 1968.

11 Khan and the plumber maintain that the procedure—which was actually to be a new connection, as opposed to the officially sanctioned and less expensive transfer—would be carried out by the BMC staff itself.

12 See Jauregui's (2014) discussion of corruption as "moral action" in her incisive analysis of the concept of *jugaad*.

13 In my research secondhand accounts were usually given by people who had also offered accounts of their own corruption-related experiences, generally as illustrations of a particular point about the pervasiveness of corruption.

14 While the water department does have water reserves in its reservoirs upstate to accommodate two consecutive failed monsoons, engineers explained that the imperative of prudence led to citywide water cuts.

15 The volume of water supplied is a function of a host of interconnected factors, including water levels in the service reservoir, pipe diameters and lengths, elevations, and friction. One engineer explained that if there are four supply zones under a service reservoir, for example, if they give a 15 percent *time* cut to the first zone, then the *volume* of water will be reduced probably a little less than 15 percent because the reservoir is full when they start—meaning water pressure is very high. But since reduced levels in the service reservoir amount to lower water pressure, administering a 15 percent time cut to the second zone will result in much greater reduction in water *volume*—maybe a 30 percent cut. The third zone will get a 40 percent volume cut, and the last zone may have a 50 percent cut. In reality the supply zones under the jurisdiction of each reservoir are much more complex, with many zones further divided into multiple subzones, coordinated by valve openings and closings. The deputy hydraulic engineer (Planning and Control) recommended that the ward-level staff simply implement a 30 percent cut in water timings across the board, "just to make it straightforward." But in practice the implementation of the water cut is in the hands of the assistant engineers and field staff in each ward.

16 The M-East Ward is often able to "borrow" tankers from the other five wards in the eastern suburban zone that use the eastern suburbs filling station. During my fieldwork the assistant engineer was sometimes able to send up to twenty-four municipal tankers per day into various areas of his ward.

17 At Rs 12 per 1,000 liters, this price is approximately four times the municipal rate for residential water supply.

18 The filling station in the eastern suburban zone, where I conducted my fieldwork, is the only one of Mumbai's twelve or so filling stations that is located inside a gated compound with security guards. Nonetheless the filling stations are also locked, the keys in the possession of the various engineers and staff charged with overseeing the distribution of emergency supplies.

19 These rates went as high as Rs 2,500 during the height of the water cuts in the spring of 2009.

20 In *The Theory of Communicative Action*, Habermas (1981) locates rationality not in the subject but in intersubjective communication. Communicative action is "that form of social interaction in which the plans of action of different actors are co-ordinated through an exchange of communicative acts, that is, through a use of language orientated toward reaching understanding" (44).

21 One builder insisted that the dynamic is quite the opposite: Mumbai is a sellers' market; groundwater providers are faced with so much demand for their supplies that builders are at their mercy. "If the water doesn't come or is late, our whole building sits idle—we can lose a fortune." For this reason, the contractor maintained, it is imperative to pay the tanker companies on time and in full. "Otherwise next time I call for a tanker they may not pick up the phone."

22   *Chai-paani* is the phrase Katekar used for "a little extra here and there." See Parry (2000) for a discussion of the gift-bribe as a continuum.

23   One senior water department engineer explained that the extra payments made by developers to engineers who agree to work overtime to process permissions ("speed money") could easily earn an engineer in the building approvals department twice his official monthly salary on a daily basis.

24   An exception to this is the construction wing of the water department, where senior sources report that competitive salaries can be earned without running oneself ragged.

25   For instance, as one engineer put it, while the department does have "supply norms," the problems of metering have led to an unofficial policy whereby "complaints of low pressure" are not "entertained."

26   Yussuf used the English word *teamwork*.

27   By "earnings" he means "unofficial charges" collected by plumbers from private parties for transfers, extra connections, or an extra turn of a valve.

28   While the mediators refer to themselves as plumbers, department staff refer to them as *dalals*, a derogatory term for "broker."

29   Korelekar, the assistant engineer of M-East Ward from 2007 to 2010, repeatedly requested a transfer to another ward since the stress of the position was adversely affecting his health. The department was unable to find a willing replacement, however, and Korelekar stayed in M-East.

30   See Hansen 2001.

CHAPTER 7: *"If Water Comes It's Because of Politics"*

1   Rafique Nagar was never declared a slum but is treated as a slum by the water department; see discussion in chapter 4.

2   A location close to the M-East Ward office.

3   The incident in Trombay described in chapter 6 was as much political performance as hydraulic intervention.

4   The water department's illegal connection-cutting actions are directed almost exclusively against PVC plastic pipes. The reasoning behind the assumption that PVC pipes are illegal, however, is unclear since the water department allows the use of PVC pipes in place of galvanized steel for household connections (between 15 mm and 80 mm). The targeting of plastic pipes seems to have a twofold reasoning. First, since PVC piping is relatively new to Mumbai, the pipes that preexist the 1995 cutoff date would necessarily be made of steel. Steel pipes thus look like old connections, while plastic pipes look new. The constant transferring of older connections, however, means that many long-existing connections have been remade with PVC piping (which is much more affordable than steel). Conversely, owners of new connections who have the means tend to opt for the more expensive steel piping, which is more resistant to cracking. The second reason is somewhat more practical: it is easier to cut plastic than galvanized steel with a hacksaw. This seemingly internalized association (plastic=illegal) was shored up with the additional motive that plastic cracks more easily and is thus vulnerable to contamination.

5   Since the neighborhood is overwhelmingly Muslim (and largely North Indian), the conversation had until this point been in Hindi/Urdu; the speech, however, was made in Marathi, which is Patil's mother tongue. My understanding of Patil's speech was based on a few fragments translated into Hindi by a sympathetic little girl standing nearby.

6   As for the cholera outbreak, it ended with the tapering of the monsoon.

7   Political aspirants are sometimes as apt to claim credit for negative as positive hydraulic outcomes. Patil's decision to stop the water department from cutting connections in Rafique Nagar seems to have been the result of an on-the-spot judgment call, in which halting the saw-wielding hand of the department was just as beneficial (and less confrontational) than having the connections cut.

8   She used a feminine verb construction, indicating that the gendered nature of the protest was intentional, choreographed.

9   Another explanation for the intentional use of women offered by a party worker was that water is not a *political* matter but rather a *domestic* issue and is thus of primary concern to women; women suffer most from water shortage, she reasoned, because they are responsible for keeping their families washed and fed.

10 Hansen's (2004) account draws on Butler's (1993:95) formulation of the "performatively constituted" character of subjectivity.

11 While the police arrested more than fifty people that day, most were quickly released; elected officials and party leaders were loaded with criminal charges and held until hefty bail payments were made.

12 In 2009 the neighborhood of Shivajinagar-Bainganwadi was represented in the Maharashtra State Legislature by a Congress Party representative, and at the city level, in BMC, primarily by Samajwadi Party representatives, who won three of the neighborhood's five seats in the 2007 corporation elections. Of the remaining two BMC seats, one was elected on a Congress ticket, and the other, widely known to be affiliated with a rival faction of Congress, was elected on an independent ticket. The MLA seat representing Shivajinagar-Bainganwadi was thus fought out among Samajwadi Party, Congress, and the independent candidate.

13 I had asked the engineer to explain the divergent outcomes of two roadblock incidents, the second of which, discussed below, resulted in the appearance of a senior water supply planning engineer.

14 "Mahanagar Palika Murdabad!"; "Pani do! Pani do! Nahi to kursi kali karo!"; "Ek do, ek do, shah engineer ko phek do!"

15 What little coverage did appear in the English-language press was nonetheless telling. A *Hindustan Times* article on the Samajwadi Party event disdainfully described the crowd as a "mob." The *Times of India* marked the Congress event with a captioned image of the ill-fated donkey.

16 Even in the case of rallies organized by NGOs, material compensation is not uncommon.

17 Rakesh spoke in Hindi but used the English word *public*.

18 For discussion, see Björkman 2014.

19 With the Congress Party in control of the government of Maharashtra, it is not a far stretch to imagine the home minister instructing the chief of police to "cooperate" with a Congress-led morcha.

20 If they do not cut the connections, Rakesh explained, the boys could make corruption complaints against the engineers, which could cause headaches for them.

21 *Hafta* translates as "weekly," indicating something of the unexceptional, routine nature of these kinds of transactions. For incisive discussions of hafta, see Anjaria 2011; Jauregui 2014.

22 Police officers maintain relationships with neighborhood informants on whom they rely for information that they need for their work. A number of water department engineers told me that they maintain such networks of "spies" in the areas for which they are responsible.

23 The Congress Party symbol is the palm of the hand.

24 While engineers insist that they do not cow to the pressures of politicians, stories abound of engineers transferred as a result of political pressures.

25 She is referring to the transfer of a particularly influential subengineer.

26 Here she seems to be referencing the rumor that the water had been diverted to Deonar Municipal Colony.

27 This account of how hydraulic authority is constituted and articulated through material performances of embodied knowledge is to be distinguished from Hansen and Stepputat's (2006) formulation, which identifies the "sovereignty" of local "strongmen" in the *regulating, disciplinary,* and *governmental* functions they perform on behalf of official state actors, a formulation that Buur (2005) characterizes as "outsourced sovereignty." Hansen and Stepputat (2006:307) write, "Police departments, civic administrations, and political parties rely on [strongmen] to govern and regulate life in slums and popular neighborhoods." My account is distinct as well from those that have pointed to how multiple articulations of postcolonial sovereignty challenge existing power structures by using occult powers (e.g., Geschiere 1997) or by drawing upon traditional, cultural resources uncolonized by state forms (as subaltern studies theorists such as Chatterjee 2004 suggest). I have shown instead how pipe politics is constitutive of authority as well as productive of the coherent-state idea.

28 *Chai-paani* is Hindi for "tea-water."

29 For an ethnographic account of how elections are constitutive of networks of authority in Mumbai, see Björkman 2014.

CONCLUSION: *Pipe Politics*

1 Nehru Nagar was constructed in 1947 as a refugee camp to house migrants from what is now Pakistan.

2 Of the thirteen elected corporators, I was personally acquainted with ten, of which six had political careers traceable directly to water-related social work. Others had built social work careers as schoolteachers, police informants or mediators, and building contractors (success at which gestures to strong networks in the municipal bureaucracy).

3 Fareed spoke in Hindi but used the English word *develop*.

4 Often referred to in international policy circles as "Asia's largest slum," Dharavi was made famous by its showcasing in the Oscar-winning film *Slumdog Millionaire*.

5 The first is the theoretical terrain of liberal theorists of clientelism, patronage, and "vote bank" politics (cf. Björkman 2014; Piliavsky 2014). The second is advanced by the "antiplan" line of theorization discussed in the introduction.

6 As we saw in chapter 3, while engineers might allow connections to unauthorized world-class constructions in reference to rules and regulations governing water supply on "humanitarian grounds," much of the infrastructural practice carried out on humanitarian grounds is not actually allowed by the parameters of this policy.

REFERENCES

Acts, Circulars, Court Orders, Government Reports

Bombay Municipal Corporation Act. 1888.

Bombay Municipal Corporation. 1984. *Report on the Draft Development Plan (Revised) (1981–2001).* Bombay.

Bombay Municipal Corporation. 1994. *Report of the Expert Committee (Water Planning) on Bombay's Future Water Resources and Improvement in Present Water Supply Scheme.* Mumbai, December.

Bombay Municipal Corporation, Department of Hydraulic Engineering Master Plan for Water Supply. 1971.

Bombay Municipal Corporation, Department of Hydraulic Engineering Master Plan for Water Supply. 1999.

Bombay Town Planning Act. 1954.

Government of India Land Acquisition Act. 1894.

Government of India, Slum Areas (Improvement and Clearance) Act. 1956.

Government of Maharashtra Land Revenue Code. 1966.

Government of Maharashtra, Regional and Town Planning Act. 1966.

Government of Maharashtra Slum Areas (Improvement, Clearance and Redevelopment) Act. 1971.

Government of Maharashtra Urban Land Ceiling Regulation Act. 1976.

Government of Maharashtra. 1964. *Report on the Development Plan for Greater Bombay.* Bombay: Government Central Press.

Government of Maharashtra. 1976. "Tackling the Slum Problem: A new deal for the urban poor." Director-General of Information and Public Relations, Government of Maharashtra, July.

Government of Maharashtra. 1999. "Chitale Committee Report."

Government of Maharashtra, Division of Relief and Rehabilitation, Department of Revenue and Forests. "Mumbai Plan." Accessed August 8, 2011. http://mdmu .maharashtra.gov.in/pages/Mumbai/mumbaiplanShow.php.

Government of Maharashtra Coastal Zone Management Authority. 2009. Meeting minutes. Mantralaya, Mumbai. May 14.

Government of Maharashtra. 1996. Urban Development (UD) Circular No. GEN-1096/45/CR—15/UD-27. March 4.

Mayor of London. 2007. "Greener London: The Mayor's State of Environment Report for London." London: Greater London Authority.

Municipal Corporation of Greater Mumbai. 2005. "Economic Profile." *Greater Mumbai City Development Plan (2005 to 2025).* Accessed January 6, 2015. www.mcgm.gov.in/irj /portal/anonymous?NavigationTarget=navurl://095e1c7b9486b1423b881dce8b106978.

———. 2007. "Project Brief: K-East Ward Water Distribution Improvement Project." Mumbai, June.

Municipal Corporation of Greater Mumbai, Department of Hydraulic Engineering. 2009. "White Paper Presented to Municipal Corporation Standing Committee." Mumbai, February.

Municipal Engineers' Association, Mumbai and Brihan Mumbai Licensed Plumbers' Association. 2008. *Water: Mumbai's Water Supply—Vision 2041*, ed. T. V. Shah et al. Mumbai: Municipal Engineers' Association.

Published Works

Anand, Nikhil, and Anne Rademacher. 2011. "Housing in the Urban Age: Inequality and Aspiration in Mumbai." *Antipode* 43 (5): 1748–72.

Anderson, B. 2006. *Imagined Communities: Reflections on the Origin and Spread of Nationalism.* London: Verso.

Angelo, H., and D. Wachsmuth. 2014. "Urbanizing Urban Political Ecology: A Critique of Methodological Cityism." *International Journal of Urban and Regional Research* 39 (1): 16–27.

Anjaria, J. S. 2011. "Ordinary States: Everyday Corruption and the Politics of Space in Mumbai." *American Ethnologist* 38 (1): 58–72.

Appadurai, Arjun. 1988. *The Social Life of Things: Commodities in Cultural Perspective.* Cambridge: Cambridge University Press.

Arabindoo, Pushpa. 2011. "Beyond the Return of the 'Slum.'" *City* 15 (6): 631–35.

Bakker, Karen J. 2003. *An Uncooperative Commodity: Privatizing Water in England and Wales.* Oxford: Oxford University Press.

———. 2005. "Neoliberalizing Nature? Market Evnironmentalism in Water Supply in England and Wales." *Annals of the Association of American Geography* 95 (3): 542–65.

————. 2010. *Privatizing Water: Governance Failure and the World's Urban Water Crisis*. Ithaca, NY: Cornell University Press.

Barad, K., 2003. "Posthumanist Performativity: Toward an Understanding of How Matter Comes to Matter." *Signs: Journal of Women in Culture and Society* 28 (3): 801–31.

Bardhan, P. 1997. "Corruption and Development: A Review of Issues." *Journal of Economic Literature* 25 (September): 1320–46.

————. 2000. *Awakening Giants, Feet of Clay: A Comparative Assessment of the Rise of China and India*. Princeton, NJ: Princeton University Press.

Benjamin, S. 2007. "Occupancy Urbanism: Ten Theses." *Sarai Reader* 7:538–63.

————. 2008. "Occupancy Urbanism: Radicalizing Politics and Economy beyond Policy and Programs." *International Journal of Urban and Regional Research* 32 (3): 719–29.

Bennett, J. 2009. *Vibrant Matter: A Political Ecology of Things*. Durham, NC: Duke University Press.

Bhaduri, Amit. 2005. "Urban Water Supply: Reforming the Reformers." *Economic and Political Weekly*, December 31.

Bhide, A. 2002. "Whither the Urban Poor?" *Combat Law* 1.

————. 2013. "Emerging Geography of Displacement and Resettlement." Unpublished manuscript.

Bijker, Wiebe E. 2007. "Dikes and Dams, Thick with Politics." *ISIS: Journal of the History of Science in Society* 98 (1): 109–23.

Björkman, Lisa. 2014. "'You Can't Buy a Vote': Meanings of Money in a Mumbai Election." *American Ethnologist* 41 (4): 617–34.

Brenner, Neil. 1998. "Global Cities, Glocal States: Global City Formation and State Territorial Restructuring in Contemporary Europe." *Review of International Political Economy* 5 (1): 1–37.

————. 2013. "Theses on Urbanization." *Public Culture* 25 (1): 85–114.

Brenner, Neil, Jamie Peck, and Nik Theodore. 2012. *Civic City Cahier 4: Afterlives of Neoliberalism*, ed. Jesko Fezer and Matthias Gorlich. London: Bedford Press.

Brenner, Neil, and Nik Theodore. 2002. "Cities and the Geographies of 'Actually Existing Neoliberalism.'" *Antipode* 34 (3): 349–79.

Budds, J., and G. McGranahan. 2003. "Are the Debates on Water Privatization Missing the Point?" *Environment and Urbanization* 15 (2): 87–113.

Butler, Judith. 1993. *Bodies That Matter: On the Discursive Limits of "Sex."* East Sussex, UK: Psychology Press.

Buur, L. 2005. "The Sovereign Outsourced: Local Justice and Violence in Port Elizabeth." In *Sovereign Bodies: Citizens, Migrants, and States in the Postcolonial World*, ed. Thomas Blom Hansen and Finn Stepputat, 153–71. Princeton, NJ: Princeton University Press.

Callon, Michel. 1998. *The Laws of the Markets*. Oxford: Blackwell.

Callon, Michel, and Bruno Latour. 1981. "Unscrewing the Big Leviathan: How Actors Macro-structure Reality and How Sociologists Help Them to Do So." In *Advances in Social Theory and Methodology: Towards an Integration of Micro and Macro-sociologies*, ed. K. Knorr-Cetina and Aaron Victor Cicourel, 277–303. London: Routledge.

Castalia. 2007. "Project Brief. K-East Ward Water Distribution Improvement Project." Unpublished manuscript.

Castells, M. [1972] 1977. *The Urban Question.* London: Edward Arnold.

Collaborative for the Advancement of the Study of Urbanism through Mixed Media (CASUMM). 2008. Accessed January 2010. www.indiawaterportal.org/articles/k-east -ward-mumbai-water-distribution-improvement-project-wdip-faqs-compiled -casumm.

Chatterjee, P. 1997. "Development Planning and the Indian State." In *State and Politics in India*, ed. P. Chatterjee, 271–95. New Delhi: Oxford University Press.

———. 2004. *Politics of the Governed.* New York: Columbia University Press.

———. 2013. *Lineages of Political Society: Studies in Postcolonial Democracy.* New York: Columbia University Press.

Chibber, V. 2013. *Postcolonial Theory and the Specter of Capital.* London: Verso.

Coalition against Water Privatization. 2004. "The Struggle against Silent Disconnections: Prepaid Meters and the Struggle for Life in Phiri, Soweto." Accessed January 2010. www.apf.org.za.

Collier, S. 2011. *Post-Soviet Social: Neoliberalism, Social Modernity, Biopolitics.* Princeton, NJ: Princeton University Press.

Corbridge, S., and J. Harriss. 2000. *Reinventing India.* Cambridge: Polity Press.

Coronil, Fernando. 1997. *The Magical State: Nature, Money, and Modernity in Venezuela.* Chicago: University of Chicago Press.

Correa, C., P. Mehta, and S. B. Patel. 1965. "Planning for Bombay." *Marg* 18 (1): 29–56.

Davis, Mike. 2007. *Planet of Slums.* London: Verso.

Deleuze Gilles, and Félix Guattari. 2004. *A Thousand Plateaus*, trans. B. Massumi. London: Continuum.

Deleuze, Gilles, Félix Guattari, and Charles J. Stivale. 1984. "Concrete Rules and Abstract Machines." *SubStance* 13 (3/4): 7–19.

Derrida, J. 1977. "Signature Event Context." *Margins of Philosophy*, 307. Chicago: University of Chicago.

de Sardan, J. P. 1999. "A Moral Economy of Corruption in Africa?" *Journal of Modern African Studies* 37 (1): 25–52.

Dossal, M. 1988. "Henry Conybeare and the Politics of Centralised Water Supply in Mid-Nineteenth Century Bombay." *Indian Economic and Social History Review* 25 (1): 79–96.

———. 1997. *Imperial Designs and Indian Realities: The Planning of Bombay City, 1845–1875.* New Delhi: Oxford University Press.

Escobar, A. 1995. *Encountering Development: The Making and Unmaking of the Third World.* Princeton, NJ: Princeton University Press.

Evans, P. 1989. "Predatory, Developmental, and Other Apparatuses: A Comparative Political Economy Perspective on the Third World State." *Sociological Forum* 4 (4).

Farías, I. 2011. "The Politics of Urban Assemblages." *City* 15 (3–4): 365–74.

Farias, I., and T. Bender, eds. 2010. *Urban Assemblages: How Actor-Network Theory Changes Urban Studies.* London: Routledge.

Ferguson, J. 1990. *The Anti-Politics Machine: "Development," Depoliticization, and Bureaucratic Power in Lesotho.* Minneapolis: University of Minnesota Press.

Foucault, Michel. 1977. *Discipline and Punish: The Birth of the Prison.* New York: Vintage Books.

Fujii, L. A. 2010. "Shades of Truth and Lies: Interpreting Testimonies of War and Violence." *Journal of Peace Research* 47 (2): 231–41.

Gandy, Matthew. 1997. "The Making of a Regulatory Crisis: Restructuring New York City's Water Supply." *Transactions of the Institute of British Geographers* 22 (3): 338–58.

———. 2005. "Learning from Lagos." *New Left Review* 33:36–52.

Geertz, C. 1980. *Negara.* Princeton, NJ: Princeton University Press.

Geschiere, Peter. 1997. *The Modernity of Witchcraft: Politics and the Occult in Postcolonial Africa.* Charlottesville: University of Virginia Press.

Ghertner, D. A. 2011. "Rule by Aesthetics: World-Class City Making in Delhi." In *Worlding Cities: Asian Experiments and the Art of Being Global,* ed. Ananya Roy and Aihwa Ong, 279–306. Hoboken, NJ: Wiley-Blackwell.

Goffman, Erving. 1974. *Frame Analysis: An Essay on the Organization of Experience.* New York: Harper and Row.

Goldman, M. 2007. "How 'Water for All!' Policy Became Hegemonic: The Power of the World Bank and Its Transnational Policy Networks." *Geoforum* 38 (5): 786–800.

Graham, Stephen, ed. 2009. *Disrupted Cities: When Infrastructure Fails.* New York: Routledge.

Graham, S., and S. Marvin. 2001. *Splintering Urbanism: Networked Infrastructures, Technological Mobilities and the Urban Condition.* London: Routledge.

Gupta, Akhil. 1995. "Blurred Boundaries: The Discourse of Corruption, the Culture of Politics, and the Imagined State." *American Ethnologist* 22 (2): 375–402.

———. 2005. "Narratives of Corruption: Anthropological and Fictional Accounts of the Indian State." *Ethnography* 6 (1): 5–34.

Habermas, J. 1981. *The Theory of Communicative Action.* London: Beacon Press.

Hansen, Thomas Blom. 1999. *The Saffron Wave: Democracy and Hindu Nationalism in Modern India.* Princeton, NJ: Princeton University Press.

———. 2001. *Wages of Violence: Naming and Identity in Postcolonial Bombay.* Princeton, NJ: Princeton University Press.

———. 2004. "Politics as Permanent Performance: The Production of Political Authority in the Locality." In *The Politics of Cultural Mobilization in India,* ed. John Zavos, Andrew Wyatt, and Vernon Hewitt, 19–36. New York: Oxford University Press.

———. 2005. "Sovereigns beyond the State: On Legality and Authority in Urban India." In *Sovereign Bodies: Citizens, Migrants, and States in the Postcolonial World,* ed. Thomas Blom Hansen and Finn Stepputat, 169–91. Princeton, NJ: Princeton University Press.

Hansen, Thomas Blom, and Finn Stepputat. 2006. "Sovereignty Revisited." *Annual Review of Anthropology* 35 (1): 295–315.

Harris, Andrew. 2012. "The Metonymic Urbanism of Twenty-First-Century Mumbai." *Urban Studies* 49 (13): 2955–73. doi:10.1177/0042098012452458.

Hart, Keith. 2010. "Africa's Urban Revolution and the Informal Economy." In *The Political Economy of Africa*, ed. Vishnu Padayachee, 372–87. New York: Routledge.

Harvey, David, 1989. "From Managerialism to Entrepreneurialism: The Transformation in Urban Governance in Late Capitalism." *Geografiska Annaler* 71 (1): 3–17.

———. 1996. "Cities or Urbanization?" *City* 1 (1–2): 38–61.

———. 2001. *Spaces of Capital: Towards a Critical Geography*. New York: Routledge.

———. 2010. *The Enigma of Capital and the Crises of Capitalism*. New York: Oxford University Press, 2010.

Heynen, Nikolas C., Maria Kaika, and Erik Swyngedouw. 2006. *In the Nature of Cities: Urban Political Ecology and the Politics of Urban Metabolism*. London: Routledge.

Huntington, S. 1968. *Political Order in Changing Societies*. New Haven, CT: Yale University Press.

Ingold, Tim. 2000. *The Perception of the Environment: Essays on Livelihood, Dwelling and Skill*. London: Routledge.

Jaffrelot, C. 2000. "The Rise of the Other Backward Classes in the Hindi Belt." *Journal of Asian Studies* 59 (1): 86–108.

Jafri, A. 2007. "World Bank Attempt to Privatise Mumbai's Water Runs Aground: Citizens Reject Report." Focus on the Global South. Accessed January 2010. www .focusweb.org.

Jauregui, Beatrice. 2014. "Provisional Agency in India: Jugaad and Legitimation of Corruption." *American Ethnologist* 41 (1): 76–91.

Joseph, D. T. 1996. "Bombay's Development Plans." In *Urban Explosion of Mumbai: Restructuring of Growth*, ed. M. D. David. Mumbai: Himalaya.

Kaïka, M. 2005. "City of Flows." *Modernity, Nature and the City*. London: Routledge.

Kanna, Ahmed. 2011. *Dubai, the City as Corporation*. Minneapolis: University of Minnesota Press.

Keane, Webb. 1997. *Signs of Recognition: Powers and Hazards of Representation in an Indonesian Society*. Berkeley: University of California Press.

Keil, R. 1995. "The Environmental Problematic in World Cities." In *World Cities in a World-System*, ed. Paul L. Knox and Peter J. Taylor, 280–97. Cambridge: Cambridge University Press.

———. 2002. "'Common–Sense' Neoliberalism: Progressive Conservative Urbanism in Toronto, Canada." *Antipode* 34 (3): 578–601.

Kidambi, P. 2007. *The Making of an Indian Metropolis: Colonial Government and Public Culture in Bombay, 1890–1920*. Hampshire, UK: Ashgate.

Klein, I. 1986. "Urban Development and Death." *Modern Asian Studies* 20 (4): 725–54.

Laclau, Ernesto. 1996. "Why Do Empty Signifiers Matter to Politics?" *Emancipation(s)*, 36–46. London: Verso.

Larkin, Brian. 2013. "The Politics and Poetics of Infrastructure." *Annual Review of Anthropology* 42 (1): 327–43.

Latour, Bruno. 1999. *Pandora's Hope: Essays on the Reality of Science Studies*. Cambridge, MA: Harvard University Press.

———. 2005. *Reassembling the Social: An Introduction to Actor-Network Theory.* Oxford: Oxford University Press.

Lefebvre, H. 1991. *The Production of Space.* Cambridge, MA: Wiley-Blackwell.

———. 2003. *The Urban Revolution.* Minneapolis: University of Minnesota Press.

Mahadevia, D., and H. Narayanan. 1999. "Shanghaing Mumbai—The Politics of Evictions and Resistance in Slum Settlements." Working Paper 7, Center for Development Alternatives, Ahmedabad.

Mamdani, M. 1996. *Citizen and Subject: Contemporary Africa and the Legacy of Late Colonialism.* Princeton, NJ: Princeton University Press.

McKinsey and Company. 2003. *Vision Mumbai: Transforming Mumbai into a World-Class City.* Mumbai: McKinsey and Company.

Merrifield, Andy. 2013. "The Urban Question under Planetary Urbanization." *International Journal of Urban and Regional Research* 37 (3): 909–22.

Mitchell, Timothy. 2002. *Rule of Experts: Egypt, Techno-Politics, Modernity.* Berkeley: University of California Press.

Mumbai Municipal Engineers Association. 2006. *Mumbai's Water: Glorious History of Bombay Water Works.* Mumbai: Sukhdeo Kashid.

Mumbai Pani. 2007. "Roll Back Water Privatisation: No to Prepaid Water Meters." Press release, November 14. Accessed January 2011. http://www.vakindia.org/pdf /Mumbai-Paani-15th-Nov2007.pdf.

Mumbai Suburban District. 2015. Accessed January 10, 2015. http://mumbaisuburban .gov.in/html/administrative_setup.htm.

Mumbai Transformation Support Unit. 2011. Accessed July 5, 2011. http://www .visionmumbai.org/aboutus.aspx#ontop4.

Nainan, N. 2012. "Lakshmi Raj: Shaping Spaces in Post Industrial Mumbai: Urban Regimes, Planning Instruments and Splintering Communities." Ph.D. diss., University of Amsterdam.

Narayanan, H. 2003. "In Search of Shelter: The Politics and Implementation of the Urban Land (Ceiling and Reservation) Act 1976 in Greater Mumbai." In *Bombay and Mumbai: A City in Transition,* ed. Sujata Patel and Jim Masselos, 183–206. New Delhi: Oxford University Press.

National Alliance of People's Movements. 2005. "The Fake Scare of Bangladeshis Taking Over Mumbai Stands Exposed." Press release, May 10.

Navdanya Research Foundation for Science, Technology and Ecology. Accessed January 2011. http://www.navdanya.org/.

Nye, J. S. 1967. "Corruption and Political Development: A Cost-Benefit Analysis." *American Political Science Review* 61 (2): 417–27.

Orlove, B., and S. C. Caton. 2010. "Water Sustainability: Anthropological Approaches and Prospects." *Annual Review of Anthropology* 39:401–15.

Pacione, M. 1981. *Problems and Planning in Third World Cities.* London: Croom Helm.

Parry, J. 2000. "The Crisis of Corruption and the Idea of India—A Worm's Eye View." In *Morals of Legitimacy: Between Agency and System,* ed. I. Pardo. Oxford: Berghahn Books.

Peck, J., N. Theodore, and N. Brenner. 2009. "Neoliberal Urbanism: Models, Moments, Mutations. *Sais Review* 29 (1): 49–66.

Peck, J., and A. Tickell. 2002. "Neoliberalizing Space." *Antipode* 34 (3): 380–404.

Phatak, V. K. 2007. "Developing Land and Real Estate Markets: The Case of the Mumbai Metropolitan Region." In *Mumbai Reader,* compiled by Pankaj Joshi, Isaac Mathew, and Ian Nazareth Rahul Mehrotra, 34–53. Mumbai: Urban Design Research Institute.

Piliavsky, A. 2014. "Introduction." In *Patronage as the Politics of South Asia*, ed. Anastasia Piliavsky, 1–37. Delhi: Cambridge University Press.

Polanyi, K. [1944] 2001. *The Great Transformation: The Political and Economic Origins of Our Time.* Boston: Beacon Press.

Polanyi, M. 2009. *The Tacit Dimension.* Chicago: University of Chicago Press.

Public-Private Infrastructure Advisory Facility. 2015. Accessed January 9, 2015. http://www.ppiaf.org.

Rademacher, Anne, and K. Sivaramakrishnan. 2013. *Ecologies of Urbanism in India: Metropolitan Civility and Sustainability.* Hong Kong: Hong Kong University Press.

Rao, V. 2006. "Post-Industrial Transitions: The Speculative Futures of Citizenship in Contemporary Mumbai." In *Mumbai Reader*, compiled by Pankaj Joshi, Isaac Mathew, and Ian Nazareth Rahul Mehrotra, 250–59. Mumbai: Urban Design Research Institute.

Robinson, J. 2002. "Global and World Cities: A View from off the Map." *International Journal of Urban and Regional Research* 26 (3): 531–54.

Rose, N. 1999. *Powers of Freedom: Reframing Political Thought.* Cambridge: Cambridge University Press.

Rose-Ackerman, S. 1999. *Corruption and Government: Causes, Consequences, and Reform.* Cambridge: Cambridge University Press.

Roy, A. 2003. *Calcutta Requiem: Gender and the Politics of Poverty.* Minneapolis: University of Minnesota Press.

Sassen, S. 1991. *The Global City: New York, London, Tokyo.* Princeton, NJ: Princeton University Press.

———. 2010. "The Global City." In *The Blackwell City Reader*, ed. Gary Bridge and Sophie Watson, 126–32. Hoboken, NJ: Wiley-Blackwell.

Schechner, R. 1985. *Between Theater and Anthropology.* Philadelphia: University of Pennsylvania Press.

Schultz, J. 2000. "Bolivia's Water War Victory." *Earth Island Journal* 15 (3).

Schumpeter, J. A. 1942. *Socialism, Capitalism, and Democracy.* New York: Harper and Brothers.

Scott, J. 1998. *Seeing Like a State: How Certain Schemes to Improve the Human Condition Have Failed.* New Haven, CT: Yale University Press.

Shaw, A. 1999. "The Planning and Development of New Bombay." *Modern Asian Studies* 33 (4): 951–98.

Simone, A. M. 2004. "People as Infrastructure: Intersecting Fragments in Johannesburg." *Public Culture* 16 (3): 407–29.

Singh, A. K. 2006. "Delhi's Watery Woes: A Cross-sectoral Analysis of the Water Crisis in Delhi." Occasional Papers, Centre for Trade and Development (Centad),

Delhi. Accessed January 13, 2015. http://www.wsscc.org/sites/default/files/india
_singh_delhis_watery_woes_2006.pdf.

Singh, G., and P. K. Das. 1995. "Building Castles in Air: Housing Scheme for Bombay's
Slum-Dwellers." *Economic and Political Weekly* 30 (40): 2477–81.

Smith, A. [1776] 2001. *Wealth of Nations*. Raleigh, NC: Hayes Barton Press.

Smith, Neil. 2002. "New Globalism, New Urbanism: Gentrification as Global Urban
Strategy." *Antipode* 34 (3): 427–50.

Swyngedouw, E. 1996. "The City as a Hybrid: On Nature, Society and Cyborg Urbanization." *Capitalism, Nature, Socialism* 7 (2): 65–80.

———. 2004. *Social Power and the Urbanization of Water: Flows of Power*. New York:
Oxford University Press.

———. 2009. "The Political Economy and Political Ecology of the Hydro Social Cycle."
Journal of Contemporary Water Research and Education 142 (1): 56–60.

Swyngedouw, E., and M. Kaika. 2008. "The Environment of the City . . . or the Urbanization of Nature." In *A Companion to the City*, ed. Gary Bridge and Sophie Watson,
567–80. Oxford: Blackwell.

Swyngedouw, E., M. Kaika, and E. Castro. 2002. "Urban Water: A Political-Ecology
Perspective." *Built Environment* 28 (2):124–37.

Thomas, N. 2009. *Entangled Objects: Exchange, Material Culture, and Colonialism in
the Pacific*. Cambridge, MA: Harvard University Press.

Totade, S. D. 2008. "Planning of Water Supply Districts in the Initial Stages." In *Mumbai Water Supply—Vision 2041* (March 24), ed. T. V. Shah et al. Mumbai: Municipal
Engineers' Association and Brinhan Mumbai Licenced Plumbers' Association.

Tsing, A. 1993. *In the Realm of the Diamond Queen*. Princeton, NJ: Princeton University
Press.

Turner, Victor. 1980. "Social Dramas and Stories about Them." *Critical Inquiry* 7 (1):
141–68.

United Nations. 2000. "Millennium Development Goals and Beyond 2015." Accessed
January 2011. www.un.org/millenniumgoals/environ.shtml.

United Nations Human Settlements Program. 2006. "The State of the World's
Cities Report 2006/2007." *The Millennium Development Goals and Urban
Sustainability*.

United Nations. 2009. *Global Report on Human Settlements 2009: Planning Sustainable
Cities*. London: Earthscan.

United Nations Human Settlements Program. 2003. *Global Report on Human Settlements 2003: Challenge of the Slums*. London: Earthscan.

Wade, R. 1985. "The Market for Public Office: Why the Indian State Is Not Better at
Development." *World Development* 13 (4): 467–97.

Wagle. 2012. "Two Tales of a City." *Indian Architect and Builder*, July. Accessed
March 9, 2012. http://issuu.com/iab_archives/docs/iab_july_2012_25.11/41.

World Bank. 2005. "Reforming Mumbai's Real Estate 'Raj': Prelude to a Business Plan."
Draft.

World Bank. 2008. "Impact Assessment of Resettlement Implementations." SR42.
Accessed January 11, 2015. http://documents.worldbank.org/curated/en/2008/09

/16609495/india-mumbai-urban-transport-project-safeguards-diagnostic-review
-impact-assessment-resettlement-implementations.

Yadav, Y. 1999. "Electoral Politics in a Time of Change: India's Third Electoral System,
1989–1999." *Economic and Political Weekly* 34 (34/35): 2393–99.

Newspaper and Magazine Articles and Television Broadcasts

Ashar. 2010. "Water Projects Will Be Focus of Mumbai's Civic Budget." *Daily News
and Analysis,* February 2.

Bharucha, N. 2009. "Woman Challenges Slum Tag for House." *Times of India,* July 6.

Finnegan, W. 2002. "Leasing the Rain." *New Yorker,* April 8.

Khetan, A. 2011. "Land Grab: And How to Make Millions." *Tehelka* 8 (21).
Accessed June 30, 2011. http://www.tehelka.com/story_main49.asp?filename
=Ne280511Coverstory.asp.

Masurkar, A. 2009. "No Temple in Your Building? You Live in a Slum!" *Mumbai Mirror,*
June 9.

"Mumbai Demanded Water, It Got Blood." 2009. *Daily News and Analysis,* December 3.

"Mumbai Water Mafia Exposed." 2010. NDT TV. January 3.

Tatke, S. 2008. "Bandra Residents Protest Hike in Water Charges." *Times of India,*
November 17.

———. 2010. "Rahul's Visit Has BMC Officials Rushing to Slum." *Times of India,* February 7.

Times of India. 2008. "Corporators Protest Water Shortage at Civic Meet." October 9.

Udwala, T. 2007. "At a Dalit Slum, a BMC Plumber Humbled NCP's Mr. Big." *Indian
Express,* February 9.

Williams, A. 2011. "In Defence of Cities." *Economist,* December 2.

INDEX

Indian Oil resettlement compound, 86–87, 91–92, 94–95, 248n25
Indonesia, 8, 47, 231
infrastructure, 2–3; embedded, 8–12; global investment capital for, 4–8, 13; knowledge about, 32, 45, 232; politics of, 12–16
Island City, 66, 91; floor space index in, 74, 76; zoning regulations of, 102

Janhit Manch (organization), 125–26
Jauregui, Beatrice, 178, 260n12
Joshi, Alok, 48–49
just-in-time management practices, 2–3, 87

Kamla Raman Nagar, 110–11, 119, 123–27, 232, 254n16; municipal raids in, 165, 178; water supply to, 145–50, 224
Kho Kho (game), 96, 190
Konkan (Maharashtrian) Muslims, 103–4
Koolhaas, Rem, 6–7
Kuala Lumpur, 57
Kumar, Subhod, 33

Laclau, Ernesto, 197
Lagos, Nigeria, 6–7
Lallubhai resettlement compound, 86–95, 158–61, 248n25, 250nn9–10, 259n23
Land Acquisition Act (1894), 65, 71, 246n6
Land Revenue Code (1966), 102, 253n4
Larkin, Brian, 12, 13
Latour, Bruno, 12, 240n25
leakage estimates, 38–39, 43–45, 48, 68, 243n24
Lefebvre, Henri, 3, 238n7, 240n26
leprosy, 173–74
Lotus Colony, 86, 103–4, 145, 199
luxury housing projects, 17, 62, 85–97, 101, 232

Maharashtra Coastal Zone Management Authority (MCZMA), 82–83
Maharashtra Housing and Area Development Authority, 75, 77, 104, 247n10, 253n7
Maharashtra Housing Board, 65
Maharashtra Metropolitan Regional Development Authority (MMRDA), 78–80; on land use determinations, 247n10; on resettlement compounds, 86–88, 91, 92, 251n16; on road improvement projects, 160

Maharashtra Navnirman Sena (MNS) Party, 216–17
Maharashtra Regional and Town Planning Act (1966), 246n6
Malaysia, 57
mandal (self-help group), 174–77, 200
maps, 12, 24, 128–31, 240n26, 257n45; availability of, 21–26, 130–32, 135, 190; knowledge not shown on, 129–32, 138–44, 176; private, 135–38, 190, 195; surveys for, 23–26, 35–37, 61, 130
marketization, 10, 25–29, 30–37, 40, 64–78; definition of, 241n5; privatization versus, 27
McKinsey and Company, 82, 99, 237n5, 249n1
meters. *See* water meters
migrants, 115, 116; Bangladeshi, 53, 121–22, 256n32; after Partition, 264n1; Sindhi, 246n3
Mitchell, Timothy, 257n45
Mitsubishi Corporation, 28
Monsanto Corporation, 28
monsoons, 45, 89, 244n35, 263n6; water shortages after, 186–87, 206
M/s Binnie (consulting firm), 29
Mumbai Pani (organization), 49–52, 54
Mumbai Urban Infrastructure Project, 248n24, 249n4

Nainan, N., 248n16
National Housing policies, 74–75, 111–12
neoliberalism, 2–7, 16–17; definitions of, 9; Foucault on, 239n19; privatization and, 26–29, 84; statecraft of, 239n18; Swyngedouw on, 239n15
Nestor's Palace, 92–97, 159
New National Economic Policy (1991), 72–73
Nye, J. S., 177

Orlove, B., 240n26
outsourcing, 29, 259n24, 264n27

Pacione, M., 65
Parry, J., 178, 260n9
Partition of India, 64, 246n3
Patil, Suresh "Bullet," 199–205, 216
Pawar, Sharad, 111, 248n18